Christopher Fry

Flora

Herbert Herbert Tree

C. Donald

J. Siddons

Irving

Brausby Williams

Terry

J. Garrick

Jannie

Sybil Thorndike

the Stalls'

Hicks

E. Kemble

Rudolph Valentino

Edward Sheam

Holn Vaulneigh

W. C. Macready

Martin Harvey

S. Siddons

J. Colman

Ellen Terry

John Tu Gud.

THEATRICAL LETTERS

THEATRICAL LETTERS

*400 years of correspondence
between celebrated actors, actresses,
playwrights, their families, friends, lovers,
admirers, enemies, producers, managers
and others*

selected & edited
by
BILL HOMEWOOD

Marginalia
PRESS

First published in 1995 by
MARGINALIA PRESS
an imprint of Ippon Books Ltd
55 Long Lane
London
N3 2HY

ISBN 1874572 119

Design & Production by Susan Richards

Printed by Redwood Books,
Trowbridge, Wiltshire

FOREWORD

I am greatly fascinated by the way the correspondence has been so cleverly arranged and researched, covering so much ground in the different periods, as well as giving very personal glimpses of the different writers; surely a most fascinating collection. I feel honoured to be included in such a distinguished company.

John Gielgud
February 28, 1995

ACKNOWLEDGEMENTS

Grateful thanks are due particularly to Dr Janet Birkett, Andrew Kirk and library staff at the Theatre Museum, Covent Garden (Victoria and Albert Museum); to Joanna Wallace of the Picture Library, Victoria & Albert Museum; to the librarians and staff of the British Library (British Museum); to Austin Hall and the Governors of Dulwich College for access to the Henslowe Papers in the Wodehouse Library; to the Actors' Centre, London; to Nicolas Soames; to Dr Frances Hughes, Arthur Kincaid, Deirdre Barber, John Casson, Sir John Gielgud, Margaret Wolfit, Lady Daubney, Christopher Fry, Mary Benson, Juliet Ackroyd, Peter Dunn, Clive Francis, Brenda Bruce, Alec McCowen, Graham Payne, Joan Hirst, Joan Plowright, Patrick Mynhardt, Arnold Wesker, Dr Homer Swander, Anne Harvey, Steve Richards, Vivien Heilbron, Gervase Farjeon, Roy Homewood, Margaret Homewood, Catherine Muttelle, Robert Crumb, Aline Crumb and Nathan Joseph for permissions, leads or for the releasing of collected or private material. My very special thanks go to Susan Richards for design and production and to Estelle Kohler for indefatigable research and support. Detailed acknowledgements of copyright material may be found in SOURCES at the back of the book.

CONTENTS

1572~1700

*In a few cases the listed name is the recipient or the subject of the letter;
often the listed name heads a section which includes other writers*

1700~1800

1800~1900

1900~1980

LIST OF PLATES
(between pages 110-111)

To
Roy and Margaret
Homewood

INTRODUCTION

'I often wish my tongue had been blistered before I uttered the words which caused you to say that thy smock should never be rubb'd by my shirt again' wrote the ardent David Garrick to the irresistible Peggy Woffington. This is one of hundreds of sentences which made me laugh aloud (a laugh quickly stifled in the cloistered and earnest silence of a museum library) during the happy course of the research and assembly of this book.

Also amusing, but extremely moving, is Edward Alleyn's letter of 1593, with which I begin the collection. This was addressed to his wife via her stepfather, Philip Henslowe: 'one of the grooms of his master's chamber, dwelling on the bank side, right over against the clink'. 'Mouse' was illiterate and dictated her loving answers to Henslowe. Their correspondence is overladen with the horrors of the plague – but Alleyn is still concerned with the colour of his woollen stockings. The other issues touched on – health, money, children and food – are among the main themes of the collection, which I have assembled for the most part chronologically, occasionally slightly out of sequence to keep family groups and exchanges together.

This is not essentially a book of famous people's letters – although many famous people feature in it. The letters have been selected for their quality of writing or intrinsic interest, making the collection a subtle kind of history: four hundred years of English-speaking theatre through the pens of its practitioners. Theatre people love language – it is, after all, our first stock-in-trade. There are many in the profession who are never 'off duty', who simply love to entertain, to please,to play with words, whose letters are moving or fun to read, and who will go on writing them come hell or high water. This is a collection of such letters.

Over the centuries there have been a number of published antholo-gies of the letters of illustrious people, with titles like 'A Treasury of Great Letters'. Without exception the elaborately-written prefaces imply tragically that they are being assembled on the death-bed of 'The Art of Letter-writing'. But, in the late twentieth century, the art flourishes. Of course many people today reach for the telephone before the pen; the act of communication on paper can be both confessional and exhibitionist, and most people need a couple of drinks before becoming either (Dr Johnson: 'In a man's letters, you know, madam, his soul lies naked'). But these telephone-grabbers are people who would always have corresponded in a perfunctory and unremarkable style; they are not our letter-writers. The good letter-writer was, is, and always will be a compulsive entertainer, and not necessarily an entertainer who can amuse face to face or over the telephone. There are as many marvellous letter-writers today as there ever were, some of them shamelessly courting posterity by publication – and why not? We read them with pleasure and foster their posterity with enjoyment.

However, letters are usually embarrassingly private and rarely circulate until years after they are written, when the embarrassment has worn off. For this reason my collection stops at about 1980, and the next generation of theatrical letter-writers waits to be unembarrassingly exposed in the twenty-first century. Lord Byron wrote: 'One of the pleasures of reading old letters is the knowledge that they need no answer.' Another pleasure is that there is no guilt in reading private thoughts in old letters. If I knew David Garrick and Peggy Woffington today, I should hate to read his extremely intimate letter to her.

You can dip into the book at any point, or you can start at the beginning. If you do, you will find that there is an underlying cat's-cradle of names – again and again the same ones crop up – which meshes the history together. Unravelling this cat's cradle has been fascinating; collecting and assembling the letters for publication has been a privilege. In the course of research two problems were occasionally frustrating: i) almost impossible handwriting and ii) actresses', and sometimes actors', coyness about their birth-dates. Neither spoiled the fun I had. What a pleasure to discover, in a rotting pile of old letters, a celebrated original; and what fun to unravel the spidery, drunken crawlings of a half-controlled quill across parchment. After study of the handwriting in question, and the context, the illegible word is often revealed by a knack of not quite focusing the eyes – rather like the technique for looking at a remote star in the sky with the naked eye. As for the actresses' birth-dates I would often find six suggestions in contemporary biography or journalistic profiles, varying by as much as eight years. This is not surprising: in the world of casting, there is a phenomenon known as the actor's 'playing age', and we all know that this may not be the same as our real age – but an admission of the second could lose us a job; this is especially true for women.

Who would not giggle with the bedroom scramblings of David Garrick and Peggy Woffington? Who would not squirm at George Bernard Shaw's brutal home-truths to a disillusioned Ellen Terry, or those in Eleanor Farjeon's letter to the hopelessly optimistic Otto, or those of Mrs Drew to her grandson Lionel Barrymore, or those of his first employer to 'Cockie' Cochran? Who would not be moved by the extraordinary letter from Scott of the Antarctic, written with frozen fingers in a fatal blizzard, asking his great friend J.M. Barrie to care for his wife and child; or by the heartfelt condolences from Charlotte Cushman to Mr Seward on the loss of his wife and daughter, or those from Shaw to Mrs Patrick Campbell on the death of her son? Who would not laugh at the furiously ironical letter from Mark Twain to No. 1356, or the one from Bernard Shaw, frozen at a matinee? ('My wife was affected to tears by the play; and her tears froze so that it took me five minutes to get her eyes open with the warmth of my hands, which are now covered in chilblains.')

All gardeners will sympathise with Edward Alleyn's anxiety about his spinach or that of Samuel Phelps about his kitchen garden. All actors, certainly, will feel a twinge of pity for Mr Woolgast, who 'went so well at Penge' – but still gets the sack.

I hope you enjoy the book.

Bill Homewood
January 1995

1572 ~ 1700

EDWARD ALLEYN

PHILLIP HENSLOWE

WILLIAM BIRDE

JAMES BURBAGE

PHILIP GAWDY

ROBERT GREENE

APHRA BEHN

THE LORD CHAMBERLAIN

THOMAS BETTERTON

AND OTHERS...

EDWARD ALLEYN (1566–1626)
PHILLIP HENSLOWE (1550/60–1616)

At the end of the sixteenth century in England the plague was killing, at its worst, thousands every week. London theatres closed. With his wife Joan's step-father Phillip Henslowe (businessman and owner of the Rose Theatre, who also had a position as 'Groom' to the Royal Court), Edward Alleyn ran the Bear Garden, an old arena near the Swan Theatre in Southwark, London. Alleyn was one of many actors forced to seek work in the provinces...

Bristol, 1st August, 1593

My good sweet mouse,

I commend me heartily to you and to my father, my mother and my sister Bess, hoping in God, though the sickness be round you, yet by his mercy it may escape your house, which by the grace of God it shall; therefore use this course:

Keep your house fair and clean, which I know you will, and every evening throw water before your door and in your back side, and have in your windows good store of rue and herb of grace... and in so doing, no doubt but the Lord will mercifully defend you.

Now, good mouse, I have no news to send you but this: that we have all our health, for which the Lord be praised. I received your letter at Bristol by Richard Couley, for the which I thank you. I have sent you by this bearer, Thomas Pope's kinsman, my white waistcoat, because it is a trouble to me to carry it. Receive it with this letter, and lay it up for me till I come.

If you send any more letters, send to me by the carriers of Shrewsbury, or to Westchester, or to York, to be kept till my Lord Strange's players come. And thus, sweet heart, with my hearty commendation to all our friends, I set from Bristol this Wednesday after Saint James his day, being ready to begin the play of *Harry of Cornwall*. Mouse, do my hearty commendations to Mr. Grigs, his wife, and all his household and to my sister Phillyps.

Your loving husband,

E. Alleyn

[Postscript] Mouse, you send me no news of any things. You should send of your domestical matters, such things as happens at home; as how your distilled water proves, or this or that, or any thing, what you will.

[Post-postscript] And, Jug, I pray you, let my orange tawny stockings of woollen be dyed a very good black against I come home, to wear in the Winter. You sent me not word of my garden, but next time you will; but remember this in any case, that all that bed which was parsley in the month of September you sow it with spinach, for then is the time. I would do it myself, but we shall not come home till Allholland tide. And so, sweet mouse, farewell, and brook our long journey with patience.

The illiterate 'Mouse' made sure her stepfather answered Edward's letter:

London, August, 1593

To my well-beloved Son, Edward Alleyn, one of my Lord Strange's Players, this be delivered with speed.

Well-beloved Son,

After our hearty commendations both I and your mother, and sister Bess, all in general doth heartily commend us unto you; and for your mouse, her commendations comes by itself, which, as it says, comes from her heart and her soul, praying to God day and night for your good health, which truly, to be plain, we do say all, hoping in the Lord Jesus that we shall have again a merry meeting…

Thanks be unto God we are all at this time in good health in our house; but round about us it hath been almost in every house about us, and whole households died, and yet my friend the bailiff doth escape – but he smells monstrously for fear, and dares stay nowhere; for there hath died this last week… of the plague 1135, which has been the greatest that came yet.

And as for other news of this and that I can tell you none, but that Robert Browne's wife in Shoreditch and all her children and household be dead and her doors shut up; and as for your joiner he hath brought you a court cupboard… and says you shall have a good bedstead; and as for your garden it is well, and your spinach bed not forgotten, your orange-coloured stockings dyed. But no market in Smithfield, neither to buy your cloth nor yet to sell your horse, for no man would offer me above four pound for him; therefore I would not sell him but have sent him into the country till you return back again.

This, like poor people rejoicing that the Lord hath encompassed us round and keepeth us all in health, we end, praying to God to send you all good health... and thanks be to God your poor mouse hath not been sick since you went.

Your poor and assured friend till death,

Phillip Henslowe,

Your loving wife till death,

Joan Alleyn

Chelmsford, 2nd May, 1593

My good sweet heart and loving mouse,

I send thee a thousand commendations, wishing thee as well as maybe, and hoping thou art in good health, with my father, mother and sister. I have no news to send thee, but that I thank God we are all well and in health, which I pray God to continue with us in the country, and with you in London. But, mouse, I little thought to hear that which I now hear by you, for it is well known, they say, that you were by my Lord Mayor's officer made to ride in a cart, you and all your fellows, which I am sorry to hear; but you may thank your supporters, your strong legs I mean, that would not carry you away, but let you fall into the hands of such Tarmagants. But, mouse, when I am come home I'll be revenged on them: tell them, mouse.

I bid thee farewell. I prithee send me word how thou dost, and do my hearty commendations to my father, mother and sister, and to thy own self; and so, sweet heart, the Lord bless thee.

From Chelmsford, the 2 of May 1593. Thine ever, and nobody's else, by God of Heaven. Farewell mecho moussin, and mouse, and farewell Bess Dodipoll,

Edward Alleyn

For my well-beloved husband Mr. Edward Alleyn, one of my Lord Strange's players; this be delivered with speed.

Well-beloved son Edward Alleyn,

I and your mother and your sister Bess have all in general our hearty commendations unto you, and very glad to hear of your good health, which we pray God to continue long to his will and pleasure: for we heard that you were very sick at Bath, and that one of your fellows were fain to play your part for you, which was no little grief unto us to hear. But thanks be to God for amendment, for we feared it much, because we had no letter from you when the other wives had letters sent; which made your mouse not to weep a little, but took it very grievously, thinking that you had conceived some unkindness of her, because you were ever wont to write with the first: and I pray ye do so still, for we would all be sorry but to hear as often from you as others do from their friends... I pray you forget not your mouse and us; for you sent in one letter that we returned not answer whether we received them or no, for we received one which you made at Saint James tide, wherein makes mention of your white waistcoat and your lute box and other things which we have received...

Now, son, although long yet at the last, I remember a hundred commendations from your mouse which... prayeth unto the Lord to cease his hand from punishing us with his cross that she might have you at home with her, hoping, hoping then that you should be eased of this heavy labour and toil.

And you said in your letter that she sent you not word how your garden and all your things doth prosper; very well, thanks be to God, for your beans are grown to high-hedge and well-codded, and all other things doth very well. But your tenants... can pay no rent, nor will pay no rent while Michaelmas next, and then we shall have it if we can get it. And likewise your joiner commends him unto you and says he will make you such good stuff and such good pennyworths as he hopeth shall well like you and content you: which I hope he will do, because he says he will prove himself an honest man.

5

And for your good counsel which you gave us in your letter we all thank you, which was for keeping of our house clean and watering of our doors, and strewing our windows with wormwood and rue, which I hope all this we do and more – for we strew it with hearty prayers unto our Lord, which unto us is more available than all things else in the world... Now, son... as for news of the sickness, I cannot send you no just note of it because there is commandment to the contrary; but as I think doth die, within the city and without, of all sicknesses to the number of seventeen or eighteen hundred in one week.

And this, praying to God for your health, I end from London the 14 of August, 1593.

Your loving father and mother to our powers,
Phillip Henslowe
Your loving wife to command till death,
Joan Alleyn

Joan eventually joined her husband on tour. Philip Henslowe continued to run the Rose Theatre and the Bear Garden, occasionally troubling his stepson-in-law and partner with worrying business matters...

London, 26th September, 1598

To my well-beloved son Mr. Edward Alleyn... at Brille, in Sussex,

Son Edward Alleyn,

I have received your letter, the which you sent me by the carrier... I understand you have considered of the words which you and I had between us concerning the Bear Garden, and according to your words you and I and all other friends shall have as much as we can do to bring it unto a good end. Therefore I would willingly that you were at the banquet, for then with our loss I should be the merrier...

Assure you I do not forget now to let you understand news, that I will tell you some, but it is for me hard and heavy: since you were with me I have lost one of my company, which hurteth me greatly – that is Gabriel; for he is slain in Hogsden Fields by the hands of Benjamin Jonson, bricklayer; therefore I would fain have a little of your counsel, if I could.

Thus with hearty commendations to you and my daughter, and likewise to all the rest of our friends, I end.

Your assured friend to my power,

Phillip Henslowe

Five years later, Alleyn left Joan at home again. 'Mouse' missed her husband tremendously. Here, she begs him to return ('... as welcome shall you be with your rags, as if you were in cloth of gold or velvet. Try and see...'):

London, 21st October, 1603

My entire and well-beloved sweet heart, still it joys me and long, I pray God, may I joy to hear of your health and welfare, as you of ours.

Almighty God be thanked, my own self, your self and my mother and whole house are in good health, and about us the sickness doth cease and likely more and more by God's help to cease.

All the companies be come home and well for aught we know, but that Brown of the Boar's Head is dead, and died very poor. He went not into the country at all, and all of your own company as well at their own houses. My father is at the court, but where the court is I know not. I am of your own mind, that it is needless to meet my father at Basing. The uncertainty being as it is, I commend your discretion. It were a sore journey to lose your labour, beside expenses, and change of air might hurt you; therefore you are resolved upon the best course.

For your coming home I am not to advise you, neither will I. Use your own discretion. Yet I long and am very desirous to see you; and my poor and simple opinion is, if it shall please you, you may safely come home. Here is none now sick near us. Yet let it not be as I will, but at your own best liking.

I am glad to hear you take delight in hawking, and though you have worn your apparel to rags, the best is you know where to have better; and as welcome to me shall you be with your rags, as if you were in cloth of gold or velvet. Try and see.

I have paid fifty shillings for your rent for the wharf – the Lord's rent. Mr. Woodward, my Lord's bailiff, was not in town but appointed his deputy who received all the rents. I had witnesses with me at the payment of the money, and have his quittance. But the quittance cost me a groat – they said it was the bailiff's fee. You know best whether you were wont to pay it; if not, they made a simple woman of me...

And so with my humble and hearty commendations to your own self, Mr. Chaloner and his wife with thanks for your kind usage, with my mother's kindest commendations... I end praying Almighty God to bless you for his mercy's sake, and so sweet heart, once more farewell till we meet, which I hope shall not be long. This 21 of October 1603.

[*Postscript*] About a week ago there came a youth who said he was Mr. Francis Chaloner's man and would have borrowed ten shillings. I enquired after the fellow and [*a neighbour*] said he had lent him a horse. I fear me he gulled him, though he gulled not *us*. The youth was a pretty youth and handsome in apparel; we know not what became of him...

And so once more in the heartiest manner farewell,

Your faithful and loving wife,

Joan Alleyn

During the worst of the Plague, Alleyn's business at the Bear Garden, where the entertainments were mainly bear-baiting and bull-baiting, ground to a standstill. However, he survived through provincial touring and, like Henslowe, who went on to build the Hope and Fortune theatres, he became a prosperous and successful man. The songwriter, actor and commentator Charles Dibdin (1745–1814) wrote: 'Alleyn's fortune proceeded no doubt from marrying three wives, each of whom brought a handsome fortune, partly from the success of his theatre, partly from his being keeper of the King's wild beasts, and master of the Royal Bear Garden, and partly from his being a most rigid and penurious economist – which character he so enjoined himself, that he was the first pensioner in his own charity.' Dibdin was a little mealy-mouthed; in fact, Alleyn was a generous and tireless philanthropist, endowing a number of charities, the greatest being the founding of Dulwich College as 'an asylum for the aged and a place of education for orphans'; he called it 'God's Gift College'.

From Richard Jones, fallen upon hard times:

[Undated; c1615]

Mr. Alleyn,

I commend my love and humble duty to you, giving you thanks for your great duty bestowed upon me in my sickness, when I was in great want. God bless you for it, Sir.

This is it: I am to go over beyond the seas with Mr. Brown and the company, but not by his means, for he is put to half a share and to stay here, for they are all against his going. Now good Sir, as you have ever been my worthy friend, so help me now. I have a suit of clothes and a cloak at pawn for three pound, and if it shall please you to lend me so much to release them, I shall be bound to pray for you so long as I live; for if I go over and I have no clothes, I shall not be esteemed of; and by God's help the first money that I get I will send it over unto you, for here I get nothing – sometimes I have a shilling a day, and sometimes nothing, so that I live in great poverty here.

And so I humbly take my leave, praying to God, I and my wife, for your health and Mistress Alleyn's, which God continue.

Your poor friend to command,

Richard Jones

RECEIVED OF MASTER ALLEYN THE – OF FEBRUARY THE SUM OF –

[Alleyn scribbled across the above]:

'Mr. Jones's letter, whereon I lent him 3.'

9

From William Birde (died in 1624) to Edward Alleyn of the Fortune Company, on the subject of a crooked 'gatherer' (box office assistant):

[1617]

Sir,

There is one John Russell, that by your appointment was made a gatherer with us, but my fellows finding often false to us, have many times warned him from taking the box. And he as often, with most damnable oaths, hath vowed never to touch. Yet, notwithstanding his execrable oaths, he had taken the box, and many times most unconscionably gathered; for which we have resolved he shall never more come to the door. Yet, for your sake, he shall have his wages, to be a necessary attendant on the stage; and if he will pleasure himself and us to mend our garments when he hath leisure, we'll pay him for that, too.

I pray send us word if this motion will satisfy you; for him, his dishonesty is such we know it will not.

Thus yielding our selves in that and far greater matter to be commanded by you, I commit you to God.

Your loving friend to command,

W. Birde

The Elizabethan Box Office: '...Those bound for the galleries paid their pennies at the theatre door, passed through the yard to the ingressus *and made additional payments there and in the rooms, according to the place selected. The custom explains itself by the arrangement between the* sharers *of companies and the* housekeepers *of theatres, which gave the latter a proportion of gallery taking in lieu of rent.*

Gatherers, appointed by the persons interested, collected the money; and although this was put in a locked box, whence the modern term "box office", there were abundant opportunities for fraud. At need, gatherers could serve as supernumeraries on the stage.' (Chambers, Vol. 2)

JAMES BURBAGE (1530/1–1597)

James Burbage was the father of Richard Burbage (1567–1619), thought of as the first leading British actor, and Cuthbert Burbage (Richard's manager) who jointly built the Globe Theatre in 1599.

Theatre Companies, with names like 'The Lord Admiral's Men' or 'The King's Men', depended on the patronage of the aristocracy and royalty, and no job was secure...

3rd January, 1572

To the right honourable *[Robert]* Earl of Leicester, their good Lord and Master,

May it please your honour to understand that forasmuch as there is a certain Proclamation out for the reviving of a Statute as touching retainers, as your Lordship knoweth better than we can inform you thereof:

We therefore, your humble Servants and daily Orators your players, for avoiding all inconvenience that may grow by reason of the said Statute, are bold to trouble your Lordship with this our Suit, humbly desiring your honour that (as you have been always our good Lord and Master) you will now vouchsafe to retain us at this present as your household Servants and daily waiters (not that we mean to crave any further stipend or benefit at your Lordship's hands but our liveries as we have had, and also your Honour's licence to certify that we are your household Servants when we shall have occasion to travel amongst our friends as we do usually once a year, and as other noblemen's players do and have done in time past) whereby we may enjoy our faculty in your Lordship's name as we have done heretofore.

Thus being bound and ready to be always at your Lordship's commandment, we commit your Honour to the tuition of the Almighty.

Long may your Lordship live in peace,
A peer of noblest peers:
In health, wealth and prosperity
Redoubling Nestor's years.

Your Lordship's Servants most bounden,

James Burbage
John Perkinne
John Laneham
William Johnson
Robert Wilson
Thomas Clarke

JOHN FIELD (died 1588)

In England, and subsequently in America, the Puritans saw Players as the Devil's accomplices. The furious John Field was a Calvinist (Presbyterian) London minister. William Shakespeare must have encountered many a John Field, and very likely had such a creature in mind when he created the hypocritical Malvolio in TWELFTH NIGHT.

JOHN FIELD TO ROBERT, EARL OF LEICESTER

[1581]

The more Satan rageth, the more valianter be you under the standard of *Him Who Will Not Be Foiled*. And I humbly beseech your honour to take heed how you give your hand, either in evil causes, or in the behalf of evil men, as of late you did for *players – to the great grief of all the godly.*

Robert Dudley, Earl of Leicester (1532/3–1588), was a courtier, a diplomat and finally a general. Thought for a time to be a potential husband for Queen Elizabeth I, he eventually sought support from the Puritans for another match, this time with Mary, Queen of Scots. This failed, too. He married twice, in each case the circumstances regarded with suspicion by his enemies. (His first wife 'fell down the stairs'; there were ugly rumours about his second wife's first husband's death.) His political connection with the Puritan movement was hard to reconcile with his generous patronage of a theatre company (whose leading man was James Burbage, q.v.).

PHILIP GAWDY

The stage has always been a dangerous place for actors – but when you go to see a play you expect to get home in one piece. In 1991 I was in a production of MACBETH at the Open Air Theatre, Regent's Park, when the blade of a sword came loose and flew into the audience during the final fight, injuring a woman seriously. Unfortunately accidents will happen; however, you certainly don't expect to get shot...

16th November, 1587

PHILIP GAWDY TO HIS FATHER

You shall understand of some accidental news here in this town though myself no witness thereof, yet I may be bold to verify it for an assured truth.

My Lord Admiral's men and players having a device in their play to tie one of their fellows to a post and so to shoot him to death... one of the player's hands swerved, his piece being charged with bullet, missed the fellow he aimed at and killed a child and a woman great with child forthwith, and hurt an other man in the head very sore.

How they will answer it I do not study, unless their profession were better, but in Christianity I am very sorry for the chance; but God's judgements are not to be searched nor enquired of at man's hands.

And yet I find by this an old proverb verified: *there never comes more hurt than comes of fooling...*

I did twice or thrice meet a silent woman there called Mrs.Tylney; she was very troublesome to my Uncle, and much fallen out with one of his men. If she reporteth any news of travellers, believe her not because her news is dire like herself...

An accident with gunpowder burned down the original Globe Theatre in 1613, when wadding from a property cannon set thatching ablaze during a performance of HENRY VIII. The audience escaped unscathed but for one man whose trousers caught fire. He is said to have put out the flames with a bottle of beer.

The Gawdys, 'of West Harling, Norfolk and London', were not a theatrical family, they were gentry. Their only theatrical connection seems to have been that an Elizabeth Gawdy married into the wealthy Hatton family in 1590 – and Lord Chancellor Christopher Hatton (1540–1591), an implacable enemy to the Puritans, was a keen amateur playwright.

ROBERT GREENE (1558/60–1592)

The playwright Robert Greene was reported by his friend the novelist and dramatist Thomas Nashe (c1567–1601) to have died after a 'surfeit of pickle herrings and Rennish wine'. An open letter of repentance, written to his wife, was found attached to his last testament, 'Greene's Groatsworth of Wit', after his death:

15th of November, 1587

The remembrance of the many wrongs offered thee, and thy unreproved virtues, add greater sorrow to my miserable state, than I can utter or thou conceive. Neither is it lessened by consideration of thy absence, (though shame would hardly let me behold thy face) but exceedingly aggravated, for that I cannot (as I ought) to thine own self reconcile myself, that thou mightest witness my inward woe at this instant, that have made thee a woeful wife for so long a time. But equal Heaven hath denied that comfort, giving it at my last need like succour as I have sought all my life: being in this extremity as void of help, as thou hast been of hope.

Reason would, that after so long wast, I should not send thee a child to bring thee greater charge: but consider he is the fruit of thy womb, in whose face regard not the father's fault so much as thy own perfections. He is yet Greene, and may grow straight, if he be carefully tendered: otherwise, apt enough (I fear me) to follow his father's folly. That I have offended thee highly I know, that thou canst forget my injuries I can hardly believe: yet persuade I myself, if thou saw my wretched estate, thou couldst not but lament it: nay certainly I know thou wouldst.

All my wrongs muster themselves before me, every evil at once plagues me. For my contempt of God, I am contemned of men: for my swearing and forswearing, no man will believe me: for my gluttony, I suffer hunger: for my drunkenness, thirst: for my adultery, ulcerous sores.

Thus God hath cast me down, that I might be humbled: and punished me for example of other sinners: and although he strangely suffers me in this world to perish without succour, yet trust I in the world to come to find mercy, by the merits of my Saviour to whom I commend thee, and commit my soul.

Thy repentant husband for his disloyalty,

Robert Greene

Foelicem fuisse infaustum.

Also from the Groatsworth of Wit (1592), an open letter of advice from Greene to his 'fellow scholars about this city' (believed to be Marlowe, Nashe and Peele) with what might be an attack on Shakespeare, the 'upstart crow':

Base-minded men all three of you, if by my misery you be not warned: for unto none of you (like me) sought those burrs to cleave: those puppets (I mean) that spake from our mouths, those antics garnished in our colours. Is it not strange that I, to whom they all have been beholding; is it not like that you, to whom they all have been beholding, shall (were ye in that case as I am now) be both at once of them forsaken? Yes, trust them not: for there is an upstart crow, beautified with our feathers, that with his tiger's heart wrapped in a player's hide supposes he is as well able to bombast out a blank verse as the best of you; and, being an absolute Johannes Factotum, is in his own conceit the only Shake-scene in a country.

APHRA BEHN (1640–1689)

Aphra Behn (who signed her letters 'Astrea'), poet, novelist and playwright, was the first English woman to earn her living solely as a writer. (OROONOKO – OR THE HISTORY OF THE ROYAL SLAVE, THE FORC'D MARRIAGE, THE ROVER). After the death in 1666 of her husband, a London merchant of Dutch extraction, she was sent by King Charles II on secret service in the Netherlands during the Dutch War.

She receives an ardent love letter from a Dutch admirer:

FROM VAN BRUIN, MERCHANT:

[Undated]

Most Transcendent Charmer,

I have strove often to tell you the Tempests of my Heart, and with my own Mouth scale the Walls of your Affections, but terrified with the Strength of your Fortifications, I concluded to make more regular Approaches, and first attack you at a farther Distance, and try first what a Bombardment of Letters wou'd do; whether these Carcasses of Love, thrown into the Sconces of your Eyes, wou'd break into the midst of your Breast, beat down the Court of Guard of your Aversion, and blow up the Magazine of your Cruelty, that you might be brought to a Capitulation, and yield up on reasonable Terms.

Believe me, I love thee more than Money; for indeed thou art more beautiful than the *Oar of Guinea*; and I had rather discover that *terra incognito* than all the Southern *incognita* of *America*: Oh! thou art beautiful in every part, as a goodly Ship under sail from the *Indies*. Thy Hair is like her flowing Pennons as she enters the Harbour, and thy Forehead bold and fair as her Prow; thy eyes bright and terrible as her Guns, thy Nose like her Rudder, that steers my desires, thy Mouth the well-wrought Mortar, whence the Granado's of thy Tongue are shot into the Gun room of my Heart, and shatter it to pieces; thy Teeth are the Grappling Irons that fasten me to my ruin, and of which I wou'd get clear in vain; thy Neck is curious and small, like the very Top mast Head, beneath which thy lovely Bosom spreads itself like the Main-sail before the Wind: thy Middle's taper as the Bolt-sprit, and thy Shape as slender and upright as the Main-mast; thy Back-parts like the gilded carv'd Stern, that jets over the Waters, and thy Belly, with the Perquisites thereunto belonging, the Hold of the Vessel, where all the rich Cargo lies under Hatches; thy Thighs, Legs, and Feet, the steady Keel that is ever under Water. Oh! that I could once see thy Keel above Water!

And is it not pity that so spruce a Ship shou'd be unman'd [sic], shou'd lie in the Harbour for want of her Crew! Ah, let me be the Pilot to steer her by the *Cape of Good Hope*, for the *Indies* of Love.

But Oh! Fair *English Woman*! Thou art rather a Fire-ship gilded, and sumptuous without, and driven before the Wind to set me on Fire; for thy Eyes indeed are like that – destructive, tho', like Brandy, bewitch-ing: Alas! they have grappl'd my Heart, my Fore-castle's on Fire, my Sails and Tackling are caught, my upper Deck's are consum'd, and nothing but the Water of Despair keeps the very Hulk from the Combustion, so you have left it only in my Choice, to drown or burn. O! for Pity's sake, take some Pity, for thy Compassion is more desire-able [sic] than a strong Gale, when we are got to the Wind-ward of a *Sally-man*; your Eyes I say again, and again, like a Chain-shot, have brought the Main-mast of my Resolution by the board, cut all the Rigging of my Discretion and Interest, blown up the Powder-Room of my Affections, and flatter'd all the Hulk of my Bosom, so that without the planks of your pity, I must inevitably sink to the bottom. This is the deplorable Condition, Transcendent Beauty, of your *Undone Vessel*,

Van Bruin

Aphra Behn, The 'Transcendent Charmer', lost no time in replying, mentioning in her Memoirs: 'To this I return'd this following ridiculous Answer, which I insert to give you a better Picture of my Lover's Intellects:'

APHRA BEHN TO MINHEER VAN BRUIN, MERCHANT:

[Undated]

Extraordinary Sir,

I receiv'd your Extraordinary Epistle, which has had extraordinary Effects, I assure you, and was not read without an extraordinary Pleasure. I never doubted the Zeal of your Countrymen in making new Discoveries; in fixing new Trades; in supplanting their Neighbours; and in engrossing the Wealth and Traffic of both the *Indies*; but, I confess, I never expected so wise a Nation shou'd at last set out for the *Island of Love*; I thought that had been a *Terra del Fuege* in all their Charts, and avoided like Rocks and Quick-sands; nay, I shou'd as soon have suspected them guilty of becoming Apostles to the *Samaoids [probably 'Samanids' or 'Samanoids', a Moslem sect in the Middle East]*, and of Preaching the Gospel to the *Laplanders*, where there is nothing to be got, and for which Reason the very Jesuits deny 'em Baptism, as of setting out for so unprofitable a Voyage as *Love*.

Hark ye, good Sir, have you thoroughly consider'd what you have done? Have you reflected on the sad Consequences of declaring your self a Lover; nay, and an old Lover too to a young Woman? To a Woman that wou'd expect all the Duties of *Gallantry*, ev'n from a young Servant; but great, and terrible Works of Supererogation from an antiquated Admirer? Have you enough examined what Degrees of Generosity *Love* necessarily inspires? That Foe to Interest? That Hereditary Enemy of your Country? Nay, have you thought whether by holding this Correspondence with Love, you may not be declar'd a Rebel, an Enemy to your Country, and be brought into Suspicion of greater Intelligence with the *French*, by entertaining their Gallantry and Love, than *de Wit*, by all his Intrigues with that *Monarch*? I confess I tremble for you.

Alas! alas! How deplorable a Spectacle wou'd it be to these eyes, to see that agreeable Bulk dismember'd by the enrag'd Rabble, and Scollops of your Flesh sold by Fish-wives for Gelders and Duckatoons!

Have you maturely consider'd the evil Example you set your Neighbours, who may be influenc'd by a Person of your Port and Figure? And shou'd the Evil by this Means spread, *Holland* were undone, for then there were some Danger of Honesty's spreading, and then good-night the best Card in all your Hands for the winning the Game and Money of *Europe*! Lord, Sir, think, what a dreadful thing it is to be the Ruin of one's Country! But, if public evils don't affect you, have you set before the Eyes of your Understanding, the Charge of fitting out such a Vessel (as you have made me) for the *Indies* of Love? and I fear the Profits will never answer the Expense of the Voyage.

There are Ribbons and Hoods for my Pennons; Diamond Rings, Lockets, and Pearl-Necklaces for my Guns of Offence and Defence; Silks, Holland, Lawn, Cambrick, &c for Rigging; Gold and Silver Laces, Imbroideries and Fringes fore and aft for my Stern, and for my Prow; rich Perfumes, Paint and Powder, for my Ammunition; Treats, rich Wines, expensive Collations, Gaming Money, Pin-Money, with a long Et-cetera for my Cargo; and Balls, Masks, Plays, Walks, Airing in the Country, and a Coach and Six, for my fair Wind. You may see by my concern for your Interest and Person, that the Approaches you have made, have not been a little successful, and if you are but as furious a Warrior when you come to storm, as you are at a Bombardment, the Lord have Mercy upon me.

But to deal ingeniously with you, I doubt your Prowess in two or three particular Retrenchments, which I fear you'll hardly be able to gain. There is first your *Age*, a formidable Bastion you'll scarce carry; then your mighty Bulk will, with the last Difficulties, be brought to treat with my Love; but what is yet more dreadful, your Treachery to *Vander Albert* is a Fort that must prove impregnable; if any thing can be so to such *Pen* and such a *Head*. But if you carry the Town by dint of Valour, I hope you'll allow me Quarter, and be as merciful to me as you are stout, and then I shall not fail of being, Extraordinary Sir,

Your Humble Servant,

Astrea

THE LORD CHAMBERLAIN

The first entrance of our Lord Chamberlain, who makes several more appearances over the next three hundred years...

In 1680 the company of players known as 'The King's Men' planned a visit to Oxford – a trip previously disallowed. They appealed to the Lord Chamberlain, who wrote discreetly to the Vice Chancellor:

Windsor Castle, May 15th, 1680

For the Reverend Doctor Timothy Haughton, Vice Chancellor of the University of Oxford:

Reverend Sir,

His Majesty's Comedians having obtained His leave to go and air themselves in the Country, now he have no need of their attendance at Court, and believing no air better than that at Oxford, having likewise prevailed with His Majesty to command me to recommend them to your Protection, that they may represent some of their good Plays for some convenient time before the University.

I do very heartily do it, assuring myself that for the Character and Privilege they have of being His Majesty's sworn servants, and for being men of letters, you will be pleased to afford them all the favour that shall be necessary towards their security, whilst they are there, which they promise they shall not abuse in any degree.

I am with much truth, Reverend Sir,
Your most Affectionate and humble Servant,
Arlington

Despite the letter, it turned out that Haughton planned to invite a different company. The King's Men appealed to the King directly and the Lord Chamberlain wrote again, rather more forcefully:

Windsor Castle

Reverend Sir,

I wrote to you on May the 15th recommending to your favour and protection His Majesty's Comedians, who having since complained to Him that there is another Company of the same Profession, whose admittance to the University will frustrate them of the Profit they promised themselves under His Majesty's name, His Majesty hath commanded me to let you know His Pleasure that He would have His own Comedians *only* gratified with this favour – they needing such an Extraordinary Encouragement to repair them for some misfortunes lately befallen them, and persuading Himself they can singly afford the University as much divertissement as their vacancy from their studies will admit of...

Your most Affectionate and humble Servant,

Arlington

THOMAS BETTERTON (1635–1710)

Thomas Betterton, actor, manager, playwright, was the most significant theatrical figure in England between the times of Burbage and Garrick (q.v.). Archbishop Tillotson of Lambeth once asked Betterton why he, an actor, appeared to move his audience more than ever the Archbishop could his congregation. Betterton replied, 'That is easily accounted for. It is because you are telling them a story, and I am showing them facts.'

Company problems were dealt with at the highest level:

Windsor Castle
May 7th, 1681

Mr. Betterton,

I did yesterday signify unto you that Mrs. Norris should be received into your Company again, and this is to explain that order.

That it is His Majesty's Pleasure that she reconcile herself unto her adversary, and submit herself to the rules and Government of the Company and upon this occasion she is to be admitted as formerly.

Arlington,
Lord Chamberlain

Windsor Castle,
March 8, 1689

Mr. Knight,

My Lord Chamberlain would have you to summon Mr. Downes, prompter at Their Majesties' Theatre, to appear on Monday morning next by Nine of the Clock, it being the time His Lordship hath appointed to hear the difference between Mr. Killigrew and Mrs. Currer.

Richard Coling
(For the Lord Chamberlain)

1700 ~ 1800

ALEXANDER POPE

JONATHAN SWIFT

DAVID GARRICK

RICHARD BRINSLEY SHERIDAN

PEGGY WOFFINGTON

KITTY CLIVE

HANNAH MORE

VOLTAIRE

DORA JORDAN

FANNY BURNEY

SARAH SIDDONS

GEORGE COLMAN

AND OTHERS...

ALEXANDER POPE (1688–1744)
DR JONATHAN SWIFT (1667–1745)

John Gay (born 1688), who wrote THE BEGGAR'S OPERA, died in 1732. Two of the greatest satirists of all time mourn the loss of a friend...

5 December, 1732

It is not a time to complain that you have not answered my two letters (in the last of which I was impatient under some fears). It is not now indeed a time to think of myself, when one of the nearest and longest ties I have ever had is broken all of a sudden by the unexpected death of Mr. Gay. Good God! How often are we to die before we go quite off this stage?

In every friend we lose a part of ourselves, and the best part. God keep those we have left! Few are worth praying for, and one's self the least of all.

I shall never see you now, I believe; one of your principal calls to England is at an end. Indeed he was the most amiable by far; his qualities were the gentlest; but I love you as well and as firmly. Would to God the man we have lost had not been so amiable, nor so good! But that is a wish for our own sakes, not for his. Sure, if innocence and integrity can deserve happiness, it must be his. Adieu; I can add nothing to what you will feel, and diminish nothing from it. Yet write to me and soon.

Believe no man now living loves you better; I believe no man ever did that.

Alexander Pope

Dublin, 1733

I received yours with a few lines from the Doctor, and the account of our losing Mr. Gay, upon which event I shall say nothing. I am only concerned that long living hath not hardened me. For even in this Kingdom and in a few days past, two persons of great merit, whom I loved very well, have died in the prime of their years but a little above thirty.

I would endeavour to comfort myself upon the loss of friends, as I do upon the loss of money, by turning to my account book and seeing whether I have enough left for my support; but in the former case I find I have not, any more than in the other; and I know not any man who is in a greater likelihood than myself to die poor and friendless.

You are a much greater loser than me by his death, as being a more intimate friend, and often his companion – which latter I could never hope to be, except perhaps once more in my life for a piece of a summer. I hope he hath left you the care of any writings he may have left, and I wish that, with those already extant, they could be all published in a fair edition under your inspection.

Jonathan Swift

DAVID GARRICK (1717–1779)

It is little known that David Garrick started out as a Wine Merchant. After his triumphant debut in Colly Cibber's version of Shakespeare's RICHARD III on Monday, Oct. 19, 1741 at Goodman's Field, David Garrick writes to his brother Peter about a change of career…

October, 1741

I received my shirt safe and am now to tell you what I suppose you may have heard of before this. But before I let you into my affair, 'tis proper to premise some things, that I may appear less culpable in your opinion than I might otherwise do.

I have made an Exact Estimate of my stock of wine, and what money I have out at interest, and find that since I have been a Wine Merchant I have run out near four hundred pounds, and trade not increasing. I was very sensible some way must be thought of to redeem it. My mind (as you must know) has been always inclin'd to the Stage; nay, so strongly so that all my Illness and lowness of Spirits was owing to my want of resolution to tell you my thoughts when here; finding at last both my Inclination and Interest requir'd some new way of Life, I have chose the most agreeable to myself; and though I know you will be much displeas'd at me, yet I hope when you shall find that I have the genius for an actor without the vices, you will think less severe on me, and not be asham'd to own me for a Brother.

Last night I played the Richard the Third to the surprise of Everybody; and as I shall make very near £300 per annum by it, and as it is really what I dote upon, I am resolv'd to pursue it. Pray write me an answer immediately.

[No signature]

[Postscript]: I have a farce, *Ye Lying Varlet*, coming out at Drury Lane.

Most people thought Thomas Sheridan (1721–1788) a reasonably talented actor and teacher; he was a respected authority on 'pronunciation'. The biographer James Boswell (1740–1795) reports, however, that one of Garrick's tutors, the scholar Samuel Johnson (1709–1784) had other opinions: 'Why, Sir, Sherry is dull, naturally dull… What influence can he have upon the language of this great country…? Sir, it is burning a farthing candle at Dover to show light at Calais.'

Thomas was the father of playwright Richard Brinsley Sheridan (1751–1815, q.v.). The first night (May 8, 1777) of 25-year-old Richard's masterpiece, THE SCHOOL FOR SCANDAL, was a triumph. The playwright only managed to gain a licence for the play through his personal friendship with the Lord Chamberlain. Sheridan reported to Lord Byron later that after the opening night celebrations he was 'knocked down and put in the watch-house for making a row in the streets, and for being found intoxicated by the watchman.'

A few days afterwards, he received some advice in this letter from David Garrick (Garrick always referred to Sheridan's wife as 'The Saint'):

DAVID GARRICK TO RICHARD BRINSLEY SHERIDAN

Mr. Garrick's best wishes and compliments to Mr. Sheridan. How is the Saint today? A gentleman who is as mad as myself about the 'School' remarked that the characters upon the stage at the falling of the screen stand too long before they speak; – I thought so too the first night: he said it was the same on the 2nd., and was remark'd by others; tho' they should be astonish'd, and a little petrify'd, yet it may be carry'd to too great a length.

All praise at Lord Lucan's last night!

I have worked with writers who adapt and change scripts throughout rehearsals. This can be either very rewarding or a considerable problem for the actor. Sheridan worked on the script of THE SCHOOL FOR SCANDAL until the last moment of rehearsal, giving the actors their parts in pieces as they were written. The last leaf of the prompter's copy of this first production is endorsed:

'Finished at last! Thank God! R. B. Sheridan.'

'Amen! William Hopkins.' *[Prompter]*

RICHARD BRINSLEY SHERIDAN (1751–1816)

In the midst of legal problems at Drury Lane Theatre, Sheridan is distracted by his youngest son's poor health. He writes to his solicitor:

R. Wilson Esq., Lincoln's Inn Fields

[Undated]

My dear Wilson,

My son will explain to you my situation. Called away a few hours after I saw you last to Polesden, where I found our sweet boy Charles in a Scarlet Fever. I am near almost hopeless of him...

Yours in great haste and fervour,

R.B.S.

[Postscript] The boy's death would kill his mother.

Richard Brinsley Sheridan was devoted to his wife. Away from home he wrote every few days, referring to himself as 'Dan' and his wife as 'Hecca'...

Devizes, July 29th, 1796
Friday

Mrs. Sheridan,
Dean of Winchester's,
St. Mary's,
Southampton,

Beloved of Dan's Soul,

I must write you a Line tho' we have parted but a very few Hours. But no Post will leave Bath tomorrow and you will think me lost. I am anxious to entreat you not to forget your promise – not to drive alone, and to ride, if ride at all, only with John and *only Pantaloon [the best horse]*. I rely on you, and am even afraid of some accident with these Precautions...

Ma'am all our Liveliness is gone since you left our Party.

Your true

R.B.S.

The Sheridans bought the mansion of Polesden, Great Bookham, advertised in the Morning Chronicle, *4 July 1796, as 'in a prime and sporting part of Surrey', for £12,384...*

1–2 August *[1796]*
Monday night.

O Ma'am, Dan is *Lemoncholy* as a yew-tree in a Church-yard. All alone – no sweet Hecca near him and no happy certainty that he can go to her in two minutes if he chose – the only feeling that can sometimes justify staying away a little. So the best I can do is to write a little to my beloved. I have been doing quantities of business today and I truly have been and truly will be sober as a Judge.

I have every hour some new reason to be satisfied with our Purchase... I hear of nothing but congratulations or envy at my Bargain. My negotiation for the lovely Farm adjoining goes on well – and we shall have the nicest Place within a prudent distance from Town in England. And sweet Hecca shall have a House after her own Fancy, and it shall be a seat of Health and Happiness – where she shall chirp like a bird, bound like a Fawn and grow fat as *[a]* little pig, and we shall get rid of all the nasty Servants and have all good and do all good round us.

The thought and plan of this is my Hope and Happiness, and puts all dismal thoughts from me, and I can never visit Bath without laying in a store of them. O me, it is a place where every Spot in it and round it leads to some interesting and melancholy recollection.

But you my Angel, you, and you only, could have done it, have brought Peace and cheerfulness to a restless and harassed Heart. You are its resting place and Delight – every hour and more...

Tuesday morn:

A thousand Thanks my own dear Wench for your Letter just arrived– Hecca's kind words make Dan's Heart Glad.

But O you little sly Beast, how you want to cajole me about your driving. So John is harassed at your skill is he? Now you little Jade if you do nothing but drive behind and follow the Track of his Curricle, what opportunity has he of seeing your Skill! I must beat you...

Yes Dearest give away the Dog if you think it best...

Tuesday night:

My own Hecca I could not get home in Time to get this Letter for the Post and now I am come from a sad melancholy Scene. You will be very sorry to hear that the Duchess of D., after suffering all sorts of cruel Operations, will certainly lose one eye...

Heaven bless and guard my Hecca!

R.B.S.

The Duchess he writes of was the Duchess of Devonshire, of whom Horace Walpole wrote (9th. Aug., 1796): 'The Duchess of Devonshire has been in great danger of losing her sight, by catching cold very indiscreetly. They have saved her eyes by almost strangling her with a handkerchief, and forcing all the blood up into her head, and then bleeding her with leeches...' (Journals and Correspondence of Miss Berry, *edited Lewis, 1865*)

PEGGY WOFFINGTON (1717–1760)
DAVID GARRICK (1717–1779)

The Irish actress Peggy Woffington's memorial in Teddington Church gives her date of birth as October 18, 1720. Most scholars believe her to have been born in 1717, some as early as 1714; she died in 1760. As a leading actress she specialised in a 'breeches' performance; her most famous rôle was that of Sir Harry Wildair in THE CONSTANT COUPLE (or A TRIP TO THE JUBILEE) by Farquhar. Charles Dibdin wrote: 'She greatly excelled in comic characters, but I cannot think it an addition to her fame, or to female delicacy, that the most prominent of these characters was SIR HARRY WILDAIR.'

Peggy Woffington writes to a young man who has caught her eye. She has heard from his father that the boy has come home, perhaps from overseas, perhaps tanned by the sun, and is to take up employment...

TO MASTER THOMAS ROBINSON AT GOODWOOD IN SUSSEX

Saturday, 19th November, 1743

[Date disputed: possibly December 18, 1742]

My pretty little Oroonoko –

I'm glad to hear of your safe arrival in Sussex and that you are so well placed in the noble family of Richmond &c.; for which I have the most profound regard and respect. Sir Thomas Robinson writes me word that you are very pretty, which has raised my curiosity to a great pitch and it makes me long to see you.

I hear the acting-poetaster is with you still at Goodwood and has had the insolence to brag of favours from me – Vain coxcomb! I did indeed by the persuasion of Mr. Swiney and his assistance answer the simpleton's nauseous letter – foh!

He did well, truly, to throw my letter into the fire, otherwise it must have made him appear more ridiculous than his *amour* at Bath did or his cudgel-playing with the rough Irishman. Saucy Jackanapes! To give it for a reason for the burning of my letter that there were expressions in it too passionate and tender to be shewn.

I did in an ironical way (which the booby took in a literal sense) compliment both myself and him on the successes we shared mutually on his first appearance on the stage, and that which he had (all to himself) in the part of Carlos in *Love Makes a Man,* when with an undaunted modesty he withstood the attack of his foes armed with cat-calls and other offensive weapons.

I did indeed give him a little double meaning touch on the expressive and graceful motion of his hands and arms as assistants to his energetic way of delivering the poet's sentiments, and which he must have learned from the youthful manner of spreading plasters when he was apprentice. There; these I say were the true motives to his burning the letter and no passionate expressions of mine.

I play the part of Sir Harry Wildair to night, and can't recollect what I said to the impertinent monster in my letter, nor have I time to say any more now, but you shall hear from me by the next post; and if Swiney has a copy of it, or I can recover the chief articles in it ye shall have 'em.

I am (my Dear Black boy)

With my duty to their Graces,

Your admirer and humble Servant,

Margaret Woffington

Saturday, November 19th, 1743

The 'Swiney' Peggy Woffington refers to in this her only surviving letter was Mr McSwiney, who afterwards became one of her most devoted admirers. He was the founder manager of the 'little house', Haymarket, a precarious Summer Theatre; he paid £5 a day rent. It is possible that the vainglorious ex-plasterer 'Jackanapes' was the actor Hallam, who sometimes played the rôle of Carlos.

Peggy Woffington enjoyed a close relationship with the great David Garrick (q.v.). As young actors, they lived together in Bow Street...

March 3

My dear never to be forgotten Peg,

Altho' we have dissolved partnership, still will the glorious attractions which accompany thy fascinating performance of the character of Sir Harry Wildair never be erased from my mind.

In the still hours of the night, when the arduous toils of the day are over, thoughts of thee will still be with me. O think, Peg, of the many

32

delicious nights we've passed together. I often wish my tongue had been blistered before I uttered the words which caused you to say that thy smock should never be rubb'd by my shirt again. I was frantic when you left me never to return.

Now dear Peg, by the remembrance of so many blissful hours we have pass'd together, forgive one who has ever had a tender memory of thee since parting.

Let bygones be bygones and bury in oblivion the past.

Send me, as thou love me, a kind answer to

Thy Repentant

David Garrick

They shared the rent and household costs, paying alternate months. During Peggy's months the entertaining was more generous; it might have been Garrick's famous parsimony that drew them apart eventually. For a while she lived in Paris, where she met Voltaire (q.v.).

KITTY CLIVE (1711–1785)

Another friend of Garrick's was the hilarious 'character actress' Catherine (Kitty) Clive, who performed at Drury Lane regularly for forty years, retiring in 1769. Tate Wilkinson (q.v.) said 'Mrs Clive was a mixture of combustibles; she was passionate, cross, vulgar, yet sensible, a very sensible woman, and as a comic actress of genuine worth – indeed, indeed she was a diamond of the first water... [she] was universally encored, and she came off the stage much sweetened in temper and manners from her first going on.' Garrick called her 'Clivy-Pivy', or just 'Pivy'...

CATHERINE CLIVE TO DAVID GARRICK

Twickenham, 1774

Sir,

I *schreamed* at your parish business. I think I see you in your church-wardenship quarrelling for not making those brown loaves big enough; but for God's sake never think of being a Justice of the Peace, for the people will quarrel on purpose to be brought before you to hear you talk, so we may have as much business upon the lawn as you had upon the boards. If I should live to be thawed, I will come to town on purpose to kiss you; and in the Summer, as you say, I hope we shall see each other ten times as often, when we will talk, and dance, and sing, and send our hearers laughing to their beds...

O jealousy, thou raging pain,
Where shall I find my peace again?

I am in a great fuss. Pray what is the meaning of a quarter of a hundred Miss Moors coming purring about you with their poems and plays and romances? [*probably a reference to playwright Hannah More, q.v.*] What? Is the Pivy to be roused, and I don't understand it? Mrs. Garrick has been so good to say she would spare me a little corner of your heart, and I can tell the Miss Moors they shall not have one morsel of it...

Here have I two letters, and not one mine – nay, you write to the Poulterer's woman rather than the Pivy, and order her to bring me the note! And the poor creature is so proud of a letter from you that it has quite turned her head, and instead of picking her Poultry she is dancing about the shop with a wisp of straw in her hand like the poor Ophelia, singing:

How should I your true love know?

And I must tell you, if you don't write to me *directly* and tell me a great deal of news, I believe I shall sing the next of the mad songs myself.

...your

Pivy Clive

CATHERINE CLIVE TO MISS POPE *[Presumably Jane Pope (1742–1818), who at 14 years old had attended Garrick's acting classes for children at Drury Lane, and whose father was barber-in-ordinary and wig-maker to the actors at Drury Lane. She played in his 1756 production of LILLIPUT, in which all characters except Gulliver were played by children, and went on to become a leading actress. Astonishingly she was in continuous employment from 1756 to 1808, except for the season 1775–6. When Kitty Clive died, 'Popy' erected a monument to her friend in Twickenham churchyard. Jane Pope was, at her death, the last surviving female member of Garrick's company.]*

Twickenham, October 17, 1784

My dear Popy,

The jack *[a contrivance for turning a spit]* I must have, and I suppose the cook will be as much delighted with it as a fine lady with a birth-day suit. I send you walnuts, which are fine, but pray be moderate in your admiration for they are dangerous dainties. John has carried about to my neighbours above six thousand, and he tells me there are as many left; indeed it is a most wonderful tree.

Mrs. Prince has been robbed at two o'clock, at noon, of her gold watch and four guineas, and at the same time our two Justices of sixpence a-piece ; they had like to be shot, for not having more.

Everybody enquires after you, and I deliver your compliments. Poor Mrs. Hart is dead – well spoken of by everybody. I pity the poor old Weasel that is left behind.

Adieu my dear Popy,

Yours ever,

C. Clive

[Postscript] The jack must carry six or seven-and-twenty pounds. The waterman shall bring the money when I know what.

A loving tribute, followed by a bit of gossip, to David Garrick:

CATHERINE CLIVE TO DAVID GARRICK

Twickenham, June 23, 1776

Dear Sir,

Is it really true that you have put an end to the glory of Drury Lane Theatre? *If it is so,* let me congratulate my dear Mr. and Mrs. Garrick on their approaching happiness. I *know* what it will be: you cannot yet have an idea of it; *but* if you should still be so wicked not to be satisfied with that *unbounded,* uncommon degree of fame you have received as an actor, and which no other actor ever did receive – nor no other actor ever *can* receive – I say, if you should still long to be dipping your fingers in their theatrical pudding (now without plums), you will be no Garrick for the Pivy.

In the height of public admiration for you – when you were never mentioned with any other appellation but Mr. Garrick the charming man, the fine fellow, the delightful creature, both by men and ladies, when they were admiring everything you did and everything you scribbled – at this very time *the Pivy* was a living witness that they did not know, nor could they be sensible of, half your perfections.

I have seen you with your magical hammer in your hand, endeavouring to beat your ideas into the heads of creatures who had none of their own. I have seen you with lamb-like patience endeavouring to make them comprehend you, and I have seen you when that could not be done. I have seen your lamb turned into a lion. By this your great labour and pains, the public was entertained; they thought they all acted very fine; they did not see you pull the wires.

There are people now on the stage to whom you gave their consequence; they think themselves very great. Now let them go on in their new parts without your leading-strings, and they will soon convince the world what this genius is. I have always said this to everybody, even when your horses and mine were at their highest prancing. While I was under your control I did not say half the fine things I thought of you, because it looked like flattering, and you know your Pivy was always proud, because I thought you did not like me then, but now I am sure you do, which made me send this letter.

Pivy Clive

Twickenham, June 10, 1778

A thousand, and a thousand, and *ten* thousand thanks to my Dear Mr. Garrick for his goodness and attention to his Pivy for the care he took in making her friends happy. Happy? That word is not high enough. *Felicity*, I think, will do much better to express their Joy when they found they were to see the Garrick – whom they had never seen before!

And yet I must tell you, your Dear busy head had like to have Ruin'd your good design, for you dated your note *Monday*, four o'clock, and *tomorrow*, you said, was to be the play. And pray who do you think set it right? Why, your blunder-headed Jemmy *[her brother]*. I did not receive your letter till Wednesday morning, so they was to set out for the play on *Thursday* – but Jemmy, poring over your Epistle, found out your Mistake, and away he flew to Mr. Shirley's with your Letter and the news paper from the Coffee house, to let the Ladies see the play was that day. This was between one and two.

Mrs. Shirley ordered the horses to the Coach that Moment, and bid the Misses fly up and dress, for they must go without dinner. Dinner? *Dinner?* Lord, they did not want dinner! And away they went... everything happened right. They got their places without the least trouble or difficulty, and liked everything they saw except the Garrick. They didn't see Much in him. (You may reverse it if you please and assure yourself They Liked Nothing Else! They think themselves under Such obligations to Me, for my goodness to them, that We are all invited to dine there today - when I shall give *you* for My toast!)

Have you not heard of the adventures of your poor Pivy? I have been *robbed and murdered* coming from Kingston! Jemmy and I were in a post. She was stopped at half past nine just by Teddington Church. I only lost a little Silver and my Senses – for one of them Came into the Carriage with a great horse pistol to Search me for my Watch! But I had it not with me. But your Jemmy lost his; he was ten times more frightened than I was, but he denies it – says it was only for Me. However, after we came home and had frighted Mrs. Mestivier, we sat down to Supper – and I don't know that I ever Laughed more in My Life!

I hope my dear Mrs. Garrick is well. I will not say anything about *you*, for they say you are in such spirits that you intend playing until next September!

Adieu My Dear Sir, be assured I am ever

Yours,

Pivy Clive

HANNAH MORE (1745–1833)

David Garrick died in January of 1779. In a letter to her sister, the poet, philanthropist and playwright Hannah More, author of SACRED DRAMAS (see also Kitty Clive), describes his funeral...

HANNAH MORE TO HER SISTER

Adelphi, February 2, 1779...

We (Miss Cadogan and myself) went to Charing Cross to see the melancholy procession. Just as we got there, we received a ticket from the Bishop of Rochester to admit us into the Abbey. No admittance could be obtained but under his hand.

We hurried away in a hackney coach, dreading to be too late. The bell of St. Martin's and the Abbey gave a sound that smote upon my very soul. When we got to the cloisters, we found multitudes striving for admittance. We gave our ticket and were let in; but, unluckily, we ought to have kept it. We followed the man, who unlocked a door of iron, and directly closed it upon us and two or three others, and we found ourselves in a tower, with a dark, winding staircase, consisting of half a hundred stone steps.

When we got to the top, there was no way out; we ran down again, called, and beat the door, till the whole pile resounded with our cries. Here we stayed half an hour in perfect agony; we were sure it would be all over: nay, we might never be let out; we might starve – we might perish!

At length our clamours brought an honest man, a guardian angel I then thought him. We implored him to take care of us, and get us into a part of the Abbey whence we might see the grave. He asked for the Bishop's ticket; we had given it away to the wrong person; and he was not *obliged* to believe we ever had one; yet he saw so much truth in our grief, that though we were most shabby, and a hundred fine people were soliciting the same favour, he took us under each arm, carried us safely through the crowd, and put us in a little gallery directly over the grave, where we could see and hear everything as distinctly as if the Abbey had been a parlour. Little things sometimes affect the mind strongly! We were no sooner recovered from the fresh bursts of grief, than I cast my eyes the first thing on Handel's monument, and read the scroll in his hand:

I know that my Redeemer liveth.

Just at three the great doors burst open with a noise that shook the roof: the organ struck up, and the whole choir, in strains only less solemn than the Archangel's trump, began Handel's fine anthem. The whole choir advanced to the grave, in hoods and surplices, singing all the way; then Sheridan, as chief mourner; then the body – alas! Whose body? With ten noblemen and gentlemen, pall-bearers; then the rest of the friends and mourners; hardly a dry eye – the very players, bred to the trade of counterfeiting, shed genuine tears.

As soon as the body was let down, the Bishop began the service, which was read in a low but solemn and devout manner. Such an awful stillness reigned that every word was audible. How I felt it! Judge if my heart did not assent to the hope that the soul of our dear brother now departed was in peace. And this is all of Garrick! Yet a very little while, and he shall 'say to the worm, Thou art my brother: and to corruption, Thou art my mother and my sister.'

So passes away the fashion of this world.

And the very night he was buried the playhouses were as full, and the Pantheon was as crowded, as if no such thing had happened; nay, the very mourners of the day partook of the revelries of the night – the *same* night, too!

As soon as the crowd had dispersed, our friend came to us with an invitation from the Bishop's lady, to whom he had related our disaster, to come into the Deanery. We were carried into her dressing room, but, being incapable of speech, she very kindly said she would not interrupt such sorrow, and left us; but sent up wine, cakes, and all manner of good things, which were really well-timed. I caught no cold, notwithstanding all I went through.

On Wednesday night we came to the Adelphi – to this house! She [*Mrs. Garrick*] bore it with great tranquillity. But what was my surprise to see her go alone into the chamber and bed in which he had died that fortnight. She had a delight in it beyond expression. I asked her the next day how she went through it? She told me, 'Very well', that she first prayed with great composure, then went and kissed the dear bed, and got into it with a sad pleasure...

VOLTAIRE (1694–1778)

The French novelist Voltaire (pen-name for François Marie Arouet) has just been apprised of the horrifying news that William Shakespeare's plays are being translated into French...

A Monsieur le Comte d'Argental

19 Juillet 1776

Mon cher ange,

I learn that the ravishing Mme. de Saint-Julien *[Voltaire idolised her, calling her his 'philosophical butterfly']* will soon be in my neck of the woods. If this is true I am all astonishment and joy; but I must at the same time in all honour tell you how implacably furious I am with a certain Tourneur *[Pierre Letourneur (1736–1788), who published his translations of Shakespeare in 20 volumes between 1776 and 1782]*, said to be 'Secretary of the National Library', who certainly does not seem to be the Secretary of Good Taste.

Have you perchance cast an eye over the two volumes this reptile has already written, in which he attempts to make us recognise one Shakespeare as the only model of Real Tragedy? He calls him *'The God of Theatre'*! He sacrifices all Frenchmen, without exception, to this idol, as we once sacrificed pigs to Ceres. He does not deign to name even Corneille and Racine; these two great men – lumped into the general bag without a mention! There are already two published works by this Shakespeare which you would take for the fairground pantomimes of two centuries ago.

This *scribbling* 'Secretary' has even persuaded the King, the Queen and the whole of the Royal Family to buy his trash!

Have you *read* his abominable scrawlings, of which there are another five volumes to come? Do you feel a sufficiently vigorous *hatred* rising in you for this impudent imbecile? Will you permit la France to be affronted thus?... No, you are too soft! In all dear France there are not insults, donkey's bonnets, or pillories enough for the punishment of such an upstart nincompoop. The blood fizzes in my veins just talking to you about him. If you, too, are not aroused to fury I take you for a passionless worm. Frightful though it seems, the monster has a following in France; and, to heap calamity on horror, it was *I* who was the first to speak of this Shakespeare; *I* was the first to show the French the few miserable pearls I found in the enormous dung-hill of his work. To think that I should live to see the day when I, Voltaire, was responsible for knocking the crowns off the noble heads of Racine and Corneille, only to see them adorning the forehead of a barbarian mummer! Try, I beg you, to share my anger; unless you do I sense I am capable of a dreadful deed.

FANNY BURNEY (1752–1840)

It is little known that the novelist and socialite Frances (Fanny) Burney (later Mme D'Arblay) wrote a tragedy in which Sarah Siddons (q.v.) and Charles Kemble (q.v.) appeared. She is chiefly remembered for her witty journal and letters. Here, she gives instruction to her sister-in-law on how to behave in the presence of Royalty…

FANNY BURNEY TO MRS BURNEY

Windsor, December 17, 1785

My dearest Hetty,

I am sorry I could not more immediately write, but I have not had a moment since your last.

Now I know what your next want is, to hear accounts of Kings, Queens and such royal personages. O no! Do you so? Well.

Shall I tell you a few matters of fact? Or had you rather a few matters of etiquette? Oh, matters of etiquette, you cry! For matters of fact are short and stupid, and anybody can tell, and everybody is tired of them.

Very well, take your own choice.

To begin, then, with the beginning… I shall give you those instructions I have received myself, that should you find yourself in the royal presence, you may know how to comport yourself.

Directions for Coughing, Sneezing or Moving before the King and Queen.

In the first place, you must not *cough*. If you find a cough tickling your throat, you must arrest it from making any sound; if you find yourself choking with the forbearance, you must choke – but not cough.

In the second place, you must not *sneeze*. If you have a vehement cold, you must take no notice of it; if your nose-membranes feel a great irritation, you must hold your breath. If a sneeze still insists on making its way, you must oppose it by keeping your teeth grinding together. If the violence of the repulse breaks a blood vessel, you must break the blood vessel – but not sneeze.

In the third place, you must not, on any account, *stir either hand or foot*. If, by chance, a black pin runs into your head, you must not take it out. If the pain is very great, you must be sure to bear it without wincing. If it brings tears into your eyes, you must not wipe them off; if they give you a tingling by running down your cheeks, you must look as if nothing was the matter. If the blood should gush from your head, by means of the black pin – *you must let it gush*; if you are uneasy to think of making such a blurred appearance, you must be uneasy, but you must say nothing about it. If, however, the agony is very great, you may, privately, bite the inside of your cheek, or of your lips, for a little relief; taking care, meanwhile, to do it so cautiously as to make no apparent dent outwardly. And with that precaution, if you even gnaw a piece out, it will not be minded, only to be sure either to swallow it, or commit it to a corner of the inside of your mouth till they are gone – for you must not spit.

I have many other directions, but no more paper... Perhaps, meanwhile, you would be glad to know if I have myself had opportunity to put in practice these receipts.

How can I answer in this little space?...

Believe me, my dearest Esther,

Most affectionately yours,

F. B.

Fanny Burney, by the seaside with His Majesty, writes to her father of bathing machines and 'Royal dippers', and records some embarrassing moments...

FANNY BURNEY TO HER FATHER, DR BURNEY...

Gloucester House
Weymouth
July 13, 1789

'Dorset Loyalty'

His Majesty is in delightful health, and much improved spirits. All agree he never looked better.

The loyalty of all this place is excessive; they have dressed out every street with labels of 'God save the King!' All the shops have it over the doors, all the children wear it in their caps, all the labourers in their hats, and all the sailors in their voices; for they never approach the house without shouting it aloud, nor see the King, or his shadow, without beginning to huzza, and going on to three cheers.

The bathing-machines make it their motto over all their windows; and those bathers that belong to the Royal Dippers wear it in bandeaux on their bonnets to go into the sea; and have it again in large letters round their waists, to encounter the waves.

Flannel dresses, tucked up, and no shoes or stockings, with bandeaux and girdles, have a most singular appearance; and when first I surveyed these loyal nymphs, it was with some difficulty I kept my features in order.

Nor is this all. Think but of the surprise of His Majesty when, the first time of his bathing, he had no sooner popped his Royal Head under water, than a band of music, concealed in a neighbouring machine, struck up 'God save Great George our King'!

One thing, however, was a little unlucky. When the Mayor and burgesses came with the address, they requested leave to shake hands. This was graciously accorded; but, the Mayor advancing in a common way, *to take the Queen's hand*, as he might that of any Lady Mayoress, Colonel Gwynne, who stood by, whispered: 'You must kneel, Sir!' He found, however, that he took no notice of this hint, but kissed the Queen's hand erect. As he passed him in his way back, the Colonel said: 'You should have *knelt*, Sir!'

'Sir,' answered the poor Mayor, 'I cannot.'

'Everybody does, Sir.'

'Sir – I have a wooden leg.'

… A thousand thanks for your home news.

I am, most dear Sir,

Affectionately and dutifully,

your F. B.

43

RALPH WEWITZER (1748–1825)
ANDREW CHERRY (1769–1812)

Ralph Wewitzer was apprenticed as a jeweller, but became actor, singer, dancer, and playwright. In his 44-year career on stage he played over 400 good supporting roles. Here he writes mysteriously to 'Friend Edwin':

Whitechapel
August 27, 1788

Friend Edwin,

I was in hopes I should have been able to come to perform tonight. I am in trouble and am afraid I shall not get out again.

I beg you will not assign the real cause to the Public, but say I am ill.

Your much distressed friend,
Ralph Wewitzer

Towards the end of his career, Wewitzer fell on hard times, and appealed to his friend Mrs Coutts (who became the Duchess of St Albans) to whom he had been a good friend during her difficult courtship with her future husband. She refused to help and he died, weakened by starvation, in a garret. She left £1,800,000 in her will to Baroness Burdett-Coutts.

At about this time an actor named Andrew Cherry, a famous Shylock, was offered work by a manager who had previously cheated him. Cherry sent the man this note:

[Undated]

Sir,

I have been bitten by you once, and am resolved that you shall not make two bites of A. Cherry.

A. Cherry

Charles Mathews the comic actor (q.v.) said of Cherry: 'In any line of comedy he is a charming actor. He is a very excellent judge of dressing, and has capital clothes, and the best wigs I ever saw.' [Until the late nineteenth century actors traditionally supplied their own costumes.]

DORA JORDAN (1761–1816)

The leading actress Dora Jordan (given name Dorothy Bland) was the mistress of the Duke of Clarence, who was crowned William IV at the age of 65 in 1830. She adopted the title 'Mrs' for propriety, and bore him ten children ennobled by the name of Fitzclarence (in addition to three more by other men). She loved him to the end – and subsidised his ruinously expensive lifestyle with her income as an actress.

Mrs Jordan requests a favour of the Duke of Clarence:

MRS JORDAN TO THE DUKE OF CLARENCE

A Sunday evening, November 1791

Sir,

How good you are in allowing for my particularities; indeed I feel at this time very awkward and silly. Do *forgive* me, you do not know how ridiculous a mortal in some respects you have to deal with. I do *not* play tomorrow. My sister leaves this house at six o'clock; may I then hope to see you any time after that hour. On Tuesday I will go with you, *where you please*.

I hope I need not say how much I am obliged to you respecting the carriage. The liveries I have made use of for some time were Mr. Ford's, and therefore I shall give them up. My *own*, before I had *his*, was dark green turned up with buff and bound with silver. The carriage cannot want any ornament, but still there is one thing I should *like*, if it is not improper – an *anchor* on the panels. *[Clarence was a naval man.]* If it is at all wrong, do not hesitate to tell me; indeed, I love everything that has the least reference to you. I do most ardently long to see you, but still it will be impossible to tell you how dearly, how fondly, I love you. You say that you have loved me eleven months; how happy should I be; and I flatter myself that dear, dear love will not abate by time. My heart and happiness is in your power. I may with truth add, my *life*, for should you cease to *love*, I must *cease to live*.

God bless you, *you do love* me, I know you *now do*, but continue to do so, for mine can never feel less ardour for you than that which now so entirely possesses my heart and soul. What love you have to me, it is more than love. Love is too faint an expression for the sensations I feel for you. May every blessing wait on you, may you ever be truly *happy* and above all may you *ever, ever love* her who is devoted to you by every dear and tender sentiment.

Your Royal Highness's dutiful Servant,

Mrs. Jordan

Eighteen years later, Mrs Jordan was on tour in her native Dublin, Ireland:

MRS JORDAN TO THE DUKE OF CLARENCE

Dublin, Saturday, 10th June, 1809

Sir,

I dined according to promise yesterday at 5 o'clock at Mrs. Lefanu's, where *hospitality* was the order of the day, but the style of living so very different from what I have been accustomed to, that I really was obliged to have recourse to my *very* best acting to conceal my surprise. We had a most plentiful dinner, of *two* courses. The soup was removed by a very *large* whole salmon, really of such a size that the tail rested in my plate, and the head in the lap of my opposite neighbour, who, happening to be an *Englishman*, was, I believe, as much astonished as myself. Two of the guests, *men*, were placed at top and bottom of the table, and when my *vis-à-vis* was asked whether he would have a bit of salmon, he very drily answered that he had *quite enough on his plate.*

With the butter and cheese came a *large silver cup* with *two handles*, filled with porter, out of which *everybody drank* but me and Lucy *[her daughter, who accompanied her on this tour].* We excused ourselves by saying we never drank most liquor...

I rehearsed today, and was addressed by a very *old man* who was standing at the wing... It was the very person that brought me on the stage the first night I ever played. He reminded me of my running off the stage behind the scenes, and his following me, and bringing me forward by *main force*. He is not a little *proud of this...*

How I dreamed of everybody at dear Bushy last night. These dreams do me *no good*. I am not well today. I should die but for poor Lucy, who hates and detests the place as much as I do.

I was forced to speak to Thomas *[a servant]* today. He abuses the

Catholics, and will get *into a scrape* if he does not take care. I pointed out the consequence to him, and I think he is *alarmed...*

Your Royal Highness's dutiful Servant,

Mrs. Jordan

Unfortunately her relationship with the Duke deteriorated until her responsibilities were no more than those of a mother to his children...

MRS JORDAN TO THE DUKE OF CLARENCE

Bushy *[Bushy House, Hampton Court]*,
Monday, 16th December, 1811

Sir,

I yesterday received Mr. Adam, and lose no time in assuring your Royal Highness that I am most perfectly satisfied with *every part* of the arrangements you have thought proper to adopt with regard to myself and your children, and shall ever remain impressed with the highest sense of *gratitude* for your additional goodness to the rest of my family, who, through me, request your Royal Highness will be pleased to accept their sincere and lasting acknowledgement.

With regard to myself, I hope I shall ever know how to *value* the sacred charge with which you have entrusted me.

It is my wish (if you have no objection) to retain Miss Sketchley, whose attachment to the dear children I think deserves it – and such of their old masters who can attend them in London; and in the event of any alterations being necessary, I should be allowed (through Sofia) to have your sanction to any new appointment of masters.

As I may now look on the arrangements as concluded, I trust you will permit me (in the course of a few days) to see George *[their son]*, who will not avail himself of the leave he has got, without your approbation. Indeed, his prudence and good sense is conspicuous in everything he does, and will, I trust in God, accompany him through life. I have every reason to be greatly pleased with Henry *[their son]*, whose conduct on the present occasion has done both his head and heart the highest honour. I have much pleasure in being able to add that all those servants that have come under my eye have, during your absence, conducted themselves with the utmost *regularity* and grateful attention to your interest.

With the most sincere and devout prayers for your health and happiness, I remain

Your Royal Highness's dutiful servant,

Mrs. Jordan

The above letter is politically courteous; even to friends she continued to defend Clarence, and to declare her affection for him:

... My mind is beginning to feel somewhat reconciled to the shock and surprise it has lately received; for could you or the world believe that we have never had for twenty years the semblance of a quarrel? But this is so well known in our domestic circle that the astonishment is the greater.

Money, money, my good friend – or the want of it – has, I am convinced, made him at this moment the most wretched of men; but having done wrong, he does not like to detract. But with all his excellent qualities, his domestic virtues, his love for his lovely children, what must he not at this moment suffer? His distress should have been relieved before; but this is *entre nous*. All his letters are full of the most unqualified praise of my conduct, and it is the most heartfelt blessing to know that, to the best of my power, I have endeavoured to deserve it.

I have received the greatest kindness from the Regent, and every branch of the royal family, who in the most unreserved terms deplore this melancholy business. The whole correspondence is before the Regent, and I am proud to add that my past and present conduct has secured me to a friend who declares he will never forsake me. My forbearance, he says, is beyond what he could have imagined! But what will not a woman do who is firmly and sincerely attached?

Had he left me to starve, I never would have uttered a word to his disadvantage. I enclose you two other letters, and in a day or two you shall have more – the rest being in the hands of the Regent. And now, my dear friend, do not hear the Duke of Clarence unfairly abused. He has done wrong, and he is suffering for it. But as far as he has left it in his own power he is doing everything *kind* and *noble*, even to the distressing himself...

The following letter from Mrs Jordan was printed in a newspaper after published attacks on her and Clarence:

Sir,

Though I did not see the morning print that contained the paragraph alluded to in your liberal and respectable paper of yesterday, yet I was not long left in ignorance of the abuse it poured out against me. This I would silently have submitted to, but I was by no means aware that the writer of it had taken the opportunity of throwing out insinuations which he thought might be injurious to a no less honourable than illustrious personage.

In the love of truth, and in justice to his Royal Highness, I think it my duty, publicly and unequivocally, to declare that his liberality towards me has been noble and generous in the *highest degree;* but not having it in his power to extend his bounty beyond the term of his own existence, he has, with his accustomed goodness and consideration, allowed me to endeavour to make that provision for myself...

This, then, Sir, is my motive for returning to my profession. I am too happy in having every reason to hope and believe that, under these circumstances, I shall not offend the public at large by seeking their support and protection; and while I feel that I possess those, I shall patiently submit to that species of unmanly persecution which a female so particularly situated must always be subject to...

I am, Sir, etc.,
Your much obliged, humble servant,
Dora Jordan

Realistically, in private, she was writing to her friend:

...When everything is adjusted, it will be impossible for me to remain in England. I shall, therefore, go abroad, appropriating as much as I can spare of the remainder of my income to pay my debts..

Clarence had dropped Mrs Jordan when he married Adelaide of Saxe-Meiningen in 1818, who was to become his queen. Her capital drained by Clarence's excesses and cheated financially by a dishonest son-in-law, Dora Jordan died an exile in Paris, virtually alone and in great poverty.

THOMAS KING (1730–1805) to TATE WILKINSON (1736–1803)

Actor, theatre manager and author Tate Wilkinson was famous for preceding his actors in his carriage (in the Summer they would walk the nine miles to the theatre), and feeding them by the roadside 'with an excellent dinner'. Poet and critic Leigh Hunt (1784–1859) wrote '…being manager of a theatre, a husband, and a ratcatcher, he would speak in his wanderings… he would interweave all at once the subject of a new engagement at his theatre, the rats, a veal-pie, Garrick and Mrs Siddons, and Mrs Tate and the doctor.' He was described by Charles Lamb (q.v.) thus: 'His acting left a taste on the palate sharp and sweet like a quince; with an old, hard, rough, withered face, like a john-apple, puckered up into a thousand wrinkles; with shrewd hints and tart replies.'

In 1796 Tate Wilkinson wrote to the actor Thomas King, suggesting that King should eat cheese sandwiches amusingly and wear lots of waistcoats to improve his comedy business as the Grave-digger in HAMLET. King was furious…

12th October, 1796

Sir,

As to your question – 'how I dress the Grave-digger' – I affect no novelty – I follow Yates [*eminent actor Richard Yates, 1745–1796, of whom Charles Dibdin wrote: 'No actor was ever more chaste, more uniform, more characteristic'*] and other *respectable* performers whom I have formerly seen.

The coat and upper waistcoat are of a greyish frieze; over which waistcoat I wear a broad belt – which coat, waistcoat and belt I take off, by the assistance of my partner, and go to work in an under thick flannel waistcoat with sleeves. When in the grave, before I dig, I also take off my hat, which is rather large and cock'd in nearly a regular triangle, and put on a cap – which cap I take from the side-pocket of my breeches, which are rather easy, *not large*.

What may have been done in former times, or may be done by mummers of the present day, I am unable to say. But I have been a member of the Theatre Royal in London and Dublin seven or eight-and-forty years, and I have never been present when Shakespeare has been degraded, and the common sense of an audience insulted, in the way you mention.

I could almost wish an actor to be confined to the eating bread and cheese for life, who could descend to using them at the grave of Ophelia; and to be divested of his last waistcoat who could so far violate propriety as to carry as many peelings as an onion, and suppose there could be merit in taking them off…

Thomas King

SARAH SIDDONS (1755–1831)

The most influential actress of her time, Sarah Siddons was born in a public house, 'The Shoulder of Mutton', Brecon, Wales. (In 1955, the 200th anniversary of her birth, the pub was re-named 'The Sarah Siddons'.) Her maiden family, the Kembles, dominated the English theatre for half a century.

Away from home, she worries about her daughter...

MRS SIDDONS TO MRS PENNINGTON

Worcester, July 26, 1798

My dear Mrs. Pennington,

Your goodness to my dear girl is what I expected, but I am not able to express my gratitude for it. Dear Soul, add still to the number of your favours by telling me every particular about her...

I know she went to the Ball. I hope it did her no harm. This weather has prevented her riding, too. Tell me about her pulse, her perspirations, her cough, everything!...

I am playing every night to very full houses, but how the people can sit to see such representations is quite wonderful, for anything so bad I never yet beheld, and I have seen strange things. The fat cakes *[lardycakes]*, however, are quite as good as formerly, only that I find *one* suffices my appetite now, and formerly, I verily believe, I could have eaten half a dozen...

God bless you and yours, and your dear charge!

Believe me, ever your grateful and affectionate

S. Siddons

GEORGE COLMAN (1762–1836)

*In 1789, dramatist George Colman took over the management of the
Haymarket Theatre from his father (also George, 1732–1794, who in 1766
wrote THE CLANDESTINE MARRIAGE with David Garrick q.v.). In 1794,
on his father's death, he bought the theatre outright. In 1797, forbidden by the
Lord Chamberlain to put plays on at the Haymarket Theatre in Lent, he found
himself very short of money...*

Sunday Night, Piccadilly

My dear Arnold,

I feel more unpleasantly than I can tell you... in writing to you on
money subjects. Take, therefore, a plain tale: though tales, nowadays,
according to Lord Bishops and Lord Chamberlains, are of ill-omen. I
am so thrown back in consequence of the failure of our Lenten entertainment (which I reckoned on as a certainty) that I am obliged to
apply to those who are more blessed with affluence than I am.

Can you, my dear Arnold, lend me two hundred pounds? For the
repayment of which, in the summer (or before), I give you the word of
an old friend and any other security in my power. I am in need of this
occasional supply to take up a bill which is soon becoming due...

Please send me a line in the course of to-morrow.

Truly yours,
G. Colman

Sadly, a few days later...

Piccadilly, March 7, 1797

My dear Arnold,

I cannot leave town... without sending you a line to thank you, my
dear Arnold, for your letter. Alas! We are two unlucky dogs! Could
you have assisted me now, it would have rejoiced me; and I am sure
you would if you could. I feel your explanations and intentions to be
most kind and friendly.

Ever truly yours,
G. Colman

But two months on...

My Dear Arnold,

... let me thank you (although I am awkward at thanks and say much less than I feel) for your goodness and real friendship on this occasion. I hate all money transactions in general; they are damned, nauseous, nasty, sour things that go against my stomach. But you have contrived to throw into your draughts such a mixture of warmth and kindness that I shall never think of it without pleasure...

I am, my dear Arnold,

Yours truly and affectionately,

G. Colman

1800 ~ 1900

GEORGE COLMAN

SARAH SIDDONS

MARY LAMB

EDMUND KEAN

MADAME VESTRIS

THE BOOTHS

CHARLES KEMBLE

FANNY KEMBLE

JOSEPH GRIMALDI

WILLIAM CHARLES
MACREADY

CHARLES DICKENS

BENJAMIN WEBSTER

CHARLOTTE CUSHMAN

VICTOR HUGO

SARAH BERNHARDT

EDWARD FITZGERALD

HENRY JAMES

ELEONORA DUSE

HENRY IRVING

THE GAIETY GIRLS

MARK TWAIN

OSCAR WILDE

ELLEN TERRY

GEORGE BERNARD
SHAW

AND OTHERS...

GEORGE COLMAN (1762–1836)
to
CHARLES MATHEWS (1775/6–1835)

Amazingly still in business at the Haymarket Theatre, actor manager George Colman tries to cast the great mimic and comic actor Charles Mathews, now playing at York...

Theatre Royal, Haymarket
14th September, 1802

Sir,

Your merits as an actor having been mentioned to me, give me leave to propose an engagement to you for next year at my theatre.

It is my intention to commence the season positively on 15th. next May, and to continue it to the 15th of the following September.

Should you think it eligible to embrace the opportunity which I now offer you, of performing for four months before a London audience, I beg you will be kind enough to inform me on what terms you will give me your assistance.

At all events, I shall thank you for a speedy answer, directed to me at Mr. Jewell's, 26 Suffolk Street, Charing Cross.

I am, Sir, your obedient servant,
G. Colman

But Mathews knew his own value. To Colman's amazement, for Mathews was not known in London, he wanted star terms: £10 and a benefit night each week...

Theatre Royal, Haymarket
8th October, 1802

Sir,

The terms which you have proposed are certainly high, and perhaps unprecedented, for a performer who has not yet felt the pulse of a London audience, but the reasons stated for thus fixing your ultimatum appear to be founded on justice, to put vanity out of the question. I waive therefore all mention of any risk incurred on my part in my new speculation and embrace your offer.

But, to prevent all mistakes, permit me to state precisely what I conceive to be the engagement. Ten pounds a week and a benefit, of which benefit you pay the usual charges. You will perform from the 15th. of May to the 15th. of September inclusive. If you engage in London after your appearance with me, you give me the preference on a re-engagement.

If you think any short legal memorandum requisite between us, I am willing to enter into it. If you conceive the letters that pass between us as sufficient, I am quite content that it should remain an agreement upon honour.

Pray send me two lines speedily, which will be conclusive. I will, when we meet in the summer, do everything in my power to contribute to your reputation with the public and your comfort in my theatre.

I am, Sir, your obedient servant,

G. Colman

[Postscript] Of course your attendance will be expected in town a week or ten days previously to opening the theatre, as I begin with novelties.

In a letter following, Colman concerns himself with Mathews' image (Mathews describes himself as a 'low comedian', and Colman presses him to elaborate on this), and on the choice of 'novelties' (publicity stunts)..

Haymarket

Sir,

... First impressions often make or mar. I remember, soon after Munden's first appearance in London, he ate, with uncommon success, a hundred pounds weight of plum puddings in *Two Strings to Your Bow*. This feat was new to a London audience. He had a good character in it, which nobody had ever seen before. Do you recollect anything in which you might make your appearance, under the same favourable circumstances?...

I am, Sir, your obedient servant,

G. Colman

In March of 1803, Colman went to York to see Mathews in action and liked what he saw. The two men became lifelong friends. Within a few years, because of family and professional debts, Colman was consigned to the debtors' prison, but continued, from there, to run the Haymarket. Mathews, by now a London star of the highest rank, one day invited Colman to dine with him at his cottage in Colney Hatch...

King's Bench Prison,
November 11th, 1808

Dear Mathews,

'I 'gin to pull in resolution.'

When I talked of holiday Sundays *[the day debtors were traditionally immune from arrest]*, I felt bolder than, upon reflection, I ought to do, with respect to the regulations of our college *[the prison]*, into which I have more particularly enquired since we met. So another day in the course of the month I will, if you please, attend you; and be kind enough to look out a moon for me, for I incline to the party of the Lunatics, and am no follower of the Prince of Darkness on the King's Highway.

So, Sheridan and Hood for ever!... God save the King! Bless the crier! Huzza! Huzza!

G. Colman

['Hood' may be a humorous and ironical reference to the successes of the popular Admiral Samuel Hood (1724–1816), who had won notable sea battles in the French Revolutionary War and occupied Corsica in 1793–4. As for 'God save the King!' why, Colman was locked up in the King's Bench Prison.]

MRS JOSEPH SUMBEL (1762–1829)
(formerly Mrs Wells)

Colman managed somehow to keep the Haymarket afloat, one of his greatest successes being an entertainment he wrote: THE ACTOR OF ALL WORK. This was a vehicle for the celebrated Charles Mathews. The show was a hot ticket...

[A hopeful] MRS SUMBEL TO CHARLES MATHEWS:

> No. 14, Newlands House,
> Portland Place
> Sept. 27, 1817

My dear Sir,

The papers inform me that you are to give your *Actor of All Work* in the manner of Mrs. Banister and Mrs. Mountain. Can you, my dear Sir, employ my poor remaining abilities to any small advantage to *myself* at the same time? It would be doing me an essential service.

I mean to offer my Imitations of Mrs. Siddons and the late Mrs. Jordan.

The very kind interest Mrs. Mathews and yourself have testified towards me alone induces me to hope you will judge favourably of the proposition.

With best compliments to Mrs. Mathews,

My dear Sir,

> Your very obliged Humble Servant,
> L. Sumbel

SARAH SIDDONS (1755–1831)

Charles Mathews was greatly admired by other actors. It can only have been an honour for him to have received the following request from the magnificent Mrs Siddons:

[*Sarah Siddons*] To – Mathews Esq., Theatre Royal, Haymarket:–

27, Upper Baker Street
August 26, 1817

Dear Sir,

I have heard so much of *The Actor of All Work*, and I have so great an admiration of your talents that I cannot resist troubling you with a request that I am sure your good nature will pardon; it is that you will have the goodness to procure a Private Box to give me that pleasure.

Allow me, Sir, to apprise you that if your compliance is likely to be attended by the least inconvenience, I shall attribute your refusal to those motives of propriety that are indispensable, and not to any disinclination to gratify.

Your Sincere Admirer,
And obliged humble Servant,
S. Siddons

[*Postscript*] Mr. Coleman [*sic*] has always been so kind as to admit me to the theatre and I flatter myself that he would not be averse to favouring me with a box any day of the week.

Sarah Siddons, in a letter to Mrs. Fitzhugh, describes a trip to Windsor...

Westbourne
January 26, 1813

I have been these three days meditating about writing you an account of my Windsor visit, which you have no doubt seen mentioned in the newspapers. But... I cannot resist the pleasure of telling you myself... Take it thus and verbatim.

On the 18th. (I think it was) I was in the middle of dressing to go and dine with Mrs. Damer, when an especial messenger arrived in the dusk with a letter from my old friend the Dowager Lady Stewart, to tell me that the Queen had ordered her to write and say 'that Her Majesty wished very much to hear me read, and desired to have an answer returned immediately to Carlton House, where the party from Windsor dined that day', which was Wednesday. I of course wrote that I should be happy to have the honour of obeying the Queens's commands, and therefore left my own house on Friday, according to appointment, and went to Frogmore...

I got there about three, and was conducted into a very elegant drawing-room, where I sat till it was time to go to the Castle and consult with Lady Stewart respecting the reading. I spent about an hour very agreeably in her apartment with herself and Princess Elizabeth, who appears the best-natured person in the world.

We concluded for some part of *Henry VIII*, some part of *The Merchant of Venice*, and to finish with some scenes from *Hamlet*. After this I dined with Madame Bechendoft, Her Majesty's confidential gentlewoman... We then parted for the night, the ladies to the Queen's card party, and I to Frogmore...

The next day the whole Royal party from Windsor, with Princess Charlotte and the Dukes of Cambridge and Clarence, dined at Frogmore. Many of the nobility and gentry were invited to the reading, and at about half-past eight I entered the room where they were all assembled.

The Queen, the Princesses and the Duchess of York all came to me, and conversed most graciously till the Queen took her place. Then the company seated themselves and I began. It all went off to my heart's content, for the room was the finest place for the voice in the world.

I retired sometimes, at Her Majesty's request, to rest; and when it was all over I had the extreme satisfaction to find that they had all been extremely delighted. Lady Stewart wrote to me yesterday that I am still the inexhaustible fund of conversation and eulogium.

When the Queen retired, after the reading, Lady Stewart brought to me a magnificent gold chain, with a cross of many-coloured jewels, from Her Majesty, and hung it round my neck before all the company. This was a great surprise, and you may imagine how so great an honour affected me. (You may conceive, too, the pleasure it gave me to be able to divert a few of those mournfully monotonous hours which these amiable sufferers, from the singularly afflicting nature of their misfortune, are doomed to undergo.)

I found the Queen had been desirous that I should not return the next day, but stay and read again to her at the Castle next night, which I was too happy to do. This reading consisted of passages from *Paradise Lost*, Gray's *Elegy* and *Marmion*. When I went into her room I found Her Majesty – with all the Princesses and the Princess Charlotte – seated, and a table prepared for me, which she (most graciously saying she was sure I must still feel fatigued from the last night's exertion) ordered me to seat myself in; when I thanked her for the magnificent favour I had received, and hoped the reading of the preceding night had not fatigued Her Majesty, for she really had a terrible cough and cold. She hoped that the keepsake would remind me of Frogmore, and said that it was impossible to be fatigued when she was so extremely delighted. I then took my leave...

I received another command from Her Majesty, and the next Sunday evening I read *Othello* to the Royal party at the Castle. And here my story ends. I have much to say if I had eyes and head; my heart, however, is still strong, and I am,

With undiminished affection,

Yours,

S.S.

CHARLES (1775–1834) and MARY LAMB (1764–1847)

In 1806, distinguished author and theatre critic Charles Lamb wrote, with his sister Mary, famous reductions of Shakespeare's plays, TALES FOUNDED ON THE PLAYS OF SHAKESPEARE. Writing them in the style of short stories, he did the tragedies while she did the comedies. In a letter he once reported: 'Mary is stuck fast in ALL'S WELL THAT ENDS WELL... and I have been obliged to promise to assist her. To do this it will be necessary to leave off tobacco.'

On September 22nd, 1796, Mary, 'worn down to a state of extreme nervous misery by attention to needlework by day and to her mother at night', had an unexpected fit of insanity and stabbed her mother to death. She was allowed to stay at home and from this time her brother cared for her, though she was periodically removed for treatment. Ten years after the calamity, during a calm period, Mary Lamb writes to her friend Sarah Stoddart:

June 2, 1806

My dear Sarah,

You say truly that I have sent you too many make-believe letters. I do not mean to serve you so again, if I can help it. I have been very ill for some days past with the toothache. Yesterday I had it drawn, and I feel myself greatly relieved but far from easy, for my head and jaws still ache; and, being unable to do any business, I would wish to write you a long letter to atone for my former offences; but I feel so languid that I am afraid wishing is all I can do...

My *Tales* are to be published in separate story books; I mean, in single stories, like the children's little shilling books. I cannot send you them in manuscript, because they are all in Godwin's hands; but one will be published very soon, and then you shall have it *all in print*. I go on very well, and have no doubt but I shall always be able to hit upon some such kind of job to keep going on. I think I shall get fifty pounds a year at the lowest calculation. But as I have not yet seen any money of my own earning, for we do not expect to be paid till Christmas, I do not feel the good fortune that had so unexpectedly befallen me half so much as I ought to do. But another year, no doubt, I shall perceive it.

When I write again, you shall hear tidings of the Farce, for Charles is to go in a few days to the Managers to enquire about it. But that must now be a next year's business too, even if it does succeed. So it's all looking forward and no prospect of present gain. But that's better than no hopes at all, either for the present or future times.

Charles has written *Macbeth*, *Othello*, *King Lear*, and has begun *Hamlet*. You would like to see us, as we often sit writing on one table (but not on one cushion sitting) like Hermia and Helena in the *Midsummer Night's Dream*; or, rather, like an old literary Darby and Joan: I taking snuff and he groaning all the while, and saying he can make nothing of it which he always says till he has finished, and then he finds out he has made something of it.

If I tell you that, you Widow-Blackacreise, you must tell me I Tale-ise, for my Tales seem to be all the subject-matter I write about; and when you see them, you will think them poor little baby-stories to make such a talk about. But I have no news to send, nor nothing, in short, to say, that is worth paying twopence for. I wish I could get franks, then I should not care how short or stupidly I wrote.

Charles smokes still, and will smoke to the end of the chapter.

Martin Burney has just been here. My *Tales* (*again*) and Charles's Farce has made the boy mad to turn Author; and he has written a Farce, and he has made the *Winter's Tale* into a story. But what Charles says of himself is really true of Martin – for *he can make nothing at all of it*: and I have been talking very eloquently this morning, to convince him that nobody can write Farces, etc., under thirty years of age. And so I suppose he will go home and new-model his Farce.

What is Mr. Turner? And what is likely to come of him? And how do you like him? And what do you intend to do about it? I almost wish you to remain single till your mother dies, and then come and live with us; and we would either get you a husband or teach you how to live comfortably without. I think I should like to have you always to the end of our lives living with us; and I do not know any reason why that should not be, except for the great fancy you seem to have for marrying, which after all is but a hazardous kind of affair.

But, however, do as you like – every man knows best what pleases him best.

I have known many single men I should have liked in my life (if it had suited them) for a husband. But very few husbands have I ever wished was mine – which is rather against the state in general. But one never is disposed to envy wives their good husbands. So much for marrying – but, however, get married, if you can...

God bless you, my dearest Sarah! I wish for your sake I could have written a very amusing letter; but do not scold, for my head aches sadly. Don't mind my headache, for before you get this it will be well, being only from the pains of my jaws and teeth.

Farewell,

Yours affectionately,

M. Lamb

EDMUND KEAN (1787/9–1833)

Like Garrick before him, Edmund Kean led a private life as complicated as his professional life was illustrious. On July 17th, 1808, he married the actress Mary Chambers in Stroud. For the first few years times were not easy...

EDMUND KEAN TO JOHN HUGHES

12, Tavistock Row, Covent Garden
December, 1811

Dear Sir,

Having travelled lately some hundred miles with a large family and very expensive baggage, I am left in London in a situation (which many of our brother professionals are acquainted with): *Non est mihi argentum.*

It is my wish, therefore, to depart by tomorrow's coach for Weymouth, but I frankly confess at present I have not the means; if, Sir, you would oblige me with the sum of ten pounds, Mr. Finch or Miss Tidswell *[Kean's Aunt]* will become answerable for my immediate appearance at Weymouth, and Mr. Hughes *[Manager of Sadlers Wells Theatre, London]* might proceed to the reduction of ten shillings per week till the debt is discharged. As I am fully sensible this is a great obligation from a stranger, it is my wish to pay interest on the money you may please to demand; and as Mr. Hughes, junior, will have the means in his hands there can be no doubt of the payment...

By 1813, Mary was finding the marriage hard work...

MARY KEAN TO MARGARET ROBERTS

September 5th, 1813

... My first step to misery was going on the Stage. My character I preserv'd pure and unsullied. I then married my husband possessed of every talent requisite for his profession, educated to give grace to that talent – and, could he have endured patiently a little longer, fortune might have rewarded his very great abilities. To forget sorrow he first took to drinking. Every dissipation followed, of course. His nights were spent with a set of wretches – a disgrace to human nature. One step led to another, till inevitable ruin was the end...

However, despite the carousing, Kean's reputation grew. His original performances were the subject of critical discussion in the press...

LETTERS TO THE EDITOR OF *THE EXAMINER*

Sir,

I am convinced that Mr. Kean's deficiency of dignity does not in the slightest degree disqualify him as a representative of Shakespeare's *Othello*. There is a delicacy about the taste and feelings of this extraordinary young actor which must be instinctive. His genius in this, as in some other of its characteristics, appears to me to bear a striking resemblance to that of Shakespeare himself. Had they lived in the same day Shakespeare would have stretched out his human hand to him and have welcomed him with delight as at least a kindred spirit.

Anonymous

An open letter to Mr. Kean:

March 1st, 1814

Sir,

I am afraid you may consider a newspaper an odd channel for the advice which I may wish to give you – which is not to mind what the newspapers say.

A morning paper says: 'The frequent smile which Mr. Kean wore in Richard destroyed the dignity that belongs to the character.' Says the Evening Editor: 'Mr. Kean forgot to diversify the sullenness he wore by the spirit of coarse merriment with which Richard contemplates the success of his projects.' A weekly publication states that 'Mr. Kean's extreme decrepitude in Shylock cast an air of imbecility over the malice of the character'; but a lively wag in a magazine writes 'Mr. Kean should not make old Shylock trip across the stage with a step light enough for Gratiano'...

If you will just allow me to remark that your tone and manner in the third scene of the fourth act of... *but why should I make remarks which I have just advised you not to attend to...?*

Yours etc.

An accident marked a turn for the worse in Kean's fortunes...

Wednesday, March 27, 1816

Dear Mr. Rae,

I shall be quite unable to play in *The Duke of Milan* this evening. I met with a damned accident yesterday, being thrown out of a gig, and besides being stunned and bruis'd, have dislocated an arm. Hoping soon to recover and with apologies to the Public,

I am yours in pain,

Edmund Kean

[Postscript] N.B. Perhaps the great W.C.M. *[William Charles Macready q.v.]* may be got.

The accident really happened, but the press accused Kean of unreliability. There were several more, less justified, cancellations, and damaging publicity concerning his affair with Charlotte Cox, the wife of a city Alderman. (She had introduced herself to Kean in Taunton by extravagantly fainting in a box, being overcome with emotion at his OTHELLO. At his command she was carried straight to his dressing room...) Kean went into hiding at the Regent Hotel in Brighton. Robert William Elliston (1774–1831), a comic actor famous for his Falstaff, and now the flamboyant manager of Drury Lane Theatre, tracked him down by subterfuge. Kean wrote to Elliston:

EDMUND KEAN TO ELLISTON

...You have employed unworthy means to disturb me in my solitude. That was neither manly nor open. It was necessary I should have repose – my health has suffered materially. Elliston, I must not be spoken to; you know what I am equal to when in vigour; but remember, also: *ad nullum consurgit opus cum corpore languet!*

You have pursued me by a trick, and I should deign you no reply. But I am here, Sir, under the direction of Sir Anthony Carlisle, and will not stir from this place until I have gone through all the routine of medicine and sea-bathing prescribed for me by that great man. The medical men of Brighton declare also that I need repose – on that question there is no dissentient voice: 'Kean must have repose'. If I am pursued either by trick or openly, I shall retire to *La Belle France* for some weeks...

I leave you in no distress. You have Macready! Macready, Elliston! Why should you be anxious about poor Kean? (Yet, a breath, I say, of Kean shall confound a generation of Youngs and Macreadys)...
[Charles Mayne Young, 1777–1856, a famous Hamlet; see Robert Keeley]

Separated from his wife, Kean became infatuated with the beautiful Ophelia Benjamin, believed by some to have been a prostitute; she was at least out to spend his money. He called her 'Mrs Kean' in company and took her to live with him. Her extravagance and rudeness led to the resignation of Phillips, Kean's private secretary of long standing...

EDMUND KEAN TO PHILLIPS

Dear Phillips,

I am shocked but not surprised. In error I was born, in error I have lived, in error I shall die – that a *gentleman* should be insulted under my roof creates a blush that I shall carry to my grave; and that you are so in every sense of the word is unquestionable, from Education, Habit and Manners. It is too true that I have fostered a worm till it has become a viper – but my guilt is on my head.

> Farewell,
> Edmund Kean

Though as celebrated by now in America as in Britain, his complicated private life certainly affected his work. On March 8, 1830, he failed to complete his first performance as Henry V, despite numerous prompts. The audience booed the play to a standstill. Kean spoke to them: '...I stand here in the most degraded situation, and call upon you as my countrymen to show your usual liberality.' Afterwards, he wrote to The Times *and to W.H. Halpin, editor of* The Star:

Sir,

Fight for me, I have no resources in myself; mind is gone, and body is hopeless. God knows my heart. I would do, but cannot.

Memory, the first of Goddesses, has forsaken me; and I am left without a hope but from those old resources that the public and myself are tired of.

Damn, God damn ambition. The soul leaps, the body falls.

Edmund Kean

Kean never attempted Henry again, but stuck to the roles he knew profoundly. He was drinking brandy heavily, and most of his fortune had slipped through Ophelia's fingers. His Aunt Tid (Miss Tidswell), now quite old, came to care for him. He went on working successfully out of London...

EDMUND KEAN TO JOHN LEE *[Theatre Manager]*

April 10th, 1831

Dear Lee,

What day do I open in Cheltenham? The stupid son of a bitch has not dated his letter. Write me Birmingham. Get as much money as you can and save it for me. I shall send you the money as soon as I get it – I won't say I wish her dead, but I'll be damned if I don't.

Yours truly,

Edmund Kean

[Postscript] Tiddy – no sausages – out of season. Capital cigars and grog.

December, 1831

Dear Mary,

Let us be no longer fools. Come home; forget and forgive. If I have erred, it was my head, not my heart, and most severely have I suffered for it. My future life shall be employed in contributing to your happiness; and you, I trust, will return that feeling by a total obliteration of the past.

Your wild but really affectionate husband,

Edmund Kean

Mary refused. Kean died shortly afterwards. He left no estate – only debts. Among his papers was a handwritten document:

Edmund Kean's last will:

The villainy of the Irish strumpet Ophelia Benjamin has undone me, and, though I despise her, I feel life totally valueless without her. I leave her my curses... My Dramatic Wardrobe with all other clothing I leave to my worthy friend John Lee. (Forgive me oh Lord and receive my soul with mercy.)

An old actor makes plans to attend what I presume, from the month and the place, must be Kean's funeral...

JOHN POWELL TO JOHN PRITT HARLEY *(1786–1858; apprenticed as a stay-maker for a draper before becoming an actor)*

Wednesday 22nd January [1832]

My dear Harley,

Pray excuse the liberty I take, but if you could by any means point out how I could get a conveyance to Richmond *inside* or *out* of a carriage, at a small expense, on Saturday next, I should feel great obligation to you.

I should be *very unhappy* if I did not pay a last tribute of gratitude to the memory of a departed friend. For God knows I have received extreme friendship from him and I hope I shall always be grateful to those who are kind to me.

I have had the *warning*, and am convinced I shall not remain long in this World, but I hope I have prepared myself for a *better*.

God bless you my dear friend and believe me with great sincerity,

Yours truly,
John Powell

[Postscript] I shall feel much obliged if you will drop me a line immediately at No. 33 Cambridge St., Edgware Road, for altho' an *old man* and very *weak*, I will crawl on my hands and knees rather than not go to my friend's funeral on Saturday.

MADAME VESTRIS (1797–1856)

Theatre Manager Madame Vestris married the son of the comic actor Charles Mathews (q.v.), Charles James Mathews, in 1838. Charles James Mathews was one of the few actors of his time who also performed in French and worked successfully in both Paris and London. They took over Covent Garden Theatre in 1839.

Eight years before this, running the Olympic Theatre, Madame dismisses an actress:

The Olympic Theatre
January 15, 1831

Madam,

I am desired by Madame Vestris to say that she is extremely sorry to be under the necessity of saying, there does not appear to be the most remote chance of any appearance for you at the Olympic Theatre, and indeed her anticipations have met with some disappointment from the nature of the recommendations she received, consequently she is obliged reluctantly to dispense with your name being attached to the Establishment from this day.

Yours &c,
N. Vining

Madame obviously meant what she said...

Olympic Theatre
Saturday evening, January 15, 1831

Madam,

I have just received a note written by you to Madame Vestris, stating that you *still* consider yourself attached to the Olympic Theatre. I am desired by Madame to say that the description she received of you by way of introduction does not in any way accord with what she imagin'd she had a right to expect, and, being so disappointed, she has been compell'd to substitute another lady for what she had originally design'd you; thus, her views have been frustrated, and Madame compell'd to adopt the measures she has done, so far as regards dispensing with the offer of your services.

Yours &c,
N. Vining

JOSEPH GRIMALDI (1778/9–1837)

The clown Joe Grimaldi was much loved by audiences and fellow professionals alike. One of his greatest friends was Lord Byron (1788–1824), who once played a practical joke on him at a high-class dinner, by suggesting Grimaldi pour soy sauce over his apple pie. The clown did so, and, uneasy in Society, was too polite to voice his true reaction to the disgusting combination. Most of the time he was a jolly man, but he never recovered from the deaths of his wife and son, and his tumbler's body became weak from innumerable stage injuries. In 1835 he tried to sell off some personal goods to raise money...

JOE GRIMALDI TO TOM ELLAR

[1835]

My Dear Friend Tom,

Answer this I pray,
Do you mean to have my instrument, say Yea or Nay.
For if I do not hear from you without more delay
In a short space of time I shall send it away.
So Dear Friend Tom, without more *Ceremony*,
Come and take the Music and bring me the *Money*.
I have something left still, for your judgement and approve-all
Which I wish to dispose of, before my remove-all,
A Case with Two Fiddles, of exquisite sound –
You shall have the Case and Fiddles for the sum of £5.
So Dear Friend Tom ever yours till I die,
The once Merry Momus, Poor Joe *Grimaldi*.
I shall quit Woolwich soon, for another *situation*,
And glad enough I shall be, to return from *Transportation*.
Once more enjoy Society, the Song, the Glee and Laugh,
Tell droll stories, think of present Times – Not forget the past,
Be merry and wise, for Time approaches fast
For Death will, you know, have the Odd Trick at last.

To a colleague in 1845:

I am sorry I shall not be able to oblige you this year even by making an appearance for an hour. I am very ill – so ill indeed that I can scarcely hold the pen in my hand to write this to you. I am rheumatised – goutised puffised – and generally done up. No more for poor Joey the larks and games, the sausages and baggy breeks, the Little Old Woman and Hot Codlins.

Eheu! My foot is swathed in bandages, my body is wrapped in flannel, and my heart is bandaged in calico. I am always in pain... I enclose the sum of Three Guineas towards your benefit. Come and see me and talk of old times when life was young and no one was happier than your old and true chum,

Joe Grimaldi

[Postscript] Come on Christmas Eve if you can.

To another friend at the same time:

My dear Friend,

I am very ill. My days of staging are nearly over. I am afflicted with rheumatism and so severely as to be scarcely able to lift this pen. Do come and see me. My poor Wife being dead I am all alone – but not kicking – unfortunately.

I feel truly miserable; I am sure my end is approaching. O for the days when I was delighting Audiences at Old Drury and the Wells!... come and see your old Friend and have an hour's chat with him. Come on Sunday. I shall have no one here but an old housekeeper. Come, dear Friend, and cheer me up. *Your honest and true Friend,*

Joey Grimaldi

Joe Grimaldi died, broken in body and spirit, on Tuesday, 31st May, 1837, after an evening in his local tavern 'The Marquis of Cornwallis'. Among his most treasured possessions he left a silver snuff box, inscribed: 'The gift of Lord Byron to Joseph Grimaldi'.

LUCIUS JUNIUS BRUTUS BOOTH (1796–1852)
EDWIN BOOTH (1833–1893)

The celebrated actor Lucius Junius Brutus Booth, father of John Wilkes Booth (q.v.) and Edwin Booth (q.v.), left his native England for America. He returned occasionally, and kept a wife in each country. In letters home he was always concerned about his family and his livestock (for a while he was a vegetarian and refused to kill his animals) ...

His dog Boatswain '...should have a run once or twice every Day and his Tub of Water always supplied (a thing very likely to be forgot as of no importance when in fact it is)...'

His children '...Pay all attention to the regularity of their diet and motions.'

To his father '...I'm sick of acting – much rather would I be home. Have the stray Hogs returned?'

To his American wife Mary Ann: 'My love for you is still undiminished. Take care of your Health and don't be dull or fretting, there's my own soul. God bless you dear Wife.'

J.B. Booth's son Edwin was as successful as his father, and toured a great deal. In 1857 he wrote a letter to a friend, Dave Anderson, on the back of a hotel washing list. He added some notes of his own to the printed side:

Don't weep
WASHING LIST
It's all I own
Mr. Booth's list of assets

0	Bosoms	
1	Drawers	
2	Stockings	
	Chemise	*oh*
	Caps	*hum*
	Dresses	*he, he*
	Night Dresses	*law!*
	Corsets	*Ha, ha, ha!*
	Capes	*I confess the cape*
	Pantalets	*De lord*
	Skirts	*jamais*

Battle House, Mobile
1857

EDWIN BOOTH (1833–1893)
JOHN WILKES BOOTH (1838–1865)

Edwin Booth's brother John Wilkes Booth was also an actor – and a political revolutionary. On 14th. April, 1865 at the Park Street Theatre, Washington, President Abraham Lincoln was watching a performance of OUR AMERICAN COUSIN. John Wilkes Booth, as an actor, knew his way about the building. He slipped past the guard, entered the President's box, and shot him in the head. Booth escaped but was soon found and shot dead on the spot. John Wilkes Booth's action was bound to affect his brother's career.

The blow came from Henry Jarrett, manager of the Boston theatre where Edwin Booth was playing at the time his brother shot the President:

Parker House, Boston, 7 o'clock a.m.
Saturday, April 15th, 1865

Edwin Booth Esquire

My dear Sir,

A fearful calamity is upon us. The President of the United States has fallen by the hand of an assassin, and I am shocked to say suspicion points to one nearly related to you as the perpetrator of this horrid deed. God grant it may not prove so! With this knowledge, and out of respect to the anguish which will fill the public mind as soon as the appalling fact shall be fully revealed, I have concluded to close the Boston theatre until further notice. Please signify to me your co-operation in this matter.

In great sorrow, and in haste,
I remain, yours very truly,
Henry C. Jarrett

EDWIN BOOTH TO HENRY C. JARRETT

Franklin Square, Boston
April 15th, 1865

Henry C. Jarrett, Esq.

My dear Sir,

With deepest sorrow and great agitation, I thank you for relieving me from my engagement with yourself and the public. The news of the morning has made me wretched indeed, not only because I have received the unhappy tidings of the suspicions of a brother's crime, but because a good man, and a most justly honored and patriotic ruler, has fallen, in an hour of national joy, by the hands of an assassin. The memory of the thousands who have fallen in the field, in our Country's defence, during this struggle, cannot be forgotten by me, even in this, the most distressing day of my life. And I most sincerely pray that the victories we have already won may stay the brand of war and the tide of loyal blood.

While mourning, in common with all other loyal hearts, the death of the President, I am oppressed by a private woe not to be expressed in words. But whatever calamity may befall me and mine, my country, one and indivisible, has my warmest devotion.

Edwin Booth

At first the plan had been merely to kidnap the President, but to John Wilkes' mind this was insufficient action. After the killing (which, in a diary entry written immediately afterwards and found with his body, John Wilkes Booth justified as 'doing what Brutus *was honored for'), he sent the following remarkable letter to the Editor of the Philadelphia Inquirer, who published it after Booth's death. (Both transcript and manuscript disappeared until 1977, when they were discovered in the USA National Archives in Washington DC.)*

My Dear Sir,

You may use this as you think best. But as *some* may wish to know *when*, *who*, and *why* and as I know not *how* to direct, I give it (in the words of your Master)

'To whom it may concern':

[A sarcastic reference to Abraham Lincoln's speech to the Confederate Commissioners at Niagara Falls, July 1864, which ended all hopes of peace.]

Right or wrong, God judge me, not man. For be my motive good or bad, of one thing I am sure – the lasting condemnation of the North.

I love peace more than life. Have loved the Union beyond expression. For four years I have waited, hoped, and prayed for the dark clouds to break, and for a restoration of our former sunshine. To wait longer would be a crime. All hope for peace is dead. My prayers have proved as idle as my hopes. God's will be done. I go to see, and share the bitter end.

I have ever held the South were right. The very nomination of Abraham Lincoln, four years ago, spoke plainly: war – war upon Southern rights and institutions. His election proved it. 'Await an overt act.' Yes – till you are bound and plundered! What folly! The South were wise. Who thinks of argument of patience when the finger of his enemy presses on the trigger. In a *foreign* war I, too, could say 'Country right or wrong', but in a struggle *such as ours*, where the brother tries to pierce the brother's heart, for God's sake choose the right. When a country like this spurns *justice* from her side, she forfeits the allegiance of every honest freeman, and should leave him untrammelled by any fealty soever, to act as his conscience may approve.

People of the North, to hate tyranny, to love liberty and justice, to strike at wrong and oppression, was the teaching of our fathers. The study of our early history will not let *me* forget it. And may it never.

This country was formed for the *white*, not for the black man; and looking upon *African slavery* from the same stand-point held by those noble framers of our constitution, I for one have ever considered it one of the greatest blessings (both for themselves and us) that God ever bestowed upon a favored nation. Witness heretofore our wealth and power, witness their elevation in happiness and enlightenment above their race elsewhere. I have lived among it most of my life, and have seen *less* harsh treatment from master to man, than I have beheld in the North from father to son. Yet Heaven knows *no one* would be willing to do *more* for the negro race than I, could I but see a way to still better their condition. But Lincoln's policy is only preparing the way for their total annihilation. The South are *not, nor have they been*, fighting for the continuance of slavery – the first battle of Bull-run did away with that idea. Their causes since, for *war*, have been as *noble*, and *greater far* than those that urged our fathers on. Even should we allow they were *wrong* at the beginning of this contest, *cruelty and injustice* have made the wrong become the *right*. And they stand now, before the wonder and admiration of the world, as a noble band of patriotic heroes! Hereafter, reading of their deeds, Thermopylae will be forgotten.

When I aided in the capture and execution of John Brown, (who was a murderer on our Western Border, and who was fairly tried and convicted – before an impartial judge and jury – of treason – and who by the way has since been made a God), I was proud of my little share in the transaction, for I deemed it my duty and that I was helping our common country to perform an act of justice. But what was a crime in poor John Brown is now considered (by themselves) as the greatest and only virtue of the whole Republican party. Strange transmigration – *vice* to become a *virtue*. Simply because *more* indulge in it. I thought then, as now, that the abolitionists were *the only traitors in the land*, and that the entire party deserved the fate of poor old Brown. Not because they wish to abolish slavery, but on account of the means they have ever endeavored to use to effect that abolition. If Brown were living, I doubt if he himself would set slavery against the Union… The South can make no choice. It is either extermination or slavery for *themselves* (worse than death) to draw from. I would know my choice.

I have also studied hard to discover on what grounds the rights of a state to secede have been denied, when our very name 'United States' and our Declaration of Independence *both* provide for secession. But there is no time for words. I write in haste.

I know how foolish I shall be deemed for undertaking such a step as this, where on the one side I have many friends, and everything to make me happy; where my profession alone has gained me an income of more than twenty thousand dollars a year; and where my great personal ambition in my profession has such a great field for labor. On the other hand, the South have never bestowed upon me one kind word – a place now where I have no friends except beneath the sod; a place where I must either become a private soldier or a beggar. To give up all of the *former* for the *latter*, besides my mother and sisters whom I love so dearly (although they so widely differ with me in opinion) seems insane. But God is my judge I love *justice* more than I do a country that disowns it. More than fame and wealth. More – Heaven pardon me if wrong – more than a happy home. I have never been upon a battlefield, but O my countrymen, could you all but see the *reality* or effects of this horrid war as I have seen them (in *every State* except Virginia) I know you would think like me; and would pray the Almighty to create in the Northern mind a sense of *right* and *justice* (even should it possess no seasoning of mercy); and that he would dry up this sea of blood between us, which is daily growing wider.

Alas – poor country. Is she to meet her threatened doom? Four years ago, I would have given a thousand lives to see her remain (as I had always known her) powerful and unbroken. And even now I would hold my life as nought, to see her what she was. O my friends, if the fearful scenes of the past four years had never been enacted, or if what has been had been but a frightful dream from which we could now awake, with what overflowing hearts could we bless our God and pray for his continued favor. How I have loved the *old flag* can never, now, be known. A few years since and the entire world could boast of *none* so pure and spotless. But I have of late been seeing and hearing of the *bloody deeds* of which she has been made the emblem, and would shudder to think how changed she had grown.

How I have longed to see her break from the mist of blood and death that circles round her folds, spoiling her beauty and tarnishing her honor. But no, day by day she has been dragged deeper and deeper into cruelty and oppression; till now, in my eyes, her once bright red stripes look like *bloody gashes* on the face of Heaven. I look now upon

79

my early admiration of her glories as a dream. My love, as things stand today, is for the South alone. Nor do I deem it a dishonor in attempting to make for her a prisoner of this man, to whom she owes so much of misery. If success attends me, I go penniless to her side. They say she has found that 'last ditch' which the North have so long derided, and has been endeavoring to force her in, forgetting they are our brothers and that it's impolitic to goad an enemy to madness. Should I reach her in safety and find it true, I will proudly beg permission to triumph or die in that same 'ditch', by her side.

A Confederate. At present. Doing duty upon his own responsibility.

It is worth remembering that John Wilkes' model, Brutus, speaking of the danger of 'the abuse of greatness' in Shakespeare's JULIUS CAESAR, Act II, Scene i, says:

> It must be by his death: and, for my part,
> I know no personal cause to spurn at him,
> But for the general. He would be crown'd:
> How that might change his nature, there's the question...
>
> And therefore think him as a serpent's egg,
> Which, hatch'd, would as his kind grow mischievous,
> And kill him in the shell.

To his mother Mary Ann, John Wilkes Booth wrote:

[1864]

Dearest beloved Mother,

Heaven knows how dearly I love you, and may our kind Father in Heaven (if only for the sake of my love) watch over, comfort and protect you in my absence. May he soften the blow of my departure, granting you peace and happiness for many, many years to come. God ever bless you.

I have always endeavored to be a good and dutiful son, and even now would wish to die sooner than give you pain. But dearest Mother, though I owe you all, there is another duty, a noble duty for the sake of liberty and humanity due to my Country. For four years I have lived, I may say, a *slave* in the North (a favored slave it's true, but no less hateful to me on that account), not daring to express my thoughts or sentiments, even in my own home constantly hearing every principle dear to my heart denounced as treasonable; and knowing the vile and savage acts committed on my countrymen, their wives and helpless children, that I have cursed my wilful idleness, and begun to deem myself a coward, and to despise my own existence. For four years I have borne it mostly for your dear sake; and for you alone have I also struggled to fight off this desire to be gone; but it seems that uncontrollable fate, moving me for its ends, takes me from you, dear Mother, to do what work I can for a poor, oppressed, downtrodden people...

Darling Mother I can not write you. You will understand the deep regret the forsaking your dear side will make me suffer, for you have been the best, the noblest, an example for all mothers. God, God bless you, as I shall ever pray him to do.

And should the last *bolt* strike your son, dear Mother, bear it patiently and think at the best life is but short, and *not at all times happy*. My Brothers and Sisters (Heaven protect them) will add my love and duty to their own, and watch you with care and kindness, till we meet again. And if that happiness does not come to us on earth, then may, O may it be with God...

Come weal or woe, with never ending love and devotion, you will find me ever your affectionate son,

John

The War Department circulated bills with the following message:

THE MURDERER
Of our late beloved President, Abraham Lincoln
IS STILL AT LARGE
$50,000 REWARD
Will be paid by this Department for his apprehension.

BOOTH is Five Feet 7 or 8 inches high, slender build,
high forehead, black hair, black eyes, and wore a heavy
black moustache, which there is some reason to believe
has been shaved off.

Shortly after John was found and shot, his brother Edwin received a letter from an estranged friend...

RICHARD STODDARD TO EDWIN BOOTH

Edwin,

When I heard of the dreadful calamity which has fallen upon us, my sorrow was two-fold – for the nation and for you. My impulse was to write you at once and say so, but I did not for several reasons.

First, I could say nothing which could for a moment mitigate your grief, or which you would not be likely to hear from others.

Second, it seemed best to me that you should be left to yourself alone with your woe and God.

Third, I knew that if you ever understood me - and I think you did once – you would understand my silence as well as my speech.

Fourth, I have always made it a rule of my life when I have lost a friend, or a friend has lost me, to take no step, and to wish none to be taken with my sanction, toward renewing the old relationship. There is no cement in this world... strong enough to mend a broken friend-ship...

Now I write to you – and why?... Because John is dead, not by the rope which he could not have escaped (and by which I would not have had him die, for your sake and your mother's and the fame of your dead father), but fighting for his life. Because it is all over with him, I write you rejoicing, though with tears, for your sake and his own. For my own part I remember him well and kindly. I saw no ill in him when I met him at your house, and shall think of him, or try to, as he seemed then, not as we are told he was later, and as we know he was at the last.

That God may sustain you and bless you and pardon him is the prayer of your once friend, never enemy.

Farewell,

Richard

In an early letter to his father, Edwin had written: 'I don't think John will startle the world... but he is improving fast and looks beautiful.'

CHARLOTTE BRONTË (1816–1855)

Charlotte Brontë and her sisters had London publishers, Mr. Smith and Mr. Williams, who had no inkling that their best-selling authors were women until she and her sister Anne (1820–1849) surprised them with a visit. The next day they all went to the Opera...

CHARLOTTE BRONTË TO MARY ['POLLY'] TAYLOR

Haworth, September 4, 1848

Dear Polly,

I write to you a great many more letters than you write to me, though whether they will all reach you, or not, Heaven knows!...

Mr. Smith said we must come and stay at his house, but we were not prepared for a long stay, and declined... as we took our leave he told us he should bring his sisters to call on us that evening. We returned to our inn, and I paid for the excitement of the interview by a thundering headache and a harassing sickness. Towards evening, as I got no better and expected the Smiths to call, I took a strong dose of sal-volatile. It roused me a little; still, I was in grievous bodily case when they were announced.

They came in, two elegant young ladies, in full dress, prepared for the Opera – Mr. Smith himself in evening costume, white gloves, etc.. We had by no means understood that it was settled we were to go the Opera, and were not ready. Moreover, we had no fine, elegant dresses with us, or in the world. However, on brief rumination I thought it would be wise to make no objections. I put my headache in my pocket, we attired ourselves in the plain, high-made country garments we possessed, and went with them to their carriage...

They must have thought us queer, quizzical looking beings, especially me with my spectacles. I smiled inwardly at the contrast, which must have been apparent, between me and Mr. Smith as I walked with him up the crimson-carpeted staircase of the Opera House and stood amongst a brilliant throng at the box door, which was not yet open. Fine ladies and gentlemen glanced at us with a slight, graceful superciliousness quite warranted by the circumstances. Still, I felt pleasantly excited in spite of headache and sickness and conscious clownishness, and I saw Anne was calm and gentle, which she always is.

The performance was Rossini's opera of *The Barber of Seville*, very brilliant, though I fancy there are things I should like better. We got home after one o'clock; we had never been in bed the night before, and had been in constant excitement for twenty four hours. You may imagine we were tired.

On Monday we went to the Exhibition at the Royal Academy and the National Gallery, dined again at Mr. Smith's, then went home with Mr. Williams to tea, and saw his comparatively humble but neat residence and his fine family of eight children. A daughter of Leigh Hunt's was there. She sang some little Italian airs which she had picked up among the peasantry in Tuscany, in a manner that charmed me.

On Tuesday morning we left London laden with books which Mr. Smith had given us, and got safely home. A more jaded wretch than I looked when I returned it would be difficult to conceive. I was thin when I went, but was meagre indeed when I returned; my face looked grey and very old, with strange, deep lines ploughed in it; my eyes stared unnaturally. I was weak and yet restless. In a while, however, the bad effects of excitement went off and I regained my normal condition...

Goodbye. God bless you. Write.

C.B.

CHARLES KEMBLE (1775–1854)

Charles Kemble was brother of John Philip Kemble and Sarah Siddons (q.v.), and father of Fanny Kemble (q.v.). He was a theatre manager and celebrated leading actor. Curiously, when he was to play the rapacious Sir Giles Overreach in the enduring success A NEW WAY TO PAY OLD DEBTS (Massinger, 1633), he was less keen to create his own interpretation than to emulate that of the actor John Henderson (1747–1785, of whom Garrick had a lower opinion, saying drily: 'I have seen the great Henderson, who has something, and is nothing – he might be made to figure among the puppets of these times.')

Kemble wrote to Mrs Inchbald, who had played Lady Allworth in Henderson's production:

[Undated, unheaded]

What kind of a hat does Mr. Henderson wear? What kind of wig, of cravat, of ruffles, of clothes, of stockings; with or without embroidered clocks, square or round-toed shoes? I shall be uneasy if I have not an idea of his dress, even to the shape of his buckles, and what rings he wears on his hands. Moroseness and cruelty seem the groundwork of this monstrous figure; but I am at a loss to know whether in copying it I should draw the lines that express his courtesy to Lord Lovel with an exaggerated or mere natural strength?

Will you take the pains to inform me in what particular points Mr. Henderson chiefly excelled, and in what manner he executed them?

Charles Kemble

FANNY KEMBLE (1809–1893)

Fanny Kemble, niece of Sarah Siddons (q.v.) and daughter of Charles Kemble (q.v.), rescued Covent Garden Theatre from bankruptcy with her sensational Juliet. Her amazing career as actress, writer, Women's Rights activist and Abolitionist in England and America spanned most of the nineteenth century. Among her friends was George Stephenson (1781–1848), the engineer and inventor, who developed the world's first public passenger train.

After a ride on 'Rocket', Fanny writes to her dearest friend Harriet St Leger...

Liverpool
August 26th, 1830

My dearest Harriet,

A common sheet of paper is enough for love, but a foolscap extra can alone contain a railroad and my ecstasies...

A party of sixteen persons was issued into a courtyard, where stood several carriages, one of which was prepared for our reception. It was a long-bodied vehicle, with seats placed across it back to back. The wheels were placed upon two iron bands, which formed the road, and to which they are fitted, being so constructed as to slide along without danger of becoming displaced.

We were introduced to the little engine that was to drag us along the rails. She (for they make these curious little fire-horses all mares) consisted of a boiler, a stove, a small platform, a bench, and behind it a barrel containing enough water to prevent her being thirsty for fifteen miles. She goes upon wheels, which are her feet, and are moved by bright steel legs called 'pistons'; these are propelled by steam, and in proportion as more steam is applied to the upper extremities (the hip joints, I suppose) of these pistons, the faster they move the wheels; and when it is desirable to diminish the speed, the steam, which unless suffered to escape would burst the boiler, evaporates through a safety valve into the air.

The reins, bit and bridle of this wonderful beast is a small steel handle, which applies or withdraws the steam from its legs or pistons, so that a child might manage it. The coals, which are its oats, are under the bench. This snorting little animal, which I felt rather inclined to pat, was then harnessed to our carriage, and Mr. Stephenson having taken me on the bench of the engine with him, we started at about *ten miles an hour!*

The steam horse being ill adapted for going up and down hill, the road was kept at a certain level, and appeared sometimes to sink below the surface of the earth, and sometimes to rise above it. Almost at starting it was cut through the solid rock, which formed a wall on either side of it, about sixty feet high. You can't imagine how strange it felt to be journeying thus, without any visible cause of progress other than the magical machine, with its flying white breath and rhythmical, unvarying pace.

After proceeding through this rocky defile, we presently found ourself raised upon embankments ten or twelve feet; we then came to a moss, all swamp on which no foot could tread without sinking, and yet it bore the road which bore us.

We had now come fifteen miles, and stopped where the road traversed a wide and deep valley. Stephenson made me alight, and led me down to the bottom of this ravine, over which he has thrown a magnificent viaduct of nine arches, the middle one of which is seventy feet high. It was lovely and beautiful beyond words. He explained to me the whole construction of the steam engine, and said he could soon make a famous engineer of me! Which, considering the wonderful things he has achieved, I daresay is not impossible!

Now for a word or two about the master of these marvels, with whom I am horribly in love. He is a man of from fifty to fifty-five years of age; his face is fine, though careworn, and bears an expression of deep thoughtfulness; his mode of explaining his ideas is peculiar and very original, striking and forcible; and although his accent indicates strongly his North-country birth, his language has not the slightest touch of vulgarity or coarseness. He has certainly turned my head!

In 1834, Fanny Kemble married Pierce Butler from Philadelphia. He owned a plantation in Georgia, where they finally moved to live in 1839...

FANNY KEMBLE TO EMILY FITZHUGH

Butler's Island, Georgia
January 9th, 1839

Dearest Emily,

We all arrived here safely on Sunday last, and my thoughts are engrossed with the condition of the people from whose labour we draw our subsistence; of which, now I am here, I feel ashamed.

The place itself is one of the wildest corners of creation. It is a sort of hasty pudding of amphibious elements, composed of a huge rolling river, thick and turbid with mud, and stretches of mud banks scarcely reclaimed from the water. The river wants *straining*, and the land *draining*, to make either of them properly wet or dry.

The island, which is only a portion of our Georgia estate, contains several thousand acres, and is about eight miles round, and formed of nothing but the deposits of the Altamaha, whose brimming waters roll round it, and every now and then threaten to submerge it. The whole island is a swamp, dyked and trenched and divided by ditches and a canal, by means of which the rice fields are periodically overflowed. A duck, an eel or a frog might find life here as in Paradise.

Yours ever,
Fanny

FANNY KEMBLE TO HARRIET ST LEGER

Butler's Island, Georgia
January 8th, 1839

Dearest Harriet,

We live here in a very strange manner. The house we inhabit is inferior to the poorest farmhouse in any part of England. The little furniture is of the coarsest and roughest description, and the household services are performed by negroes who run in and out, generally bare-footed and always filthy. This unlimited supply of trained savages (for that is what they really are) is anything but a luxury for me. Their ignorance, dirt and stupidity seem to me as intolerable as the unjust laws which condemn them to be ignorant, filthy and stupid. I had desired very earnestly to have the opportunity of judging this matter of slavery for myself; not, of course, that I ever doubted that to keep human beings as slaves was in itself wrong, but I suppose that I might discover at any rate circumstances of palliation in the condition of the negroes. Hitherto this has not been the case. The wrong strikes me more forcibly every hour I live here; and the evil effect of such a state of things upon the *whites*, who inflict the wrong, impresses me as I did not anticipate it would, with still more force.

The negroes here, who see me row and walk in the hot sun, lift heavy burthens and make various exertions which are supposed to be their peculiar *privilege*, frequently remonstrate with me, with the remark, 'What for you do work, Missis? You hab niggers enough to wait upon you!' You may suppose how agreeable such remonstrances are to me!

Ever your affectionate

Fanny

[On one of our American tours with FANNY – THE LIFE AND TIMES OF FANNY KEMBLE, Estelle Kohler and I visited Butler's Island in Georgia, now barely cultivated; we found Pierce Butler's rice mill and the remains of an 'English Garden' Fanny Kemble had planted herself.]

The irascible Charles Macready (q.v.), was famous for his death scenes and his 'pauses' (he once confided terrifyingly in his journal: '... the prompter, in every pause I made in a scene where the pauses are effects, kept shouting 'the word' to me till I was ready to go and knock him down.' On another occasion a young actor trod on his outstretched hand after his death in MACBETH. Macready jumped to his feet, roared 'Beast of Hell!' at the poor wretch, and repeated the death for the audience. A hot-tempered but sincere tragedian with a reputation on both sides of the Atlantic, Macready's career in North America was ruined by his celebrated feud with the American tragedian Edwin Forrest (1806–1872).

Fanny Kemble had a famous stage partnership with Macready, though she rarely enjoyed it...

February 18th, 1848

Dearest Harriet,

I have been this morning to a rehearsal of *Macbeth — which Mr. Macready did not attend...* I have another rehearsal tomorrow at which it is to be hoped he will attend, as otherwise my being there is quite a work of supererogation...

February 19th

I had a three hour rehearsal this morning, and Macready was there... He is not courteous or pleasant, or even well-bred, remains seated while one is standing talking to him; and a discussion having arisen as to the situation of a table which he wished on the stage and I wished removed, he exhibited considerable irritability and ill humour.

He is unnecessarily violent in acting, and I congratulated myself that as Lady Macbeth I could not possibly suffer from this; but was astonished and dismayed when, at the exclamation 'Bring forth men-children only', he seized me ferociously by the wrist and compelled me to make a demi-volte or pirouette such as I think that lady did surely never perform before...

God bless you, dear,
Ever yours,
Fanny

To another friend on the same subject...

King Street,
Wednesday, February 23, 1848

Dear Hal,

The staircase I have to go up to my dressing-room at the Princess's Theatre is one with which you are unacquainted, my dearest Hal, for it is quite in another part of the house, beyond the green room, and before you come to the stage...

Not only had I this inconvenient distance and height to go, but the dressing room appointed for me had not even a fireplace in it; at this I remonstrated, and am now accommodated decently in a room with a fire, though in the same inconvenient position as regards the stage...

Mr. Maddox assured me that Macready poisoned every place he went into, to such a degree, with musk and perfumes, that if he were to give up his room to me, I should not be able to breathe in it. With my passion for perfumes, this, however, did not seem to me so certain; but the room I now have answers my purpose quite well enough...

Macready is not pleasant to act with, as he keeps no specific time for his exits or entrances, comes on while one is in the middle of a soliloquy, and goes off while one is in the middle of a speech to him. He growls and prowls and roams and foams about the stage in every direction, like a tiger in his cage, so that I never know on what side of me he means to be; and keeps up a perpetual snarling and grumbling like the aforesaid tiger, so that I never feel quite sure that he *has done*, and that it is my turn to speak.

I do not think fifty pounds a night would hire me to play another engagement with him; but I only say 'I don't *think*...' Fifty pounds a night is a consideration, four times a week! And I have not forgotten the French proverb, '*Il ne faut pas dire: "Fontaine, jamais de ton eau je ne boirai."*'

I do not know how Desdemona might have affected me under other circumstances, but my only feeling about acting it with Mr. Macready is dread of his personal violence. I quail at the idea of his laying hold of me in those terrible, passionate scenes; for in *Macbeth* he pinched me black and blue, and almost tore the point lace from my head. I am sure my little finger will be rebroken, and as for that smothering in bed, 'Heaven have mercy upon me!' as poor Desdemona says. If that foolish creature wouldn't persist in *talking* long after she has been smothered and stabbed to death, one might escape by the off side of the bed, and leave the bolster to be questioned by Emilia, and apostrophised by Othello. But she *will* uplift her testimony, after her death, to her husband's amiable treatment of her and even the bolster wouldn't be stupid enough for that.

Did it ever occur to you what a witness to Othello's agony in murdering his wretched wife his inefficient clumsiness in the process was – his half-smothering, his half-stabbing her? *That* man not to be able to kill *that* woman outright, with one hand on her throat, or one stroke of his dagger. How tortured he must have been, to have bungled so his work!

I wish I was with you and Dorothy at St. Leonards instead of struggling here for my life – livelihood, at any rate – with Macready; but that's foolish. He can't *touch* me tonight, that's one comfort, for I am Queen Katherine.

Farewell, believe me,
Ever yours most respectfully,
Fanny

King Street
Friday, February 28, 1848

Dear Hal,

I got through Desdemona very well, as far as my personal safety was concerned; for though I fell on the stage in real hysterics at the end of one of those horrible scenes with Othello, Macready was more considerate than I had expected, did not rebreak my little finger, and did not really smother me in bed. I played the part fairly well, and wish you had seen it. I was tolerably satisfied with it myself, which, you know, I am not often...

I really believe Macready cannot help being as odious as he is on the stage. He very nearly made me faint last night in *Macbeth*, with crushing my broken finger, and, by way of apology, merely coolly observed that he really could not answer for himself in such a scene, and that I ought to wear a splint! And truly, if I act much more with him, I think I shall require several splints, for several broken limbs.

I have been rehearsing *Hamlet* with him this morning for three hours. I do not mind his tiresome particularity on the stage, for though it all goes to making himself the only object of everything and everybody, he works very hard, and is zealous, and conscientious, and laborious in his duty, which is a merit in itself. But I think it is rather *mean* (as the children say) of him to refuse to act in such plays as *King John, Much Ado about Nothing*, which are pieces of his own, too, to oblige me; whilst I have studied expressly for him Desdemona, Ophelia, Cordelia, parts quite out of my line – merely that his plays may be strengthened by my name. Moreover, he has not scrupled to ask me to study new parts in new plays which have been either written expressly only for him, or cut down to suit his peculiar requisitions. This, however, I have declined doing. Anything of Shakespeare's is good enough, and too good, for me...

I shall have a nausea of fright till after I have done singing in Ophelia tomorrow night.

Ever yours,
Fanny

JOANNA BAILLIE (1762–1851)

Joanna Baillie wrote poetry, nine plays on the Passions and a tragedy which was produced at Drury Lane Theatre with leads played by Charles Kemble (q.v.) and Sarah Siddons (q.v.). W.C. Macready (q.v.) wrote disparagingly of her literary technique in his journal (ed. Trewin, Longmans 1967): 'There is a stiffness... a sort of brocaded style, a thick kind of silk, that has no fall or play – it is not flexibility of nature.'

Perhaps her mentor, the poet and critic Samuel Rogers (1763–1855), had something to do with this...

[Undated]

JOANNA BAILLIE TO SAMUEL ROGERS

My dear Mr. Rogers,

You once called me, and not very long ago, an ungrateful hussy, and I remember it the better because I really thought I deserved it. But whether I did or not...

Do you remember when I told you, a good while since, of my intention of looking over all my works to correct them for an edition to be published after my decease, should it be called for, and you giving me a hint never to let a *which* stand where a *that* might serve the purpose, to prefer the words *while* to *whilst*, *among* to *amongst*, etc.? I acquiesced in all this most readily, throwing as much scorn upon the rejected expressions as anybody would do, and with all the ease of one who from a natural taste has always avoided them.

If you do, you will guess what has been my surprise and mortification to find through whole pages of even my last dramas, 'whiches', 'whilsts' and 'amongsts', etc., where they need not have been, in abundance. Well, I have profited by your hint, though I was not aware that I needed it at the time when it was given, and now I thank you for it very sincerely. I cannot imagine how I came to make this mistake, if it had not been that, in writing songs, I have often rejected the words in question because they do not sound well in singing. I have very lately finished my corrections, and now all my literary tasks are finished...

Very truly and gratefully yours.
J. Baillie

[Fanny Kemble (q.v.) said of Samuel Rogers: 'He certainly had the kindest heart and unkindest tongue of anyone I ever knew.']

WILLIAM CHARLES MACREADY (1793–1873)

Macready, a big-hearted, industrious and passionate man, whose journals make hilarious and moving reading (ed. J.C. Trewin, Longmans 1967), took over from Edmund Kean as London's leading actor. Throughout his career in England and America, Macready fought for a return to Shakespeare's texts as written (many of them were commonly played in altered form). His playing opposite the marvellous Helen Faucit was powerful, and his platonic though profound friendship with her the subject of much speculation. However, Fanny Kemble (q.v.) found him impossible to work with ('He growls and prowls and roams and foams about the stage in every possible direction').

The mighty tragedian considers the repertoire, and advises the playwright:

5, Clarence Terrace, London
August 16th, 1840

My dear Serle,

From some mistake of that most blundering copyist, I have only got the 2nd., 3rd. and 5th. acts of *Master Clarke* – which I have read most attentively, piecing out with my memory as best I could the movement in the opening and 4th. acts.

I have also read *The Spanish Maid* again, following clearly your Red letters – well: I do not like to make a choice – I think both safe – only I do not quite like the ending of *Master Clarke*, I think it is tame – and I don't *quite* like the *single* appearance of the Monk in the last scene of *The Spanish Maid* – with that exception I think *The Spanish Maid* the more interesting play. But I think *both* will go well.

Therefore you had better see Webster [*Benjamin Webster – q.v.*] without delay, and say that we wait his directions to begin. The reasons on both are so nearly balanced, that it would be dangerous to decide on differences so nice, especially as that uncertain thing, the feeling of the audience, may overturn all our calculations. Which-ever therefore you choose, I am ready for – only let us two work in earnest.

Too much time has been lost. There is very charming writing in *The Spanish Maid* – the only rub is the rather *clumsy* entrance of the Monk

– the Beefeater commanding them all in the King's name to drop their swords and daggers – I think it is so very sweet a play, that it would be your best interest to keep it and remedy that defect.

I would not otherwise touch it – and so throw yourself for the present on our friend Clarke. Only please be stirring – with all good hopes and wishes,

Ever and always, dear Serle,

Yours,

W.C. Macready

CHARLES DICKENS (1812–1870)

The novelist Charles Dickens loved the theatre and theatricals, and saw himself as something of an actor. He was a better writer, and in that profession had no equal, though perhaps he was looking over his shoulder – a successful songwriter called Henry Russell was complaining to Dickens one night at the Lyceum Theatre that another man, one John Smith, was claiming authorship of his songs. 'Never mind, Russell,' replied Dickens, 'Every man has his Smith.'

Dickens writes to Charles Macready on sartorial matters, 1845:

Sir,

You once – only once – gave the world assurance of a waistcoat. You wore it, Sir, I think, in *Money*. It was a remarkable and precious waistcoat, wherein certain broad stripes of purple disported themselves – as by a combination of extraordinary circumstances too happy to occur again, I have seen it on your manly chest in private life. I saw it, Sir, I think, the other day in the cold light of morning, with feelings easier to be imagined than described.

Mr. Macready, Sir, are you a father? If so, lend me that waistcoat for five minutes...

I will send a trusty messenger at half-past nine precisely in the morning. He is sworn to secrecy. He durst not, for his life, betray me, or swells in ambuscade would have the waistcoat at the cost of his heart's blood.

Thine,
'The Unwaistcoated One'

Charles Dickens, very fetched by 'a piece of womanly tenderness', to Macready:

Office of *All the Year Round*,
A weekly journal conducted by Charles Dickens,
26, Wellington Street,
Strand,
London W.C.

Thursday, 19th February, 1863

My dear Macready,

I have just come back from Paris, where the readings *Copperfield*, *Dombey*... and *Carol*... – have made a sensation which modesty (my natural modesty) renders it impossible for me to describe. You knew what a noble audience the Paris audience is!! They were at their noblest with me.

....Fechter doing wonders over the way here *[Lyceum Theatre]* with a picturesque French drama. Miss Kate Terry, in a small part in it, perfectly charming. You may remember her making a noise years ago, doing a boy at an inn in *The Courtier of Lyons*? She has a tender love scene in this piece which is a really beautiful and artistic thing. I saw her do it at about 3 in the morning of the day when the Theatre opened, surrounded by shavings and carpenters and (of course) with that inevitable hammer going; and I told Fechter 'That is the very best piece of womanly tenderness I have ever seen on the stage, and you'll find that no audience can miss it.'

It is a comfort to add that it was instantly seized on and is much talked of...

Yours most affectionately,
Charles Dickens

[The Fechter Dickens mentions was Charles Fechter, 1823/5–1879, who trained as a sculptor before becoming an actor, working in England, France and Germany. A critic in Blackwood's Magazine *of 1861 wrote: 'I think his Hamlet is one of the very best, and his Othello one of the very worst, I have ever seen...']*

BENJAMIN WEBSTER (1797–1882)

Actor and dramatist Benjamin Webster (the most famous Webster of an illustrious family) started his career as a pit violinist. He described his first professional engagement as follows:

'...I had others to support... I resolved to walk to Croydon, ten miles every day, to rehearsal, and back to Shoreditch on twopence a day – one pennyworth of oatmeal and one pennyworth of milk – and I did it for six weeks, Sundays excepted, when I indulged in the luxury of shin of beef and ox-cheek. The gentlemen in the gallery pelted the orchestra with mutton pies. At first indignation was uppermost, but on reflection we made a virtue of necessity, and collecting the fragments of the not very light pastry, ate them under the stage...'

Webster became a successful actor and playwright. He was also manager of the Haymarket from 1837–1853. Today agents do the hard negotiating for us. Here is an insight into how it was done in 1845. Webster writes to the Scots actor James Anderson:

Theatre Royal Haymarket
23 September, 1845

My dear Anderson,

I have heard from Miss Faucit *[Helen Faucit, leading actress, 1817/20–1898; see Macreudy].* Maddox told her that Mac *[Macready, q.v.]* positively commences on the 13th. October, and she wishes to begin as soon after as possible. Can you play on or before 20th. October? Make an effort, as I want to take the wind out of Mac's sails!

The plays she names at present are *Lady of Lyons, Romeo and Juliet, The Hunchback, As you like it* and, if I like, *The Patrician's Daughter,* but I don't know the play. She is also ready in *Macbeth* if required. There is my budget and now for the reward of merit:

It is understood between us that you are to have One Hundred Pounds for twelve nights, to be played off at three nights a week, and a clear third of a benefit.

Wishing you well through it, and expecting an answer by return,

I remain, Yours truly,
B. Webster

16 High Street, Camden Town
September 24, 1845

My dear Webster,

I will write to Manager Simpson to let me off my Liverpool engagement, which I have no doubt he will for a consideration; then I am
yours. Mind, everything must be on a fair 'give and take' principle. If it
is left to be supposed that I am engaged merely to support Miss Faucit,
I must decline the engagement altogether. I am thus explicit to prevent
any further misunderstanding. No one can have more respect for
Helen Faucit, or a greater admiration of her talent, than myself; yet I
must have assurance that there will be no partiality shown, no difference in the announcement of either in play bills and advertisements, or
in any other way.

Your reply in the affirmative will finish the business, the remunera-
tion part of the affair being perfectly understood.

Yours faithfully,
J .R. Anderson

Theatre Royal, Haymarket
September 25, 1845

My dear Anderson,

You shall have a clear stage and no favour, so set your heart at rest.
Miss F. merely mentioned what she would wish to be done. In the
announcings and all you shall have fair play.

Yours truly,
B. Webster

ROBERT KEELEY (1794–1869)

In 1852, Mr Robert Keeley (famous for his joke to a smallish Chelmsford audience at curtain call: 'Why is the Chelmsford Theatre like a half-moon? D'ye give it up? Because it's never full!') and his wife (who had played the Nurse to Fanny Kemble's début as Juliet at Covent Garden) negotiated their joint contract with Benjamin Webster at the Haymarket Theatre:

19 Brompton Square
March 23, 1852

To B. Webster, Esq.

My dear Webster,

Our last engagement with you was in these words:

> *Memorandum.* Mr. and Mrs. Keeley are hereby engaged to Mr. Benjamin Webster, to perform. Mr. Keeley at the Theatre Royal, Haymarket, and Mrs. Keeley at the Theatres Royal Haymarket and Adelphi for three seasons – viz. (here the seasons are specified) at the Salary of Twenty pounds each per week, playhouse pay. Mrs. Keeley's playing at the Adelphi to be subject to her approval of the part she plays.

I am willing to make these words the basis of our present engagement, substituting the dates of the remainder of the present season of 1852 – the seasons of 1852/3 – and of 1853/4; and, doing so, I should wish it also to be understood between us:

> That all new pieces in which you think it desirable that either of us should play shall be perused by us before they are cast publicly, that we may have an option of declining to perform such parts as we do not think suitable to our professional abilities.

> That if there be any names of performers made prominent in the play–bills or in the posters, our names shall be equally conspicuous.

> That late hours be as much as possible avoided; but if the run of the business should render them unavoidable that our performing in the pieces played last in the evening shall be alternated with other performers.

I think your agreement to these conditions would prevent the possibility of misunderstanding between us.

In reference to the engagement of my daughter Mary, it would be payable only when her services were required – with the understanding that if she played on any *one* night in any one week she would be entitled to the full week's salary for that one night's performance. Period of Engagement the same as our own, and Salary Four Pounds per week available for either of the Theatres Haymarket or Adelphi but not at both on the same night.

I think I have enumerated all the points that could possibly arise between us, and have written in as explicit and understandable a manner as I can to prevent mistake. If you think so too, we will exchange to that effect.

> I am, my dear Webster,
> Very truly yours,
> R. Keeley

In view of the above it is worth recording H. Barton Baker (Our Old Actors):

> ...As we have seen, Hart's salary was only £3 per week; Betterton's and his wife's only £5 (the two). In a list of 1708/9 there is no salary above £6. Mrs. Oldfield's was only £4. But their benefits realised from £150 to £200. In 1729 Mrs. Oldfield's salary had been raised to £12 12s.. Mrs. Porter's was £266 per annum. Mrs. Woffington's and Mrs. Pritchard's were 10s., Clive's £15 15s.. Their benefits averaging about £200 each. Throughout the century, salaries continued to increase. From a Drury Lane list, 1801/2, we find Bannister received £17; King £16; Wroughton £15; Dowton £8; Suett £12; Charles Kemble £10; Mrs. Jordan £31 10s.; Miss de Camp £12; Mrs. Pope (Miss Younge) £12.
>
> There were twenty–five principal gentlemen and twenty ladies at £3 and upwards. Cooke never received above £20 a week in England, and went to America for £25. A few years afterwards even Charles Young was paid £50 per night.

In fact, the 'overpaid' Charles Mayne Young was a much-admired actor. Edmund Kean said of him: 'I had never seen Young act! Every one about told me he could not hold a farthing rushlight to me; but he can! He is an actor; and though I flatter myself that he could not act Othello as I do, yet what chance would I have in Iago after him, with his personal advantages and his damned musical voice?... I tell you what, Young is not only an actor such as I did not dream him to have been, but he is a gentleman!'

JENNY LIND (1820–1887)

'I don't, and won't admire Jenny Lind, whose success has been of a kind to make all such triumphs ridiculous. She is an accomplished singer, and second-rate actress; we have had so many better!' wrote the critic Anna Jameson (1794–1860).

In 1850 the celebrated 'Swedish Nightingale', Jenny Lind, was presented in America by the showman P.T. Barnum (1810–1891). The year before, taking a 'cure' in Ems, Germany, she wrote to her old tutor, the dramatist Charlotte Birch-Pfeiffer (1800–1868, once a successful actress and theatre manager in Vienna and Munich).

Jenny Lind describes her search for 'true nobility', the need to earn money for her 'beneficent acts' – and longs for boiled noodles...

Ems

8th August, 1849

Most honoured Mother Birch,

I received your *beautiful* letter the night before last, but very late, so that after all the activities that I must now engage in, I was exceedingly tired and did not want to begin this letter until I could find a quiet time for it. Yesterday, I went out to Stolzenfels with several Swedish friends who are also taking the cure here. So yesterday I didn't write it either. Now, I began this morning with a heavy headache, but my good Josephine said I simply must read that big packet from Berlin, that perhaps through this my headache might get better. So I did just that. I stayed very quietly in bed, and I must confess that after I had read your loving lines, I felt quite well and healthy once more. And now, I simply have no choice but to write my thoughts to you immediately. Dearest Mother, thoughts that once again were wakened in my breast by your letter.

I was *deeply touched* by everything that you tell me in it. And the good old days in Berlin came back most vividly before my eyes. In my imagination I savoured again with pleasure those boiled noodles. I heard you talking once more, saw my good aunt and little sister and the two little dogs, one of which was always so funny. Do you remember my song on the tree in the courtyard...? Yes, dear God! It is so beautiful to live again in all those wonderful memories...

103

You ask me, 'Well, now, are you really going to be married?' I answer, 'Absolutely not!' I have, indeed, greatly wished for it, for few people have a truer feminine feeling than I, the feeling of a loving woman, and it would have been a blessing for me to be able to call a child *my very own*. I was actually very close to marrying recently in England, dear Mother; but although the young man possessed many good qualities that I admired exceedingly, he was really much too young for me, and he had the softness of a girl, but not the strength of a man. Besides, his mother wanted to put a bridle on me as an artist, so to speak; but thank you very much! – such a narrow, prejudiced woman will never be able to influence my aims in life. I am really sorry, however, for the young man. He was quite attached to me, although my art was completely lost on him, for he had no interest in it at all. Now I know you are asking: 'But, Jenny, how could you fall in love with such a person?' But, my dear Mother, I love the English character *with all my heart*. The young man was very religious and as pure as gold, and just at that time I felt myself to be very much *alone*, for, as you know, I have no *joy* of my father and mother, and I am happiest when I am far away from them. I must turn to someone with this overflowing heart of mine.

I decided to part with the young man when I saw that, in him, I would merely have one more person to look after, and this certainly was not my purpose in marriage! Well, this whole affair flowed over my soul like a beneficial stream that melted all the hardness in my nature and led the way to many a green clearing in the lovely sunlight. As a result, now I am always green with the most beautiful hopes and see quite clearly how infinitely much I still have to do before I achieve true nobility. I have only one fervent prayer: that I will be able to present to the Lord a pure soul, the education of which no one undertook when it was still easy to do, for I was always a good child...

I should so like to come to Berlin, but I cannot promise it... The doctor urges me very insistently to take a grape-juice cure... and therefore I will not be ready before the middle of October. But can I – dare I – hope for an invitation to your house for boiled noodles?

Next spring, I must try once more to earn a great deal of money, because the beneficent acts I am planning are very expensive. I am like a bird; I don't feel a day older – quite the contrary in fact – and the *summa summarum* is (as you told me you yourself had experienced it) that I have gained the greatest profit from both *external* and *internal* unhappiness, and thank God that I am familiar with grief. After all, in the end everything happens for the best! *God is not dead*, dear Mother.

Otherwise, I am cheerful, happy, and thankful from morning till evening. I manage to keep myself very pleasantly occupied; I don't feel at all alone; nor do feel any trace of boredom, but I find that the day goes by quietly and pleasantly. I have a gladness in my soul that strives towards Heaven!...

Well, now, I have written you this long letter so that you might know that my inner life is much more cheerful and more happy than it formerly was. Please forgive it for being so long and verbose, and do not doubt the sincerity of

Your grateful and devoted

Jenny Lind

P.S. I visited Mme. Mendelssohn-Bartholdy in Kreuznach, and I came away from her quite refreshed. Oh, what a lovely person!

P.P.S. How remarkable, dear Mother, that you had begun letters to me... and then didn't dispatch them. I always forget that one can become a victim of false modesty, so that one is not conscious of the mistrust that one feels for one's self.

CHARLOTTE CUSHMAN (1816–1876)

In 1879 a Miss Elizabeth Peabody described the American actress Charlotte Cushman's Queen Katherine (in Shakespeare's HENRY VIII) and her great humanity ('There was swimming-room for all the world in her heart'), in a letter to Emma Stebbins, Cushman's friend and biographer:

ELIZABETH PEABODY TO EMMA STEBBINS

...I need not say how I enjoyed her splendid impersonation throughout, but especially the death scene. It was perfectly wonderful how she blended the infirmities of dying with the majesty of her spirit. But especially I was struck anew with the miraculous genius of Shakespeare as evinced in that last speech to Cromwell, in which Queen Katherine characterised Wolsey, in those sharp, heavily thought-freighted sentences, which it was obvious must be just so concise and terse, because the fast-coming death so overcame her power to utter that it was only by the intense will she could utter at all, and so was forced to concentrate in the first few words of each sentence. Then in the very death she did not seem to struggle much, did not evince physical pain, only torpor of organs. She went out of the body almost visibly, while the song of angels was sung behind the scenes.

When she returned again in 1860 she gave me a season ticket, and I went down from Concord to Boston, and saw her through the whole, constantly surprised to new admiration by each impersonation. I do not know, but I thought Rosalind the most marvellous of all. Her wit and grace and make-up making her seem but twenty-eight; and changing my former idea of a petite Rosalind into the new one of so fine and large a figure, which of course I saw Rosalind must have been, to match the force of character that conceived her bold enterprise.

Another seven years passed before I saw her in Rome, and experienced the generous friendship and hospitality which made those five months so rich in opportunities of enjoyment. But even amid the glories of Rome there was nothing that I studied with more interest and intensity than herself. Such simplicity and directness and humility of heart was to me most touching and wonderful in a person of such magnificent executive powers. You remember the conversations at those delightful breakfasts, to which she invited me every morning? Never was my own mind in such an intense state of activity... Principles seemed to rise up over the rich scenery of human life, like the white peaks of the Alps over the Swiss valleys, which were to me the most exciting and transporting objects in nature... for they carry one beyond the limits of the finite...

What golden hours those were when such grand receptive hearts and imaginations bettered one's thoughts in the reply! And were not some of those evenings symposia of the gods? Do you remember one when she read *The Halt Before Rome* to Lord Houghton, Lothrop, Motley, Bayard Taylor, yourself and me? Can you, or anybody with mortal pen, describe so that readers could realise the high-toned, artistic, grandly moral, delightfully human nature, that seemed to be the palpable atmosphere of her spirit, quickening all who surrendered themselves to her influence? What sincerity, what appreciation of truth and welcome of it (even if it wounded her); what bounteousness of nature; and how the breath of her mouth winnowed the chaff from the wheat in her expression of observed character and judgement of conduct!...

One of the last times I saw her I remember her earnest affectionate appeal to a young friend to forget herself and her appearance to others, in the noble unconsciousness that springs unbidden from surrendering one's self to some generous idea, and the sweet impulse of making others happy and appreciated. It must have waked an echo that will forever repeat itself, for I think it may have been the last time the young girl ever saw her...

Ah! What a loss she is to me, who in comparison with you and her family only touched the outside of her circle at an occasional tangent!... I never knew a person so ready, and even ardent, to help and further the efforts and works of others! There was swimming-room for all the world in her heart! She was one of the prophets of the unity of the human race – a proof of it, indeed!

I enclose you a letter; the only one in which she speaks of herself at any length, for generally her letters were only full of her correspondents' interests or affairs.

[LETTER FROM CHARLOTTE CUSHMAN TO ELIZABETH PEABODY]

Your letter has done me good, dear friend, and not the least part of it that which speaks approvingly of my beloved art, and all that it takes to make an exponent of it. It has been my fate to find in some of my most intimate relations my art 'tabooed', and held in light esteem. This has always hurt me; but my love for my friends has ever been stronger than my pride in anything else, and so my art has been 'snubbed'. But no one knows better than myself, after all my association with artists of sculpture or painting, how truly *my* art comprehends all the others and surpasses them, in so far as the study of mind is more than matter! Victor Hugo makes one of his heroines, an actress, say, 'My art endows me with a searching eye, a knowledge of the soul and the soul's workings, and in spite of all your skill, I read you to the depths!' This is a truth more or less powerful as one is more or less truly gifted by the good God.

You must keep it in a golden box, for I value it above all things else she ever gave me...

Elizabeth Peabody

Throughout her career, Charlotte Cushman had been known for encouraging and supporting her colleagues and friends. When her friend Mrs Seward died, followed by the death of her daughter Fanny Seward, Charlotte Cushman, travelling in Italy, wrote to Mr Seward...

Rome
[Undated]

CHARLOTTE CUSHMAN TO MR SEWARD

How can I ever tell you of the sadness which filled my soul at the intelligence which reached me on my return to Rome last Saturday night. No words can express what I feel for you all, how truly my heart goes out to you in your great sorrow and bereavement, and how deeply with that sorrow for you is mingled a grief for my own loss, which I find it so difficult to realise. I ask myself every hour, 'Can it be possible that my sweet young friend has passed away, and shall I never see her more?' This is hard to believe. I have heard from her so constantly this summer, that I have known of her failing health; but her last letter brought me so much better tidings that I was comforted much, and therefore the suddenness of the announcement shocked me more than words can tell. Alas! poor, dear child! how short has been her separation from the mother she adored, and what terrible sacrifices have you, my noble and sorely-tried friend, been called upon to lay upon the altar of your country! How more than hard has been your way! how terrible your pain! how little your seeming reward! but:

> He who ascends to mountain-tops shall find
> The loftiest peaks most wrapped in clouds and snow.
> He who surpasses and subdues mankind
> Must look down on the hate of those below;
> Though high above the sun of glory glow,
> And far beneath, the earth and ocean spread,
> Round him are icy rocks, and loudly blow
> Contending tempests on his naked head;
> And thus reward the toils which to those summits led.

My heart bleeds and aches for you as each successive blow falls upon you. I find myself awe-stricken, wondering how it can be possible that you should endure still more and live! You have had to bear so much in every way, that it seems to me you must be more than mortal if you are not broken in pieces...

I know it is hard, but I shall be so glad of a word from among you that I venture to ask it, trusting to the goodness and kindness you have always shown me. I regret more than ever that I am unable, through illness, to get to America this summer; it would have been a great joy to me then, and a great consolation to me *now*. But it was not to be. Ah, my friend, truly God's ways are not as our ways!

That He may bless and comfort you, prays ever
Your faithfully-loving friend,
Charlotte Cushman

WILKIE COLLINS (1824–1889)

A great friend of Charles Dickens (q.v.), the novelist and occasional playwright Wilkie Collins (THE WOMAN IN WHITE, THE MOONSTONE) writes to Miss Lydia Foote...

9, Melcombe Place,
Dorset Square, N.W.
December 17th, 1866

Dear Miss Foote,

I cannot allow *The Frozen Deep* to disappear from the bills of the Olympic Theatre without congratulating you sincerely on your performance of the part of 'Clara'.

In the first act especially, you played with a truth, grace, and simplicity – and you managed the difficult transitions from one section to another with an artist-like subtlety – which fulfilled, and more than fulfilled, the highest expectations I had formed of you.

Whatever reasons I may have seen on the stage for the disastrous result of the experiment from which we had all hoped so much, I saw nothing in *your* performance that disappointed me – and I thank you as heartily as if we had achieved a great theatrical success.

Very truly yours,
Wilkie Collins

After Sir Godfrey Kneller (1646–1723)

THOMAS BETTERTON
(1635~1710)

*'You are telling them a story,
and I am showing them facts'*

Plate
i

DAVID GARRICK
(1717~1779)

*'Last night I played Richard the
Third to the surprise of
Everybody'*

Portrait by Johann Zoffany (1735-1810)
Lithograph by Lowes Cato Dickinson (1819-1908)

Plate
ii

Peggy Woffington
(1717~1760)

*'Sir Thomas Robinson writes me
word that you are very pretty,
which has raised my curiosity to
a great pitch...'*

Anon. oil on canvas

Plate
iii

Charles Mathews
(1775/6~1835)

IN THE CHARACTER OF
THE OLD SCOTCH LADY, AS
REPRESENTED BY HIM WHEN
'AT HOME'

LYCEUM THEATRE, 1818

'Ten pounds a week and a benefit…'

Plate
iv

JOSEPH GRIMALDI
(1778~1837)

A SILVER CRUET SET DEPICTING THE
GREAT CLOWN
LYCEUM THEATRE, 1818

'I am rheumatised – goutised – puffised – and generally done up'

Plate
v

FANNY KEMBLE
(1809~1893)

'Anything of Shakespeare's is good enough,
and too good, for me'

Portrait by Thomas Sully (1783–1872)
Courtesy of Pennsylvania Academy of Fine Arts

SARAH BERNHARDT
(1844~1923)

'Your words are my food, your breath my wine'

Original photograph London Stereoscopic Company, Cheapside

Plates
vi a & b

EDWARD WILLARD
(1853~1915)

as Cyrus Blenkarn in
THE MIDDLEMAN

*'The clay owl… [he] hoped I wouldn't
mind baking it for him in my oven'*

Plate
vii

EDWIN BOOTH
(1833~1893)

'…the suspicions of a brother's crime'

HENRY IRVING
(1838~1905)

*'In all humility…mine is the
only great Shylock'*

ELLEN TERRY
(1847~1928)

*'Sir Henry is not at all
a terrible person'*

Unattributed photographs from *The Life & Art of Edwin Booth
and his Contemporaries*, Boston 1886

Plates
viii a, b & c

DION BOUCICAULT (1822–1890)

However, an experienced Miss Foote received advice and criticism, too, from the great Dion Boucicault. Boucicault was an Irish actor-manager and playwright who was only 19 when he saw his comedy LONDON ASSURANCE put on at Covent Garden in 1841. He is believed to have written 400 plays, of which at least 180 were produced on the London stage.

Globe Hotel, Glasgow
[Undated]

My dear Lydia,

I enclose your cheque for this last week and next.

I was delighted with you last night.

It will do.

You must take *more* courage and broaden out the character a little more. (The outline is quite correct.)

Give the audience your full face a little more – your profile is charming (I always admired it) but your full face is very pleasant too.

You are a very good girl. Consider yourself kissed.

Very sincerely,
D. Boucicault

An interesting insight into the nineteenth-century playwright's struggle for existence, which has timeless resonances for all writers, may be gleaned from the following wry article by the prolific Boucicault in The North American Review, *Sept. 1877:*

> ... the usual price received by Sheridan Knowles, Bulwer, and Talfourd at that time for their plays was £500. I was a beginner in 1841, and received for my comedy *London Assurance* £300. For that amount the manager bought the privilege of playing the work for his season. Three years later I offered a new play to a principal London theatre. The manager offered me £100 for it. In reply to my objection to the smallness of the sum he remarked, 'I can go to Paris and select a first-class comedy; having seen it performed, I feel certain of its effect. To get this comedy translated will cost me £25. Why should I give you £300 or £500 for your comedy of the success of which I cannot feel so assured?' The argument was unanswerable and the result inevitable. I sold a work for £100 that took me six months' hard work to compose and accepted a commission to translate three French plays at £50 apiece. This work afforded me child's play for a fortnight. Thus the English dramatist was obliged either to relinquish the stage altogether or to become a French copyist.

VICTOR HUGO (1802–1885)
SARAH BERNHARDT (1844–1923)

In 1877, French novelist Victor Hugo (LES MISERABLES, HERNANI, THE HUNCHBACK OF NOTRE DAME) saw Sarah Bernhardt in the revival of HERNANI at the Théâtre Français, Paris. The following morning she received a silver pendant in the form of a teardrop, with a letter:

Madame,

You were grand and enchanting. You moved me – me, the old soldier! – and, at a certain moment, while the enchanted public applauded you with emotion, I wept. This tear, which fell for you, belongs to you. Please allow me to offer you it.

Victor Hugo

Sarah Bernhardt wore the silver tear on stage until her death forty-six years later. At the age of 70 she had one leg removed but carried on with a triumphant tour of Europe and America. The day before she died, at 78, she was filming.

One of her greatest passions was Victorien Sardou (1831–1908), the poet-playwright (author of FEDORA). After their deaths, their love-letters were published.

SARAH BERNHARDT TO VICTORIEN SARDOU

[Undated]

Wonderful boy,

Where are you tonight? Your letter came only an hour ago – cruel hour – I had hoped you would spend it with me here.

Paris is a morgue without you; before I knew you, it was Paris, and I thought it was heaven; but now it is a vast desert of desolation and loneliness. It is like the face of a clock, bereft of its hands.

All the pictures that hung in my memory before I knew you have faded and given place to our radiant moments together.

Now I cannot live apart from you; your words – even though bitter – dispel all the cares of the world and make me happy; my art has been suckled by them, and softly rocked in their tender cradle; they are as necessary to me now as sunlight and air.

I am as hungry for them as food. I am thirsty for them, and my thirst is overwhelming. *Your words are my food, your breath my wine. You are everything to me.*

Your Sarah

SAMUEL PHELPS (1804/6–1878)

Actor Samuel Phelps, an actor of immense range, was famous as Bottom the Weaver in Shakespeare's A MIDSUMMER NIGHT'S DREAM, and as Malvolio in TWELFTH NIGHT. He opened the Sadlers Wells Theatre in 1844, and for 20 years, against all the odds, made Shakespeare pay — including a celebrated revival of ANTONY & CLEOPATRA in 1849.

While playing THE SCHOOL FOR SCANDAL in Bradford, he writes home on much more important matters...

Victoria Hotel, Bradford

Tuesday Evening *[Postmarked April 12, 1868]*

My darlings,

We got on all right last night. The house was very good and the play went off immensely...

I have had my rooms changed to the opposite side of the hotel, for those infernal cats were at it again this morning and would not let me sleep after daylight.

I should like to take the kitchen garden, you may tell Stevens, but I will not buy the fruit trees without seeing them. If they are there when I return and I think them worth the money I'll have them, but they are not to keep them on my account.

Nell may as well look out and have ready the things for Mr. Oakley as it is *possible* I may send for them. The weather here is cold, but if it was not for the horrid smoke would not be unpleasant... I will write again after we have played *The School For Scandal* tomorrow night.

God bless you my darlings,

Samuel Phelps

FANNY KEMBLE (1809–1893)

Fanny Kemble's much-publicised divorce had led to the publication of her journal, setting out her feminist attitudes and her anger at slavery in America. She was forced to return to England, leaving her small daughters behind. She did not see them again until they were grown up.

On tour in the United States with our play SHAKESPEARE LADY – THE LIFE & TIMES OF FANNY KEMBLE, Estelle Kohler and I met descendants of Fanny Kemble and were taken to the (Horace Howard) Furness Room at the Annenberg Museum to see, amongst other Kemble memorabilia, 'a pair of Shakespeare's gloves'.

Here, aged 65, re-united with her daughters and touring America with her 'Dramatic Readings' of Shakespeare, Fanny discusses Home Rule for Ireland, the cost of living in Philadelphia, Women's Rights – and the gloves...

> 1812 Rittenhouse Square, Philadelphia
> Good Friday, April 3rd., 1874

My dearest Harriet,

I not only am not likely to prefer Home Rule in Ireland to Colonel Taylor's Conservatism, but have a general idea that Irish rule, at home or abroad, is very nearly synonymous with *no* rule or *misrule*.

Oh! If you could have heard the account given me this morning by the poor matron of a children's hospital of her Irish 'help' – that is, the eleven hindrances (maid-servants) under her immediate control (*un*control) – you certainly would have wondered, as I often do here, whether the Irish alphabet and multiplication table are the same as those used anywhere else in the world: they seem so incapable of any but what I think must be called Irish conclusions, i.e. *confusions*... Surely the political progress of England and Ireland must be very manifest when the speeches of such a Tory as your nephew remind you of the Whig speeches of former days...

Young Mr. Furness, the son of my dear and venerated spiritual pastor and master, the editor of Shakespeare, comes occasionally with his wife and passes an evening with me. I was so much pleased with the enthusiastic devotion to his laborious task of his Variorum Shakespeare that I gave him the pair of Shakespeare's gloves Cecilia

Combie left me in her will, and which had come to her mother, Mrs. Siddons, from Garrick...

That precious bequest of Shakespeare's gloves reached me one evening while I was giving a reading in Boston, and occasioned me such an emotion of delight and surprise that one of the few times when I made blunders in my text was when I resumed my reading after finding them in the room to which I retired for rest in the middle of my performance. My Boston audience were my friends; and I think if I had told them the cause of the mistakes I made, when I resumed my seat and my book, they would have sympathised with and pardoned me. Perhaps they would have liked me to show them the gloves, which I never showed to any American that he did not directly put his hand into one of them.

The one exception to this was my dear and reverend Dr. Furness, who hardly seemed to dare to touch them; but 'reverence, the angel of this world', had blessed him with its influence...

I have no idea what your prices in Dublin for the necessities of life are, but here everything is exorbitant. We pay thirty-two shillings a ton for the commonest kind of coal, and three pounds a cord for wood for the one grate in the house where I burn it – which is my dressing room, and has andirons – in what is called a Franklin stove. My tea costs seven shillings a pound, and that which they drink in the kitchen four shillings, and so on with every item of household expenditure; in spite of which, the wife of the gardener at Butler Place comes into town and visits Ellen, with her little girl dressed up in white Marseilles piqué, all trimmed with needlework, and a broad sash of rich sky-blue silk, and ribbons in her hair to match, fit for a duke's daughter.

I hear nothing at all of the Woman's Right question in this country. Fanny Cobbe [1822–1904, English philanthropist and moralist] wrote me word, that the new state of things in England was favourable to it, and spoke of how many votes they hoped to get in the new Parliament in favour of woman's suffrage. I have no doubt that women, both here and in England, will eventually obtain the right to vote, if they persist in demanding it; and probably, by slow degrees, what I covet more for them, a better, perhaps even a tolerably good, education.

Fanny Cobbe always seems to me to be misled by the very amiable modesty of supposing that other women are her equals, her intellectual and moral peers; and I believe the women she talks to are conceited enough to take her at her word.

I divide my evening between Patience and knitting, and having done so until ten o'clock, read for about an hour before going to bed; but I am terribly afraid of using up my remains of eyesight.

Ever yours,
Fanny

EDWARD FITZGERALD (1809–1883)

Edward Fitzgerald (given name Edward Purcell, translator of THE RUBAIYAT OF OMAR KHAYYAM) amuses Fanny Kemble:

October 4, 1875

Dear Mrs. Kemble,

I duly received your last legible Letter. for which all Thanks... I return the expected favour (*Hibernice*) with the enclosed Prints, one of which is rather a Curiosity: that of Mrs. Siddons by [*Sir Thomas*] Lawrence when he was aetat. [*aged*] 13. The other, done from a Cast of herself, is only remarkable as being almost a Copy of this early Lawrence – at least, in Attitude, if not in Expression. I dare say you have seen the Cast itself.

And now for a Story better than either Print: a story to which Mrs. Siddons' glorious name leads me, burlesque as it is.

You may know there is a French Opera of *Macbeth* by Chelard. This was being played at the Dublin Theatre – Viardot [*Louise Héritte Viardot*], I think, the Heroine. However that may be, the Curtain drew up for the Sleep-walking Scene; Doctor and Nurse were there, while a long mysterious Symphony went on – till a Voice from the Gallery called out to the Leader of the Band, Levey: 'Whisht! Lavy, my dear – tell us now – is it a Boy or a Girl?' This Story is in a Book which I gave 2s. for at a Railway Stall, called *Recollections of an Impresario*, or some such name [*'The Enterprising Impresario' by Walter Maynard, publ. T.W. Beale, 1867*]; a Book you would not have deigned to read, and so would have missed what I had read and remembered and written out for you...

Your hot Colorado Summer is over: and you are now coming to the season which you – and others beside you – think so peculiarly beautiful in America. We have no such colours to show here, you know: none of that Violet which I think you have told me of as mixing with the Gold in the Foliage...

I have just been telling some Man enquiring in 'Notes and Queries' where he may find the beautiful foolish old Pastoral beginning –

My Sheep I neglected, I broke my Sheep-hook, &c.

117

– which, if you don't know it, I will write out for you. Mrs. Frere of Cambridge used to sing it as she could sing the Classical Ballad – to a fairly expressive tune: but there is a movement (Trio, I think) in one of dear old Haydn's Symphonies almost made for it. Who else but Haydn for the Pastoral! Do you remember his blessed Chorus of 'Come, gentle Spring,' that opens *The Seasons*? Oh, it is something to remember the old Ladies who sang that Chorus at the old Ancient Concerts rising with Music in hand to sing that lovely piece under old Greatorex's Direction! I have never heard Haydn and Handel so well as in those old Rooms with those old Performers, who still retained the Tradition of those old Masters.

Now it is getting Midnight; but so mild – this October 4 – that I am going to smoke one Pipe outdoors – with a little Brandy and water to keep the Dews off. I told you I had not been well all Summer; I say I begin to 'smell the Ground' which you will think all Fancy.

But I remain, while above Ground,

Yours sincerely,

E.F.G.

Edward Fitzgerald remained 'above ground' for another 8 years.

HENRY JAMES (1843–1916)

Fanny Kemble died in 1893.

Her old friend the author Henry James (WASHINGTON SQUARE, THE HEIRESS, THE TURN OF THE SCREW) writes to Sarah, her daughter…

January, 1893

Dear Mrs. Wister,

I stood by your mother's grave this morning – a soft, kind, balmy day, with… a few of those friends who have survived her, and were in town, and were not ill – as all the world lately has been. The number is inevitably small, for of all of her generation she is the last, and she had made no new friends, naturally, in these last years.

She was laid in the same earth as her father, and buried under a mound of flowers, which I don't like, but which many people – most people – do. It was all bright, somehow, and public, and slightly pompous. I thought of you…'far away on the billow', as it were – and hoped you felt, with us here, the great beneficence and good fortune of your mother's instantaneous and painless extinction. Everything of the condition, at the last, that she had longed for was there – and nothing that she dreaded was.

And the devotion of her old restored maid, Mrs. Brianzoni, appears to have been absolute – of every moment and every hour. She stood there this morning with a very white face and her hands full of flowers. Your mother looked, after death, extraordinarily like her sister…

I mention these things to bring everything a little nearer to you. I am conscious of a strange bareness and a kind of evening chill as it were in the air, as if some great object that had filled it for long had left an emptiness – from displacement – to all the senses. It seemed, this morning, her laying to rest – not but what I think, I must frankly say, the act of *burial* anything but unacceptably horrible, a hideous old imposition of the church – it seemed quite like the end of some reign or the fall of some empire.

But she wanted to go, and she went when she could, at last, without a pang. She was very touching in her infirmity all these last months – and yet with her wonderful air of smouldering embers under ashes. She leaves a great image – a great memory.

Henry James

LIONEL TENNYSON (1854–1886)
[Son of Alfred, Lord Tennyson, 1809–1892]

Fanny Kemble had been great friends with Lord Tennyson. The Poet Laureate's younger son goes to the Lyceum to see his father's play, QUEEN MARY, and 'picks holes'...

Bath Hotel,
Arlington Street,
Piccadilly
12.00 p.m., April 29th, 1876

My dear Papa, Mama, Hallam, etc.,

I have just returned from *Queen Mary*. Mrs. Crowe is certainly *most pathetic* in the first Acts. One cannot deny that there is something wanting in her acting – it is really, I suppose, want of power. She is a woman but not a queen – she is excited but not grandly passionate – and never calmly tragic; her acting is wanting also in variety of conception; she begins in a tremendous way, and leaves no room for climax. In her scenes with Philip she has no reserved dignity in the demonstration of her love, but is almost servile. But the last Act is splendid and I believe if I went every night for 3 weeks I should be moved to tears by it. There are just one or two little mannerisms that jar upon one – such as instead of ending a sentence with 'death', she says 'de - a - th'. There is an entire absence of sensationalism from her acting; her death is perhaps even a little tame. I suppose what is wanting in her acting is a sense of reserved power. Salvini has it – but no one else that I ever saw.

It was a great disappointment – we had, instead of Irving, Swinbourne. But even he was better than usual. Brooke in Renard is very clever but is rather too much of the 'stage cunning man' to please me quite; he forms angles with his body in various parts of the stage which is an unpleasing process. His face is wonderful. Elizabeth is clever, but the Bateman pipe is apparent, and she has no real dignity.

There is much more good acting in *Queen Mary* than I have ever seen at the Lyceum, but of course one can't help picking holes... The acting of such of the characters I have mentioned is a study.

And now for the audience: they were not a very applausive

audience, but their applause was very much appreciative – and Mrs. Crowe was called before the curtain after each Act – and perfect silence was maintained throughout the acting. In the last Act the hush was wonderful. The house was by no means an empty one; the boxes were not full, but the stalls and pit crammed and the galleries nearly full.

I am sure Papa would be pleased with the acting of it, and I do hope he will come up on Tuesday. I must go again... As it stands at present it is more of a domestic tragedy than a historical drama; the mounting is tasteful but by no means splendid and how anyone unacquainted with the whole play could make out the story in the acted play I can't conceive. No one can deny the distinctness of the characters or the *go* of the play.

I am very tired so good-night.

Your loving

L. Tennyson

Lionel Tennyson died in the Red Sea while returning from India in 1886.

EDWARD WILLARD (1853–1915)

Edward Willard was as popular an actor in the United States and Canada as he was in Great Britain. While playing in THE MIDDLEMAN, a play featuring an impressive oven on stage (see Plate vii), he received an unusual request (this letter may be seen as absolute proof of the phenomenon of 'suspension of disbelief'!)...

EDWARD WILLARD TO RICHARD LEE

Shaftesbury Theatre,
Shaftesbury Avenue,
London W.
[Undated]

My dear Lee,

I'm so sorry I neglected to bring *that letter* with me this evening, altho' I placed it ready.

However, I can give you the particulars...

The clay owl you saw last night came carefully packed, accompanied by a letter in a schoolboy's hand, setting forth that the writer had seen *The Middleman*, and had since been trying to bake his modelling in the kitchen oven. He found he couldn't do it, and hoped I wouldn't mind baking it for him in my oven. I was to please let him know when it was done, as he wanted to give it to his mamma.

He wound up by saying '*The Middleman* is a stunning piece. I *should* like to know how you work the stairs.' (He meant the stepladder in Act 2.)

Yours in haste,
Edward Willard

GENEVIEVE WARD (1833/8–1922)

American actress Genevieve Ward (The Countess de Guerbel) started her career as an opera singer, using the name Madame Guerabella. After losing her voice on tour in Cuba, she successfully took up acting in Europe, beginning as Lady Macbeth at the Theatre Royal, Manchester, continuing with a brilliantly successful show, FORGET ME NOT, with which she toured the world, giving over 2000 performances, and ending as one of Irving's most famous leading ladies.

GENEVIEVE WARD TO THE CRITIC CLEMENT SCOTT:

Olympic Theatre
Genevieve Ward,
'Forget Me Not'
27th February, 1883

Dear Mr. Scott,

I was so disappointed not to see you Saturday morning for 'Nance', *[Nance Oldfield]* but perhaps 'tis all the better – we shall all be *dans la peau de nos personages* next Saturday – when I hope you will come.

Medea plays an hour and a half; you won't mind that much tragedy, will you?

Yours sincerely,
Genevieve Ward

ELEONORA DUSE (1859–1924)

Italian actress Eleonora Duse was the lover of poet and playwright Gabriel d'Annunzio (1863–1938). The exceptional work of her travelling theatre company was an inspiration to British and American actors. Bernard Shaw (q.v.) was a great admirer, and Sybil Thorndike (q.v.) said she 'worshipped her'.

In 1884 Duse wrote this philosophical letter to the Marchese d'Arcais, from a quiet retreat in the Piedmontese Mountains, Italy:

I am alone here, sitting at a lattice window under which I have fixed, as a window-sill, something that seems to have been once part of a balcony, so that I may support my elbows and my thoughts on it. It is a wretched day; it rains and rains and rains. The mountains have withdrawn themselves, and the valleys of Ivrea and Chiusella are only patches of mist. Are they no longer there? What if after waiting and waiting for something to happen, I should after all see never again the scattered houses leading down to the village, nor the little street, nor the dark lake beside Castello di Montalto, nor the Dora stream, which is like a long, long serpent? Whenever from up above I catch sight of the village and the tiny peasant houses and see the signs of habitation, a feeling of pity comes over me, a pity beyond tears, because it is quite without solace. These houses apprehensively huddled together fill me with a sense of our poverty, our feebleness of life, and in facing life. I can well understand that these people should huddle together, for they suffer, and most people are afraid of being alone.

When I think that I must go back to that distracted and chaotic life, sometimes I feel the same pity for myself that I have for the people here. And yet, when I am well again... who knows, I may be the first myself to want to go back? At present I can frankly assure you that I have almost forgotten the stage. I could almost say that to me it is as if I had never acted in a theatre.

Acting – what an ugly word! If it were merely a question of 'acting', I feel that I could never have done it, and could never do it again. But the poor women in the plays I have acted so got into my heart and mind that I had to think out the best way of making them understood by my audience, as if I were trying to comfort them... But in the end it is generally they who comfort me. How and why and when this inexplicable reciprocity of feeling between these women and myself began; that story would be far too wearisome – and difficult as well – if I were to tell it fully. But this I can say: though everybody else may distrust women, I understand them perfectly. I do not bother whether they have lied, betrayed, sinned, or whether thay have been lost from their birth, once I feel that they have wept and suffered while lying or sinning or loving. I stand by them, I stand for them, and I burrow, burrow into them, not because of any thirst for suffering, but because women's capacity for sympathy is greater and more many-sided, gentler and more perfect than man's.

HENRY IRVING (1838–1905)

Henry Irving studied law and was called to the bar but never practised. After playing 500 small parts in ten years he was engaged by Dion Boucicault (q.v.) to play a lead in Manchester. He soon became the most powerful actor-manager of his day. Among his triumphs was an OTHELLO with American actor Edwin Booth (q.v.) in which they alternated the roles of Iago and Othello, and a Shylock of which Irving said in later years: 'In all humility ...mine is the only great Shylock.' He gave many of his greatest performances opposite Ellen Terry (q.v.). He was knighted in 1895 – the first ever Knight of the Theatre – and buried in Westminster Abbey.

Henry Irving had an ambivalent relationship with the English theatre critics. He wires an ironical telegram before an overseas tour...

POST OFFICE TELEGRAPHS
LIVERPOOL VICTORIA STREET
Handed in at the SOUTHAMPTON Office at 4.30 p.m..
Received here at 4.41 p.m..
TO: E.R. Russell, Liverpool Daily Post, Liverpool

ADIEU ADIEU REMEMBER ME
HENRY IRVING

SQUIRE BANCROFT (1841–1926)

In 1879 the Haymarket Theatre went under new management yet again. The new tenant was actor-manager Squire Bancroft (knighted in 1897). He began his career on a guinea a week, but on retiring was described in 'The Green Room Book' of 1907 as 'with the single exception of David Garrick, the only actor who has realised a fortune solely in his own theatre, without the aid of provincial or American tours'. He was an outstanding manager and certainly wily; during the negotiations, the old tenant, John S. Clarke, had trouble arranging meetings...

Haymarket Theatre
October 15, 1879

Dear Bancroft,

I called at the Haymarket yesterday to learn that Mr. Bancroft had just left by the stage door, and afterwards at the Prince of Wales's to be informed that Mr. Bancroft had just gone by the front door. A plague o' both your houses, thought I. I will try to look in at the stage door of the Prince of Wales's about 12.45 tomorrow, and take my chance of finding you.

But if Mr. Bancroft shall have left by the window, I shall go on and take my chance at both doors of the Haymarket.

Yours sincerely,
J.S. Clarke

THE GAIETY GIRLS

Patronage takes many forms... A diamond ring for the daughter of Mr Bertrand, ballet master, Empire Corps de Ballet, Gaiety Theatre:

[c 1889]

Dear Miss Bertrand,

Will you accept the enclosed little present as an appreciation of your artistic ability, by an admirer?

Yours faithfully,

X

My Lord,

Will you accept the enclosed 'present' back as an appreciation of your damned impertinence.

From

<u>HER FATHER</u>

At a luncheon party in 1973, ex-Gaiety Girl Ruby Miller (1889–1976), a marvellously glamorous 84, regaled me with the following stories, also recorded in her autobiography Champagne From my Slipper *(Jenkins, 1962) and in* The Gaiety Years *(see Sources).*

A titled admirer sent her a bunch of orchids with a £5 note wrapped round each stem. The stage door-keeper returned the money: 'I'm sorry, m'Lord, but Mr Edwardes does not allow his young ladies to receive gifts of money.' The next night his Lordship sent Ruby a Fabergé emerald and diamond bracelet.

A Russian Grand Duke threw a party for her at Romano's. He asked for her slipper; he filled it with champagne and drank it all. She complained, 'That was a charming gesture, Sir, but it has left my slipper somewhat damp.'

A few days later, she received six pairs of slippers from H. and M. Rayne, with a note:

Dear Miss Ruby Miller,

That was the best champagne I ever drank. Thank you for the loan of your slipper.

X

Actress Marion Hood wanted £200 a week for a tour with the Gaiety Company. The Manager, Edwardes, offered her £100, adding: 'Rajahs, Jams and Nabobs are in the habit of presenting stage favourites with ropes of pearls and rubies.' She wrote to him:

Dear Mr. Edwardes,

If you accept my terms you can have the Rajah's rubies.

Marion Hood

MARK TWAIN (1835–1910)

In 1887, the manager of a touring company dramatised Mark Twain's TOM SAWYER, and offered Twain a free ticket to the performance, as payment for the liberty of using his name in the advertising. Mark Twain (given name Samuel Langhorn Clemens) did not mince his words...

Hartford, Sept. 8, 1887

Dear Sir,

And so it has got around to you, at last; and you have also 'taken the liberty'. You are No. 1365. When 1364 sweeter and better people, including the author, have tried to dramatize 'Tom Sawyer' and did not arrive, what sort of show do you suppose you stand? That is a book, dear sir, which cannot be dramatized. One might as well try to dramatize any other hymn. *Tom Sawyer* is simply a hymn, put into prose form to give it a worldly air.

Why the pale doubt that flitteth dim and nebulous athwart the forecastle of your third sentence? Have no fears. Your piece will be a Go. It will go out the back door on the first night. They've all done it – the 1364. So will – 1365. Not one of us ever thought of the simple device of half-soling himself with a stove lid. Ah, what suffering a little hindsight would have saved us. Treasure this hint.

How kind of you to invite me to the funeral. Go to; I have attended a thousand of them. I have seen Tom Sawyer's remains in all the different kinds of dramatic shrouds there are. You cannot start anything fresh. Are you serious when you propose to pay my 'expence' – if that is the Susquehannian way of spelling it? And can you be aware that I charge a hundred dollars a mile when I travel for pleasure? Do you realise that it is 432 miles to Susquehanna? Would it be handy for you to send me the first $43,200 first, so I could be counting it as I come along; because railroading is pretty dreary to a sensitive nature when there's nothing sordid to buck at for *Zeitvertreib*.

Now as I understand it, dear and magnanimous 1365, you are going to recreate *Tom Sawyer* dramatically, and then do me the compliment to put me in the bills as father of this shady offspring. Sir, do you know that this kind of compliment has destroyed people before now? Listen.

Twenty-four years ago, I was strangely handsome. The remains of it are still visible through the rifts of time. I was so handsome that human activities ceased as if spellbound when I came in view, and even inanimate things stopped to look – like locomotives, and district messenger boys and so on. In San Francisco, I was often mistaken for fair weather. Upon one occasion I was travelling in the Sonora region, and stopped for an hour's nooning, to rest my horse and myself. All the town came out to look. A Piute squaw named her baby for me – a voluntary compliment which pleased me greatly.

Other attentions were paid me. Last of all arrived the president and faculty of Sonora University and offered me the post of Professor of Moral Culture and Dogmatic Humanities; which I accepted gratefully, and entered at once upon my duties. But my name had pleased the Indians, and in the deadly kindness of their hearts they went on naming their babies after me. I tried to stop it, but the Indians could not understand why I should object to so manifest a compliment. The thing grew and spread and spread and became exceedingly embarrassing. The University stood it a couple of years; but then for the sake of the college they felt obliged to call a halt, although I had the sympathy of the whole faculty.

The president himself said to me:

'I am as sorry as I can be for you, and would still hold out if there were any hope ahead; but you see how it is: there are a hundred and thirty-two of them already, and fourteen precincts to hear from. The circumstance has brought your name into the most wide and unfortunate renown. It causes much comment – I believe that that is not an over-statement. Some of this comment is palliative, but some of it – by patrons at a distance, who only know the statistics without the explanation – is offensive, and in some cases even violent. Nine students have been called home. The trustees of the college have been growing more and more uneasy all these last months – steadily along with the implacable increase in your census – and I will not conceal from you that more than once they have touched on the expediency of a change in the Professorship of Moral Culture. The coarsely sarcastic editorial in yesterday's *Alta* – headed 'Give the Moral Acrobat a

Rest' – has brought things to a crisis, and I am charged with the unpleasant duty of receiving your resignation.'

I know you only mean me a kindness, dear 1365, but it is a most deadly mistake. Please do not name your Injun for me.

Truly yours.

We have all written raging letters we found we could not post. In this case, Twain kept the above letter in his desk and instead sent the following:

New York
September 8, 1887

Dear Sir,

Necessarily I cannot assent to so strange a proposition. And I think it fair to warn you that if you put the piece on the stage, you must take the legal consequences.

Yours respectfully,
S.L. Clemens

Thirteen years later, a Mr Kester asked permission to dramatise the book, and this was Mark Twain's philosophical but peppery reply:

[Sir],

I should *like* to see *Tom Sawyer* staged. You need not submit the play to my approval... Turn the book upside down and inside out if you want to. If you wish to add people, incidents, morals, immorals, or anything else, do so with a free hand. My literary vanities are dead and nothing I have written is sacred to me.

Sincerely yours,
S.L. Clemens

OSCAR WILDE (1854–1900)

Oscar Wilde, brilliant novelist and playwright (THE PICTURE OF DORIAN GREY,THE IMPORTANCE OF BEING ERNEST, LADY WINDERMERE'S FAN) writes to his friend the artist Will Rothenstein (1872–1945, knighted in 1931). Wilde's new play SALOME, written in French in 1892, was being rehearsed for performance in London, with Sarah Bernhardt in the lead, when it was prohibited by the censor:

51 Friedrich's Promenade
Bad-Homburg
1892

My dear Will,

The *Gaulois*, the *Echo de Paris* and the *Pall Mall [Gazette]* have all had interviews. I hardly know what new thing there is to say. The Licenser of Plays is nominally the Lord Chamberlain, but really a commonplace official – in the present case a Mr. Pigott – who panders to the vulgarity of the English people, by licensing every low farce and vulgar melodrama – he even allows the stage to be used for the purpose of the caricaturing of the personalities of artists, and at the same moment when he prohibited *Salome*, he licensed a burlesque of *Lady Windermere's Fan* in which an actor dressed up like me and imitated my voice and manner!!!

The curious thing is this: all the arts are free in England, except the actor's art; it is held by the Censor that the stage degrades and that the actors desecrate fine subjects – so the Censor prohibits not the publication of *Salome* but its production: yet, not one single actor has protested against this insult to the stage – not even Irving, who is always prating about the art of the actor – this shows how few actors are artists. All the *dramatic* critics except Archer of *The World* agree with the Censor that there should be a censorship over actors and acting! This shows how bad our stage must be, and also shows how Philistine the English journalists are.

I am very ill, dear Will, and can't write any more.

Ever yours,
Oscar Wilde

In 1895 Wilde was publicly accused of Homosexuality by the Marquess of Queensberry (1844–1900), who devised the 'Queensberry Rules' for Boxing and was father of Wilde's lover Bosie (Lord Alfred Douglas, poet, 1870–1945). Wilde took Queensberry to court, lost the case and was sentenced to Reading Prison for two years. He was bankrupted. Unhappy in England after his release, he left for France.

Before its inclusion in a published collection in 1930 (limited publication of 550 copies) the following letter from a poverty-stricken Wilde to Rothenstein was described by the novelist André Gide (1869–1951) as 'the most important unpublished Wilde letter' he knew of. Wilde heads the letter with the pseudonym he occasionally used:

From: M. Sebastian Melmoth

(Hotel de la Plage)
Berneval-sur-Mer
Dieppe
Wednesday *[June 9th, 1897]*

My dear good friend,

I cannot tell you how pleased I was to get your kind and affectionate letter yesterday, and I look forward with real delight to the prospect of seeing you, though it be only for a day. I am going into Dieppe to breakfast with the Stannards, who have been most kind to me, and I will send you a telegram from there, so that you and your friend can dine and sleep here. There is no one in this little inn but myself, but it is most comfortable, and the chef – there is a real chef – is an artist of great distinction; he walks in the evening by the sea to get ideas for the next day. Is it not sweet of him? I have taken a chalet for the whole season for £32, so I shall be able I hope to work again, and write plays or something.

I know, dear Will, you will be pleased to know that I have not come out of prison an embittered or disappointed man. On the contrary. In many ways I have gained much. I am not really ashamed of having been in prison: I often was in more shameful places: but I *am* really ashamed of having led a life unworthy of an artist. I don't say that Messalina is a better companion than Sporus, or that the one is all right and the other all wrong: I know simply that a life of definite and studied materialism, and philosophy of appetite and cynicism, and a cult of sensual and senseless ease, are bad things for an artist: they narrow the imagination, and dull the more delicate sensibilities. I was all wrong, my dear boy, in my life. I was not getting the best out of me. *Now*, I think that with good health, and the friendship of a few good, simple, nice fellows like yourself, and a quiet mode of living, with isolation for thought, and freedom from the endless hunger for pleasures that wreck the body and imprison the soul, well, I think I may do things yet, that you all may like. Of course I have lost much, but still, my dear Will, when I reckon up all that is *left* to me, the sun and the sea of this beautiful world; its dawns dim with gold and its nights hung with silver; many books, and all flowers, and a few good friends; and a brain and body to which health and power are not denied – really I am *rich* when I count up what I still have: and as for money, my money did me horrible harm. It wrecked me. I hope just to have enough to enable me to live simply and write well.

So remember that you will find me in many respects very happy – and of course by your sweetness in coming to see me, you will bring me happiness along with you.

As for the 'silent songs on stone' *[Wilde's name, plagiarised from Whistler, for Rothenstein's lithographs]*, I am charmed at the prospect of having society of yours. It is awfully good of you to think of it. I have had many sweet presents, but none shall I value more than yours.

You ask me if you can bring me anything from London. Well, the soft air kills my cigarettes, and I have no box in which to keep them. If you are in a millionaire condition and could bring me a box for keeping cigarettes in, it would be a great boon. In Dieppe there is nothing between a trunk and a 'bonbonniere'. I do hope to see you tomorrow (Thursday) for dinner and sleep. If not, well Friday morning. I am up now at 8 o'clock regularly!

I hope you will never forget that *but for me* you would not be *Will* Rothenstein R.A.. It is one of the most important facts in the history of art. I look forward greatly to seeing Strangman. His translating *Lady Windermere* is delightful.

Your sincere and grateful friend,
Oscar Wilde

Will Rothenstein, Esquire, Artist,
53 Glebe Place, Chelsea, S.W.,
Londres, Angleterre

Tragically, Wilde never regained his joie-de-vivre and a few years later died penniless in Paris of meningitis.

C.B. COCHRAN (1872–1951)

C.B. 'Cockie' Cochran, who became the most powerful impresario/'showman' of his day, started out with other intentions..

24 Limekiln Street, Dover

September 15, 1891

My dear Mother,

I promised yesterday (feeling quite confident of success) to let you know how I got on last night. I do so now and must say, speaking briefly, that I was a

DISMAL FAILURE

I sang my three songs and at the end received scarcely a clap and cannot say I deserved one. I was not to the slightest degree nervous, but I seemed unable to put the 'go' that I have always prided myself on in the songs. During the evening I received the following note from the Proprietor:

> I find that you are wholly incompetent for the duties for which you were engaged and I hereby dismiss you under Rule 11 of your Contract.

You can scarcely imagine my feelings – I felt then, if ever I did, that I would do something desperate – but after a mighty conflict in my mind I turned into bed.

All that life seemed to me worth living for (FAME and popularity) had vanished, and I felt that I cared for nothing. However I slept and this morning after my breakfast strolled on the Admiralty Pier (where the Calais and Ostend boats come in) and after a great battle within myself realised that one of the great questions of my life had been answered: 'Was I to be a music-hall singer?' and the verdict was 'No'; and so I gradually came round to the fact that I must abide by that decision, although I feel sure had I the money to look round and see all the principal songwriters and wait till I got a good thing before purchasing, the result would have been different. You who know not the sweets of applause cannot imagine the blow I received after having been sought after so much in Brighton and received as though I was a genius – and also my really fine reception at Worthing.

Yesterday marks an epoch in my life and the next thing is to decide what to do now.

I must certainly better my present position at Neales' and I am determined to get riches or fame or perhaps both in some way.

The weather down here is grand and the old Town extremely picturesque. I shall start tomorrow to walk home, putting up, if possible, at friends on the way. It will be a nice trip.

I do not regret in the least having tried (although it has cost me a lot and left me in debt) as I should never have settled to anything while I was under the impression that there was money and popularity awaiting me at the stage door.

I remain,
Your loving son,
Charles

[Postscript] Please do not show this letter 'up and dahn and rahnd the tahn' but only to the family.

But two days later 'Cockie' was still in Dover, ego intact.

24 Limekiln Street, Dover
September 17, 1891

My dear Mother,

When I last wrote to you I was in one of my well-known temporary fits of insanity. I do not know what I said but I am sure it was senseless and idiotic.

Of course I am very sorry that I failed, but it has only given me renewed energy to go in and retrieve my lost repute which I am sure I can do.

I managed to catch a nasty cold in London, arrived at Dover late, dressed in a hurry and was a bit worried about a little matter in Town, and then small wonder I failed, as lots of people now in the front rank have done before me on the occasion of their debut.

However, I will wait to see you before doing anything.

Hoping you are well,
I remain,
Your loving son,
Charles

Not long afterwards, Cochran set off for New York, where he set up as a producer. Things did not go smoothly at first...

The Royal Hotel,
53 Princes Street,
Edinburgh
27th October, 1897

My dear Min,

I have only just arrived here after a very rough passage, and found your letter waiting for me. I can hardly thank you sufficiently for the enclosures – it was really brickish of you to respond so readily, but I must confess that the tone of your letter surprised me.

In the first place, what do you mean when you say 'there must be something more you can tell me, for you seem to be in such straits'? If you think that I am in any trouble in New York, I assure you it is not so and, as for being 'in straits', I'm as well off as I ever was – I never had money when I was out of an engagement – I've never been able to save any. Then again you say 'the big position you held so long with Richard Mansfield ought alone to help you.' In what way, my dear girl, do you mean it should help me? Surely not in borrowing money to tide me over my difficulties with – I could borrow money from my friends in New York, yes, lots of it, but you must remember that I'm a very well-known figure in New York life – during the past few months I have been spoken of more kindly by the press than almost any man I can remember for a long time, and this in spite of what you say about me not being able to 'afford to ride the big horse'.

It would, however, never do to let my pals in NY know my true financial position as I hope to return to America before long and, in that country, when a man is 'broke' he is down – very much down. As it was, I went to a friend I could trust and borrowed my fare from NY – a matter of thirty-five dollars (£7)...

Now to the real drift of this very lengthy scrawl. Why may I not come to Brighton for a day or so and see my parents and my brothers and sisters?... Of course I shouldn't let anybody at Brighton know that I was hard up and, as I'm pretty well dressed, I don't think for one minute that they would imagine such was the case. In spite of what you say about my making others miserable, I still have some feelings left... However, having accepted your money, I am, as it were, on a parole d'honneur to you and shall not move without your permission. Grant it and I promise to be discreet.

I am leaving for London tonight, and will let you know as soon as I secure rooms. For the present address me c/o Low's Exchange, London.

Now, my dear Mins, with more thanks,

I remain,

Your loving brother,

Chas.

PS After writing this... I learned that Mr. Beerbohm Tree was in Edinburgh, and as I knew him very well, having met him lots of times in America, I called to pay my respects. He was most charming and promised to do all in his power for me upon his return to London next week. This assistance was volunteered – not asked for – as I chatted to him in his dressing room whilst he was making up for Svengali.

PPS: 28th October. I've had a busy day and not a fruitless one... Miss Mabel Beardsley is also exercising herself greatly in my behalf and she knows everybody.

Cochran rose eventually to immense power in the profession, and a knighthood. He died as a result of scalding; osteo-arthritis in his hip prevented his reaching to turn off a running hot tap in a bath.

ELLEN TERRY (1847–1928)

In 1925 Ellen Terry was honoured with the Grand Cross of the Order of the British Empire. Her obituary in The Times *read 'She was a woman of genius; but her genius was not that of the brain so much as of the spirit and of the heart. She was a poem in herself a being of an exquisite and mobile beauty.'*

Her first rôle was in 1856 as the boy Mamilius in THE WINTER'S TALE for Charles Kean (actor-manager, son of Edmund Kean q.v.), and she went on, from 1878, to become Henry Irving's (q.v.), and Britain's, favourite leading lady. For thirteen years the two dominated the London theatre.

In later years she conducted a famous correspondence with the playwright and critic George Bernard Shaw (q.v.). In a letter to him in 1896 she described her first kiss (at 16).

Of course, there's kissing and kissing. I'm a very kissing person. But some girls kiss in 'conservatories' (Oh, don't you know what I mean – the dancer they have met an hour ago, the next one, probably, and the next – ad lib). I never could have done that. Very many women kiss two men at the same time. Pigs!

I'll never forget my first kiss. I made myself such a donkey over it, and always laugh now when I remember. Mr. Watts kissed me in the studio one day, but sweetly and gently, all tenderness and kindness, and then I was what they call 'engaged' to him and all the rest of it, and my people hated it, and I was in Heaven for I knew I was to live with those pictures.

'Always' I thought, and to sit to that gentle Mr. Watts and clean his brushes, and play my idiotic piano to him, and sit with him there in Wonderland (the Studio).

Then I got ill, and had to stay at Holland House – and then – he kissed me – DIFFERENTLY – not much differently but a little, and I told no one for a fortnight, but when I was alone with Mother... I told her I MUST be married to him NOW because I was going to have a baby!!! And she believed me!! Oh, I tell you I thought I knew everything then... I was SURE THAT KISS MEANT GIVING ME A BABY!

At the age of sixteen, Ellen Terry actually married 46-year-old Mr. Watts (George Frederic Watts, celebrated painter and sculptor, 1817–1904, who in 1852 offered to decorate the great hall of Euston Station, London, for the cost of the materials alone); the marriage failed immediately. She subsequently eloped with the architect Edward Godwin, with whom she had two children.

Ellen Terry became passionately involved with the family life of her son, the innovative stage designer Gordon Craig (1872–1966) – 'I try to perceive things feelingly, not thinkingly... thinking comes afterwards...' After he had left his wife May in 1897 for another woman, Jessy, and then threatened to leave her, too, Ellen poured her heart out in a letter to him:

Amuse me?... You Flat-Iron – you idiot —— I can find no name to tell you what I think of your intelligence. You are doing your best to miss your salvation – your fortune that lies before you – your whole happiness (by that I mean J.) & with all of it at your feet you are —— so blind, with jealousy, vanity, discontent and *obstinacy* you don't see it —— you refer I suppose, when you speak of *'amusing'* me, to the evening when I laughed at your saying I had no love for you? If you could only have known the weight you lifted from me, as you said that, for then I knew that you were *jealous* and *feeling wretched, which indeed* you *should* feel at the work your foolish obstinacy has done in simply driving J. from you — I felt when you said *that* (she 'had no love for you') that *all* was not yet lost —— that you *did* love her — and were not callous as *she* thinks, but only *jealous* without knowing it. Now consider – she has done everything a woman can do for three years to prove her love for you – in spite of your outrageous ungentleness and selfish inconsiderateness. She longs for you to be with her – I can't get a word from her upon any other subject but you – you – you and no one but a really unintelligent person could fail to know her entire devotion and adoration of you (I am blind sometimes but not *so* blind as not to see this laid out like a Map before me)...

Amuse me – *you*! You *torture* me – as you have the other poor souls who have loved you – for all the heartbreak you have caused & are causing me — you have never appreciated *any* of the love you have had thickly thrown upon you...

141

When I used to pour out *just what I thought of you* – with intent for your happiness *solely* before my eyes —— you simply *fled*. That was your usual pretty unreasoning trick to avoid anyone's implorings or advice. Then, knowing how words of any kind but *flattering* words, make you *impatient* (& I *wouldn't* give those) *then* I tried to be not so serious with you – avoided speaking of your affairs & only just *shouldered your difficulties* time after time you ungrateful son – hoping you might take the chances of love & fortune that have presented themselves before you, & which you have only blindly *kicked aside* – & *after all*, and the last few months intenser suffering than I have ever experienced for *myself* you think you *'amuse'* me!! If you could *see* my ragged old heart – Do you know *nothing* – have you *no* perception?...

Unless you will be plain with me & tell me what to do for you —— point out the way *you can see* for me to help you – in *business*, with regard to J. , with regard to *anything on earth* for you and your better having – I'm getting very doddery so I'll end – one thing: don't dare to say or even *think* that *I* say or *think lightly* for one moment about you...

> You are all heart of my heart – breath of my body –
> Mother

In a letter to the critic Clement Scott (see Genevieve Ward) marked 'PRIVATE', Ellen Terry agonises over the rôle of Lady Macbeth:

After feeling miserable a bit, about what you were *going to say* (for of course I *guessed* it – having just about enough wit to keep myself warm) I must confess I laughed, when I read what you did say. You have hit the blot! – 'an empty and barren cry' – *indeed it was, when I* called on the spirits to unsex me – I acted that bit just as badly as anybody could act anything...

It was most kind of you to *suppose* that I *could* act Lady M. – you write from that point of view, which itself is a very great compliment. For my own part I am quite surprised to find I am *really* a useful actress – for I *really am*! To be able to get *through* with such difficult parts as:

Ophelia – Olivia – Beatrice – Margaret – & Lady M. –

& my aim is *usefulness* – to my lovely art, & to H.I. *[Henry Irving, q.v., playing her Macbeth]*. This is not a very high ambition – is it? But long ago I gave up *dreaming* & I think I see things as they are (especially see myself as I am, Alas!) & off and on the stage only aspire to *help* a *little* —— Mind you though Mr. Clement, although certainly I know I cannot do what I *want* to do in this part, I don't even *want* to be a 'fiend' – and *won't* believe for a moment – *can't* believe for a moment that she did conceive that murder – that *one* murder of which she is accused. Most women break the law during their lives, few women realise the consequences of *that they do today*.

In my memory I have *facts*, & I use them for (not for my *'methods'* in my work – that's where I fail dismally in this – but for) reading women who *have* lived, & can't speak & tell me – *I am quite top full of* – (not direst cruelty I hope but) – *women's secrets* – (& I have *my own*!!!) & my women – my friends – were *not* wicked – & *you say I'm* not – !!!

I do believe that at the end of the banquet, that poor wretched creature was brought through agony & sin to repentance & was *just forgiven*.

Surely she did not call on the spirits to be made bad, because she knew she was *not* so *very* bad? *I'm* always calling on the spirits to be made *good*, because I know I'm not good – not *strong* in good, although all the while desiring it above all else. No – she was not good, but not much worse than many women you know – me for instance. My hankerings are not for blood, but I think I *might kill* for my child, or my love *blindly* – & see & regret & repent in deepest sincerity after – You would have laughed the other night though – the man at the side put the paint – 'blood'– on my hands, & in the hurry & excitement I didn't look, but when I saw it I just burst out crying.

I don't believe you think I'm very bad – I am. Perhaps when I tell you I loved, you won't believe it, when at the *same time* I tell you I broke the law *& forged* for my love – I tell you I *did* love, & forged – said money was owed by him to me when it was not – in order to get it again *for him* of course. Do you think I thought that wicked *then*? I thought it was *right* – I couldn't have done it with my baby at my breast if I had seen it *as I see it now* – you won't say I can't be Lady M.

143

whilst all the time you see I am quite as bad —— Don't have me hanged drawn & quartered after this —— You are quite right I can't play Lady M. – but it's because my *methods* are not right. & oh, nothing is right about it yet. To be consistent to a conviction is what I'm going to *try* for.

If you don't put this into the fire *this moment* may my eternal cuss fall on you!... I wish I didn't act, or you didn't *write*, then perhaps I might see something of you. Forgive this horrid scrawl which is written to *assure* you I am a *real* bad person, & yet somehow in the person of Lady M. have contrived, with evident subtlety, to make you think I can't *assume* bad, 'cos I'm good! Don't you think it's all rather humorous?...

I wish I could have seen Helen Faucit in the part – I do believe *she* was the *rightest* – although not to be looked by the side of the portrait of Siddons as a singly effective figure. Can you ever forgive me, or can I ever forgive myself, this long horrible scrawl?

Ah, but I do wish you and yours a happy new year –

Ellen Terry

[Postscript] Fire – Fire – *Fire!*

GEORGE BERNARD SHAW (1856–1950)

Ellen Terry and Bernard Shaw corresponded affectionately over many years, though they did not meet until old age...
Ellen Terry writes for advice, after receiving a worrying begging letter...

28th February, 1897
Margate

Forgive my enclosing this queer letter and oblige me by reading it. I have not so many £10's flying about unappropriated as some folk think, so I'm obliged to tear up most of the hundreds of letters of the kind which I receive. But I could not tear this up somehow.

I'm sure you won't mind troubling to read it for me. Don't bother yourself to give me any reason but just say Yes or No to me. Would you or would you not (if you were me) send him the money?

I think the poor fellow is 'off it', but I feel so ill myself, and if he is mad just from ill-health, why, how terrible. But I'm laughed at for being constantly deceived, 'taken in' as they say, that I'm sure I must be the uncleverest person in the world. I had such a beautiful birthday yesterday. Fly away time! Some rest I hope at last!

Yours, my Bernie,
E.T.

GEORGE BERNARD SHAW TO ELLEN TERRY

[Undated; approx. 1st March, 1897]

Your letter has just come. Of course you know my advice beforehand – DONT *[sic]*. The gentleman is not slimy like the usual begging letter writer: his frank opening 'I wish you would lend (*'lend'* mark you!) me £10' is so good that I am half disposed to advise you to send him five shillings as a tribute to his cheek, and tell him why. But he betrays himself later on. There is no mistaking the approach of death and the longing for it, followed by 'I trust in God I shall yet live to etc. etc.'And the clergyman's letter, and the want of food and so on!

No, dear Ellen: if you want to spend £10, get ten sovereigns and skid them out from the beach into the sea: they will do no harm then, and they will twinkle prettily in the sun if you make them ricochet successfully. Or, if you want to 'do good' with them, send them to one of the heaps of people who are disinterestedly in that business, and know how to do it. But *never* give it to a beggar, especially a beggar who begs well (practice being the secret of excellence in that as in other departments of acting). You need have no remorse in this instance: the gentleman's cant is unmistakable: he wont [sic] starve and he wont die; and I dont mind wagering that he wont work either. As to his sanity, I guarantee it. You cant [sic] even answer him, because if you lecture him, you must send him the money to shew that you are not taking a moral attitude to save your own pocket; if you write kindly, your sympathy is mere hypocrisy without the money: if you write 'Dear Sir – No – yours truly, Ellen Terry,' which would be quite proper, you will hardly feel that to be an improvement on silence. The waste paper basket is the proper place for all such appeals...

What birthday did you say? 59th was it?

G.B.S.

1900 ~ 1980

HERBERT BEERBOHM TREE	JOHN GIELGUD
MAX BEERBOHM	NOEL COWARD
W.B. YEATS	GEORGE KAUFMAN
ELLEN TERRY	ATHENE SEYLER
HENRY IRVING	SYBIL THORNDIKE
NELLIE MELBA	DONALD WOLFIT
GEORGE BERNARD SHAW	BERNARD MILES
J.M. BARRIE	EDITH SITWELL
MARTIN HARVEY	LAURENCE OLIVIER
RUTH GORDON	KENNETH TYNAN
THE LORD CHAMBERLAIN	RALPH RICHARDSON
THE BARRYMORES	HAROLD PINTER
	TENNESSEE WILLIAMS

AND OTHERS...

HERBERT BEERBOHM TREE (1853–1917)
MAX BEERBOHM (1872–1956)

In 1900, at the age of twelve, Olivia Truman fell in love with the established actor Herbert Beerbohm Tree (knighted in 1909). At thirteen, she wrote him a love letter:

OLIVIA TRUMAN TO HERBERT BEERBOHM TREE

1901

I am thirteen and never loved so passionately before.

At fourteen she went to see Tree, already an obsession, as the evil Svengali in Paul Potter's melodrama TRILBY. She wrote to her former governess, Miss Mackay (I have left the spelling as written):

June 25th, 1902

...I went to *Trilby* on Saturday, cold and all – nothing on earth could have kept me away, and oddly it made me no worse, it was Sunday I got it so bad. I enclose a paper on the play full of 'gass' and programm, please be careful of the sacred articles and return at an early date. I have always adored Mr. Tree because he was so soft and sweet and such a great artist, but I don't think I have ever really thought him an extraordainry actor beyond his versitility, till Saturday. Of the 9 plays I've seen him in, he has never played with the depth, the feeling, the power, the subtle masterfullness of Svengali in fact I never guessed he had it in him. It is the greatest masterpiece of acting I've ever seen, speaking unpredudied it is pure and simple *genius* it is *wonderful* his make up is extraordainry he looks ultra devilish, when in the wretched Paris studio in his rags, in the darkness with only a blue light on his face declares he is his own god, then nearly dies and prays, and in the end in his rich clothes in the magnificent opera house with a green light on his white face with its big nose and streaming black hair, flung across a table with his head hanging down the effect is super-human!!! except perhaps for Sherlock Holmes I never enjoyed a play so much it is the first time Trees acting has convinced me, moved and touched me, and the devilish horror of it froze me with terror, and oh! the divine applause how I loved them they were wonderful, how I clapped!! We all liked it, but I got cross with the darling Tree, at the end he waited till everyone was nearly out of the house then the curtain went up, and 'Trilby' and *he as himself in evening dress stood on the stage*!! imagine my feelings!!!!!!!! and as I was behind the barrier near the door, and had to stand on tip toe to see him at all, he was so far off I could see very little of his face (shall I put an adjective?) and that only a second. Dada hustled me off, oh I could have yelled, the *brute* why did he not come on before?!!!!

In no time at all she was forcing answers to her letters...

August 8, 1902,
1, The Albany, London.

Dear Miss Truman,

I am sorry you are worried lest I should be angry. How could I be? Whatever you did could only have been meant kindly, and the intention is all – or nearly all – when one is young.

I am very sensible of your kindness, and if I have not acknowledged your various letters, it is because it would not be fitting that I should encourage you to write to me. I am writing this in order that you may know I am not annoyed at anything you have done...

I am also writing to return to you some postal orders which you sent me and which I could not accept, so please do with them as you think fit.

Some time ago you were fearful that I might worry about failure and consequent money loss – these things trouble me not at all, and I am always in high spirits during stormy times (you see, misfortune is my native element – perhaps, like Herod, I was born "neath a wild moon by the sea'.) Nor am I troubled about 'honours', I rate myself far too highly for that. (Forgive this personal note.) I am very happy in your good opinion, and I hope you will always be sensible and strong-minded (in the womanly way).

I am sure your mother won't mind my writing this – so please tell her.

Yours sincerely,
Herbert Beerbohm Tree

OLIVIA TRUMAN TO MISS MCKAY

22nd March, 1903

Stafferton Lodge, Maidenhead

Dearest Lady,

How incompatable this dolorous edge is with the wild mad joy at my heart! Never, never have I been so wild about seeing him before. I suppose because it was put off once, and all this week I have been ill, yes really ill with excitement I could not eat. I felt so sick, was always trembling and was besieged with fears it might go wrong again, anyhow it was with difficulty I restrained a collapse. (I can hear you say 'little ass'. But Miss Mackay once you were my age, you must know, you must understand!)...

Ultimately I went to tea at Stella's... Well there I met a young man who is thinking of going on the stage, and seems very much in the 'know' about H going to rehearsals there ect: Four years ago at the dress rehearsal of *King John*... H finished a magnificent tableau. About 50 of his friends were there. He asked one 'What do you think of it?' 'It might be improved' was the answer. Then H turned to his wife 'Well, my dear and what do *you* think of it?' 'I agree with Mr. So-and-so' she answered... that wicked woman wounded his very soul, weary as it was – he cried on the stage! I had much to do to keep from doing so too when this was told me.

Ah! my dear this is one scene of many, poor heart, poor heart, after 19 years she has not taken the trouble to understand him, but I know all it means to him, I went back, my mind full of pain and longing for him, it haunted me all night.

The next day I wrote to him unsigned, unaddressed, I asked him if moments never came when after all his dreaming and toiling others, to show their knowledge tho' they could not excel what he had created, because they were jealous disparaged it, did he never ask then does *no one* understand? I told him I was coming to him on Saturday that I at least in that vast audience knew what it meant to him, I asked him if the knowledge that at moments when he felt that no one else on earth understood, that I did, was any help to him, to send an unaddressed note to the Box Office where I could call for it after the performance, that he was only to send it if from his heart he found that I who knew all it meant to him, was a real help to him being in the audience.

Miss Mackay he sent it!!!

You have no idea all it means to me, it is no silly craving for a love letter, it means that I, I, I insignificant little me, really am some use to that great man, that I help the one I adore, a thing I thought impossible, indeed dreamed the reverse. And that is not all it means, he addressed it to 'Miss Truman' – guessed whom his letter was from tho' my writing is quite different from when I first wrote him 'billet-doux'!...

It was the proof of a photograph of himself as the handsome dashing soldier making love to Lena Ashwell as the young innocent girl, he is about to kiss her – it was signed by himself. That was all there was – no other word: it was enough, don't you see what it means, why he should have chosen that particular picture? because, because he places me in the young girls place, she is a type of me, – it means, it means he would kiss me!!!!!!!!!! his forgiveness for the old wrong, his gratitude for my present understanding, his kiss for the future!!! The one thing I have hoped and longed and prayed for, of which he has given no indication before has come to pass! You will ask what colour my cheeks are when I say the realisation of that kiss is all I ask better, and now perhaps some day it may! are you surprised I am crazy with joy?

I send you a critic on the play it was very difficult to do, it is quite true they don't believe what they say, and he doesn't, I know when he doesn't because he strikes attitudes at once, but I was very deeply touched when he said and meant it 'Love is everything'. 'The only true happiness in life is to live for others' he looked very handsome, and played with an air of quiet, powerful distinction that was extraordainery. I have never seen him make every day love before, he was EXQUISITE so natural and such a gentleman, I nearly died of jealousy, he did it so well, raining kisses on her, mine was *real* jealousy, not like

Mrs. Trees afraid he may not pay enough attention to her in public and so hurt her pride, not because she cares about him, *I* envied every embrace...

Your Olivia

P.S. Please return critic.

P.P.S. Of course you will regard all this in strictest confidence, but I had to let it out or I should have been ill, the suppression of the last week has been awful.

Her campaign was effective, though for some time his replies remained properly formal...

April 28th, 1903

My dear Miss Truman,

I hardly know how to write to you. I do deeply appreciate the kind and beautiful letter you sent me, and am very proud to think that I should have been the means of inspiring such sweet and noble thoughts in you. I have not written because I did not think it right to enter into a correspondence with you, and so encourage a feeling which is only a passing phase and which I hope will in time give place to a great-hearted devotion to someone who is worthy of it. I only wish to assure you that I am not indifferent to your kindness, for I should indeed be ungrateful if I did not appreciate it.

I would most gladly see you if your mother were with you. I will send the picture for which you asked me.

I have been much worried and preoccupied of late. I am delighted to think that *Resurrection* has appealed to you in the same way that it appealed to me – it has been a rare joy to give it to the people.

With all my heart's best wishes,

I am,

Yours sincerely,

Herbert Beerbohm Tree

When Herbert was overseas, Olivia wrote anxiously and regularly to Herbert's step-brother Max Beerbohm (knighted in 1939), the celebrated caricaturist and dramatic critic, who also became a friend. He dealt with her beautifully:

48, Upper Berkeley Street
London
Tuesday

Dear Olivia,

I have been really quite ill... and am so far restored that I feel worthy to write to you... but I reject as false and grotesque your suggestion that I am 'the best dressed individual' that you know. That is what the Hottentot lady said to the missionary... but coming from you to me, it won't do.

I haven't heard from Herbert, since he went to Marienbad – but I have no doubt he is enjoying himself very much there: he loves the place; and, though you may doubt it, he really is quite capable of looking after himself; he isn't half so vague as he seems; when it rains he seeks shelter under a tree or a roof; when food is placed before him he somehow manages to insert it into his mouth with a fork or a spoon; he always emerges undrowned from his morning bath; he never puts his coat on inside-out, or his hat on upside-down. Some good fairy watches over him all the time, believe me. Set your mind at rest. Of course he *may* be shipwrecked on the way home...

Please give my remembrances to your mother.

Yours ever,
Max

...and, even more wickedly...

August 9th., 1906

My dear Olivia,

I have sent in my resignation to the Editor of the *Saturday Review*, enclosing your letter, so that he shall understand exactly why I have taken this step.

How blind I have been all these years! As you say, 'an attack on the stage in any form is, in his (Herbert's) great position, indirectly an attack on him'. And to think I had never thought of that: – all the while that I was criticising this and that actor or theatre unfavourably I was incidentally stabbing Herbert in the back – lowering his profession in the eyes of the world, and thus lowering him. I can't forgive myself. Nothing can wipe out the hideous past. How he must have suffered. Yet he never uttered a groan. Well, I shall gnaw no longer at his vitals. The theatre will know me no more. Not the least painful part of the matter is that you – et tu Bruta – acknowledge as 'in the main true' what I said about the regrettableness of the public's attitude towards mimes in general. (*Mimes*, by the way, is a good old English word, not in the least derogatory; and used by me always to save the space that would be wasted by 'actors and actresses'. Give me another noun of common gender, and I will use that instead. But I forget: it is too late now.)

'In the main true'! Oh Olivia, say oh say that this was a slip of the pen. A treacherous private endorsement from you makes my crime seem doubly hideous. Don't send me any more such 'buttonholes' to wear with my sack-cloth and ashes.

Before your letter arrived I had written a short obituary article on Toole [*J.L. Toole, 1832–1906: farceur and theatre manager*]. I wired to the *Saturday* to withdraw it; but too late. It is very painful reading in print. Of course, it is 'in the main true' that actors are mortal and must sooner or later go the way of all flesh. But 'it was not for an actor's brother' to have drawn the public's attention to that horrid fact. If only your letter had arrived a day or two earlier!

If you will promise never to refer to this or anything else in my unfortunate and false position, I shall be indeed delighted to come to Efford. Will you ask your mother whether I might come on Saturday, 18th?

Yours ever,

Max

Olivia continued to write to her beloved H.B. Tree, her letters a mixture of adoration and perceptive criticism (though her spelling barely improved). By 1906 she had become his confidante and friend...

August 9, 1906
Garrick Club

...When may I come to you? Will you kindly let me know whether it will be convenient to your mother? I hope to get my motor on Monday next...

All goes well with the rehearsals of *Winter's Tale* and Viola is a great joy to me. I have really good inspiration for *Antony and Cleopatra*. I am beginning the play with a vision of the Sphinx in the desert, the stars shining in the dark sky. Slowly the vision vanishes, and Antony and Cleopatra are seen sailing in the barge just as it is described by Enobarbus – they land and speak of love. The end of the play is the same as the beginning – passion has raged its brief day – battles have been fought – Antony and Cleopatra are both dead – and Caesar has come and gone in triumph, night has fallen again, and through the darkness we see once more the vision of the calm Sphinx – the embodiment of Fate; the eternal stars are still shining, indifferent to the fret and strife of human passions.

I quite understand your brother's feelings about our people, but you know we are not ignoble entirely, and we have enormous power for good if we only care to exercise it – have we not? With the decline of dogma in religion, our stage will become stronger and stronger. How blind are the bishops!

It always delights me when you write about yourself – that was a splendid touch of femininity when you spoke of the dream in which you saw blood streaming *'on the white sating dress'* of milady!

I hope you will be glad to get my little letter – give my kindest regards to your mother and believe me always yours in ardent homage,

H.B.T.

They became lifelong correspondents and friends, despite his marriage and a mistress with six children by him (May Pinney, mother of Carol Reed the film-maker and grandmother of the actor Oliver Reed). When Herbert Beerbohm Tree died, his widow wrote to Olivia: 'Herbert spoke of you so much and loved the flowers and things you sent him. I know you grieve for him and understand my grief.'

WILLIAM BUTLER YEATS (1865–1939)

The poet, dramatist, critic and theatre director William Butler Yeats, who
extraordinarily produced his greatest work between the ages of 50 and 75
(EASTER 1916, THE TOWER, THE WINDING STAIR, etc.), writes to the
actress Mrs Patrick Campbell (q.v.):

18 Woburn Buildings,

Euston Road

[Undated – probably 1901]

Dear Mrs. Patrick Campbell,

I was anxious to ask if I might see you after the performance today
to tell you how much I admired you in it. But I did not like to do so, as
I... feared that the sight of my card would make you expect irrelevant
conversations about impossible things.

You will permit me, however, to thank you by letter for the performance of today. Your acting seemed to me to have the perfect precision
and delicacy of every art at its best. It made me feel the unity of the
Arts in a new way. I said to myself 'That is exactly what I am trying to
do in writing. To express oneself without waste, without emphasis. To
be impassioned and yet to have a perfect self-possession. To have a
precision so absolute that the slightest inflection of the voice, the slightest rhythm of sound or of motion plucks the heart strings!'

But do you know that you acted too well? You made me understand
a defect in Bjornson's play *[BEYOND HUMAN POWER, Royalty*
Theatre] which I had felt but had not understood when I read it.
Bjornson's hero could only have done those seeming or real miracles
by having a religious genius. Now the essence of genius, of whatever
kind, is precision; and that hero of his has no precision. He is a mere
zealous man, with a vague sentimental mind. The kind of man who is
anxious about the housing of the working classes but not the kind of
man who sees what Blake called 'The Divine Vision and Fruition'.

I happened to have in my pocket *The Revelation of Divine Love* by
'The Lady Julian' – an old mystical book; my hand strayed to it all
unconsciously. There was no essential difference between that work
and your acting. Both were full of fine distinctions, of delicate logic, of

that life where passion and thought are one. Both were utterly unlike Bjornson's hero. The actor played him to the life but I was miserable until he was off the stage. He was an unbeliever's dream of a believer, an atheist's Christian.

But nowhere is it a fine play.

Again thanking you,
I am, yours sincerely,
W.B. Yeats

LADY GREGORY (1852–1932)

Playwright and author Lady Isabella Augusta Gregory, W.B. Yeats (q.v.) and dramatist J.M. Synge (1871–1909 – THE PLAYBOY OF THE WESTERN WORLD, DEIRDRE OF THE SOROWS) were the first Directors of the Abbey Theatre, Dublin. Lady Gregory writes to W.B. Yeats immediately on learning of Synge's death:

Coole Park, County Galway
Wednesday, 24th March, 1909

Dear Willie,

I have just had Henderson's wire – it is terribly terribly sad. That sudden silence is so awful. Yesterday you could have asked him his wishes and heard his thoughts – today, nothing. I wonder if the doctors told him the end was near – It is most wrong when they do not, there would always be some last word to say.

You did more than any for him, you gave him his means of expression – You have given me mine, but I would have found something else to do, tho' not coming near this, but I don't think Synge would have done anything but drift but for you and the theatre – I helped him far less – just feeding him when he was badly fed, and working for the staging of his plays, and in other little ways – and I am glad to think of it, for he got very little help from any other except you and myself – I wonder if he was ever offered a meal in Dublin except at the Nassau?

Let me know what changes there are in programme – I am glad you were in Dublin as I couldn't be there; it seems a very lonely death indeed.

Yours aft,
A.G.

The next day Lady Gregory wrote again to Yeats:

...What a quiet end that was! No struggle or disturbance, just what he would have wished. And what a pity you could not have seen him after he knew death was coming – It would have been happier for him if he had talked things over with you – I feel very downhearted for it is such a break in our very small group of understanding friends – which indeed has been little more than a triangle – One never had to re-arrange one's mind to talk to him – I had got to know him much better in his last year's illness when I was with him every day – It is I who ought to have gone first – Health is a mysterious thing...

ELLEN TERRY (1847–1928)

AUTOGRAPH

from <u>Ellen Terry</u> ≈

<u>For the Stage</u> – imagine first, & observe afterwards!

E.T.

On notepaper headed:

PROVINCIAL TOUR, 1901
HENRY IRVING
MISS ELLEN TERRY
and
THE LYCEUM COMPANY

ELLEN TERRY TO MRS NETTLESHIP

Birmingham
Monday, March 22, 1901

Dear Nettle – If you can send me 2 *big* bows of *velvet* (1 for hair – one for front of dress) for *Nance Oldfield* to the Coronet Theatre, Notting Hill Gate – by Monday afternoon ≈ you know the pretty bright colour (this is dirty and faded – but just to remind you!) I shall be much obliged.

I'm dead beat but have promised my son to play for him for *one* week. (Rehearsals of *Coriolanus* all the time!) – Can't get the drawings! Can't begin anything extra until Coronet week is over – I think *I'll* be 'over' then also!

Yours affectionately,
E.T.

HENRY IRVING (1838–1905)

Note from Ellen Terry to an autograph hunter, regarding her co-star:

Sir Henry is not at all a *terrible* person and I think you must ask him yourself for his signature.

SIR HENRY IRVING TO DAVID HEILBRON

Adelphi Hotel
Liverpool,
4th December, 1904

David Heilbron Esq.,
72 Bath Street,
Glasgow

Dear Mr. Heilbron,

Thank you for the promptness with which you have fulfilled my order. Your 'King's Liqueur' whisky is certainly most excellent and it only requires to be known to have a remarkable vogue.

Believe me,
Faithfully yours,
Henry Irving

[David Heilbron was grandfather to actresses Vivien and Lorna Heilbron]0

HERBERT BEERBOHM TREE (1853–1917)

H. B. Tree objects to a cartoon...

TO MR SHORTER, EDITOR OF *THE TATLER*

HIS MAJESTY'S THEATRE

October 17th, 1904

My dear Mr. Shorter,

I thank you for your pleasant assurances of good-will. I trust I am not devoid of a sense of humour, and I am often greatly amused at satire at my own expense, but the page to which I took exception seems to me quite outside the pale of humour and decency... I have glanced at the other pictures by the same artist, and though they are not in exquisite taste, they are not informed by that bitterness which has inspired the cartoon on the subject of myself.

Leaving out of consideration the first two sketches, the third represents me as a vulgar showman, animated by base motives in putting on Shakespeare's *Tempest*, and contains a very objectionable reference to my young daughter. The fourth represents me in my every day clothes as wearing corsets; and to my astonishment, I now hear that a firm calling itself 'The London Corset Company' has received your permission to advertise this objectionable print as an advertisement for their wares!...

The sixth represents me in the invidious position of bowing my back in anticipation of a knighthood, but I hope I have never mistaken honours in the plural for honour in the singular. This cartoon seems to be lacking in taste.

It is impossible to conceive that any lady could commit such grossness unaided, and I think I was not unreasonable in supposing that the cartoon was not devoid of masculine inspiration. There are some people so vile that if they saw one give a penny to a lame beggar girl, they would attribute it to an immoral purpose...

If I might venture a suggestion, it would be that there would be no loss of dignity to yourself if a suitable expression of regret were inserted in your next issue. It did not need your expressions to assure me of your personal good-will towards me and my work, but I think you will sympathise with my attitude and with my strong condemnation of the publication in question.

Yours sincerely,

Herbert Beerbohm Tree

In a different mood to the same Editor:

HIS MAJESTY'S THEATRE

May 23rd, 1906

My dear Mr. Shorter,

Of course a couple of seats are being reserved for you for the first performance of *Colonel Newcome*.

Many thanks for your friendly note on *The Daily Mail* attack. It certainly was outrageous to criticise a play in advance. I have known nobody yet to approve of such a curious form of journalism, but as you say it at least serves as an advertisement. Wonderful are the ways of the *The Daily Mail* group!

Yours very truly,

Herbert Beerbohm Tree

ELEONORA DUSE (1859–1924)

The tempestuous Sarah Bernhardt (q.v.) was quoted in an English magazine as saying Duse was 'a great actress', but not 'an artist'. In 1905 she offered Duse a contract to play at her Paris theatre. This was Duse's reply...

Nothing is forgotten in my heart.

This, for you, Madame, is my first thought – sent with the greatest respect – in these few words scribbled within an hour of my arrival in Paris.

Your graciousness I have never forgotten and shall never forget; in bygone days your kindness and goodness to me knew no bounds, and thus I became accustomed to a gentle trust, which developed, on my part, into a deep and respectful tenderness.

Alas – why, Madame, why can my heart no longer reach out to yours? What is an honest, gracious and dignified soul to feel?

I cannot ignore at this time the opinion you have expressed on my art – I cannot ignore it, or admit it, or forget it – for we do not like to forget that which causes the most fertile of forces to vibrate within us. But... the painful memory of your judgement of my work does not eclipse that or your first great kindnesses; for each hour has its own treasured value in our lives, and I prefer, at this moment, to remember what you were once to me: perfect and good.

So what shall we do?

I repeat, Madame, these fond words: Nothing is forgotten in my heart. The recollection of one thing, the memory of another – I store them all.

I beg you, Madame, to remember, in your turn, my boundless admiration and my infinite gratitude.

Paris, 20 février, 1905

Eleonora Duse

[Duse did not accept the offer.]

163

NELLIE MELBA (1861–1931)

In 1883 a young Australian mother, Nellie Armstrong (born Helen Porter Mitchell), wrote to her old singing teacher Pietro Cecchi in Melbourne to tell him of her decision to turn professional. She was to become Dame Nellie Melba (DBE in 1918), regarded as the successor to the great soprano Adelina Patti (1843–1919).

NELLIE ARMSTRONG TO PIETRO CECCHI

...Now to business. My husband is quite agreeable for me to adopt *music* as a profession. I do not mind telling you that times are very bad here, and we are as *poor* as it is possible for anyone to be. We have both come to the conclusion that it is no use letting my voice go to waste up here, for the pianos here are all so bad it is impossible to sing in tune with them. Not only that, the heat is so intense that I feel my voice is getting weaker every day. So you will understand that I am anxious to leave Queensland as soon as possible. I *must make some money*. Could you not form a small company and let us go touring through the Colonies, for of course I should like to study for the Opera, but would have to be earning some money at the same time. My husband will accompany me, and my baby will be quite big enough to leave in Melbourne with my sisters. Madame Elmblad *[a pianist]* would join us, I am sure.

Do you think we could make some money? I shall wait anxiously for a letter from you, for I am very unhappy here, where there is no music, no nothing.

We spoke of August next year; let it be much earlier than that if you could possibly arrange it, for I believe I shall be *dead* by then. I shall be advised by what you say in this. I hope what I say will be agreeable to you. I hope you will answer this letter as soon as you receive it, so as to let me know what ought to be done. Remember, whenever you are ready for me I can come at once, for there is nothing to detain me now that Mr. Armstrong is agreeable. I want you to keep this quite a secret from my sisters and friends. Do not mention it to anyone until everything is settled...

Nellie Armstrong left her husband and an unhappy marriage, took the child and travelled by ship to Melbourne, via Brisbane and Sydney. She worked hard and became internationally successful.

In 1903, at the height of her fame, she returned from European triumphs only to be accused, in a magazine called Truth, *of drunkenness – by an unscrupulous, oddly-motivated and dishonest English journalist called John Norton. Norton had himself once been discovered in a harem in Constantinople – the Master of the harem giving him the option of either leaving by the mail steamer or being trussed in a weighted sack and dropped into the Bosphorus; he opted for the ship.*

Norton enjoyed the misery he caused…

TRUTH – SUNDAY, 28th. MARCH
OPEN LETTER TO NELLIE MELBA

Concerning her Champagne Capers, Breaches of
Public Faith, Outrages Against Good Manners, and
Insults to Australian Citizens!

Madame –

Marvellous Melba, Mellifluous Melba, Supreme Singer Crowned Cantatrice, and Monarch of Matchless Music though you be, your public and private conduct during your short six months sojourn in Australia makes it compulsory that you should be told the truth.

Genius is mostly eccentric; the eccentricities of genius are generally pardoned – up to a certain point. You have great genius, which is only excelled by your eccentricity. The public have heard too little of the first, and a great deal too much of the last. The turpitude of a talented termagant can be forgiven ten times ten, but there is a limit of licence which cannot be condoned. You have so often transgressed that limit that the public has at last become tired of your truculent tricks and vicious vagaries. Public patience is exhausted; public opinion exasperated; and in that style of language to which you have shown that you are not a stranger, you have to be told, on behalf of an abused and outraged community, that 'It's time you took a pull,' or were 'Pulled up with a round turn'.

Your scandalous breaches of public faith and private propriety are

165

no longer to be borne without protest. That protest I now make; and if you resent it, I invite you to vindicate yourself by civil or criminal process in a Court of Law.

You are in the heyday of your culture, ripened powers, at the zenith of your fame; and occupying, of right, the position of proud pre-eminence formerly filled by the peerless Patti... What woman with a heart or soul would rashly risk such rich gifts and golden opportunities as yours by wantoning in wine? The careers of great divas – some of whom have died drunk and destitute – who have caressed the cup and drowned their songs in strong drink, should cause you to look upon champagne with a shudder, and to shun it with a shiver so long as God shall give you leave to sing. Your voice will not last forever; it should be cherished like chastity, and not submitted to the risk of ruin that banquets and drinking bouts entail. Divas as divine and delightful as yourself have been dethroned and damned by Drink before today. That you can escape their fate, if you follow in their footsteps, is not in the Providence of God, who gave you your great gift of song, in trust for the gratification of the highest instincts of your generation...

Surely you have made enough money out of your offended and outraged countrymen and countrywomen, and given so little of your easily gotten superfluity to the deserving charities of your native land, to enable you to deal not only fairly but liberally with the few second rate artists who accompany you...

Madame, I've done with you for the meantime...

> Goodbye, Nellie, I must leave you,
> Give up swigging dry champagne;
> Else your friends will surely leave you
> In disgust and poignant pain.

> John Norton

Melba could hardly fight back...

> [Memo] They say what they say. Let them say.
> <u>Nellie Melba</u> July 12th 1914

Isn't it disgusting? The people say I am drunk. What can be done about it?

Yours, heartbroken,

Nellie Melba

McKay got Melba's note published in the Sydney Morning Herald. *It helped briefly, but Norton's campaign was ruthless; in her lifetime she never repaired her undeservedly damaged reputation in her own country, despite her popularity in Europe and America. She retired in 1926 and became President of the Melbourne Conservatoire.*

BRANSBY WILLIAMS (1870–1961)

The following is a letter many of us have had to write in our time, probably no more coherently than the great 'character impersonator' Mr. Bransby Williams (given name William Pharez Williams) whose speciality was to apply wigs and greasepaints as the audience watched (on one glorious day in 1904 before the King and Queen at Sandringham). Perhaps Mr. Williams's postscript says it all....

BRANSBY WILLIAMS

London Address
'Rosemary'
Rodenhurst Road,
Clapham S.W.

Telephone No. 874 Battersea

January 14, 1908

To Mr. King

Dear Sir,

Regrets that have not been able to answer your letter earlier but so busy etc. – I appreciate your long letter and your confidence and can thoroughly understand you and your position – I assure you I fear to attempt to advise anyone with regard to the stage when I see the poverty – even the starvation – in the profession. I know so well – as [I] have so many calls upon me – I myself was to have embarked upon a theatrical tour but it is in such a terrible state. I am remaining at least another year upon the music halls and every week we have more *actors* and actresses coming into the music halls. I cannot recommend an agent, although I know them all – but I also know how your letter would be treated.

I really cannot think how to advise you – feeling an interest after reading your letter – were I to give the ordinary – oh yes do it – I should be assisting to do you harm.

Apply to some manager – such as F.R. Benson – as you have to me, is about all I can say, or join a Sketch Co..

I cannot do more – Best wishes,

Yours always,

Bransby Williams

[Postscript] Beware! There are very few Prizes but lots of disappointments

Williams refers to F.R. Benson (1858–1939, knighted in 1916); an actor-manager who in 1900 is said to have advertised for a recruit as follows:

> 'WANTED – for leading Theatrical Company, young Actor with Classical Training, to play Laertes, Cassio, &c. (Medium-pace bowler preferred)'

VIOLET VANBRUGH (1865/7–1942)

Leading actress Violet Vanbrugh is more encouraging. Here, she advises the mother of an aspiring actress to send her daughter to a particular academy (now known illustriously as 'The Royal Academy of Dramatic Art', founded by Herbert Beerbohm Tree, q.v., in 1904)...

Queen's Hotel,
Southport
Telephone No. 1404 (Two lines)
Telegrams: Queen's Southport
[No year]
Thursday

Via Miss Chappell,
Victoria Buildings, Rhyll, N.W.

Dear Mrs. Lawrence,

I will send you the particulars you ask for – shortly. I have sent to my secretary for them. *The Actor's School of Acting in 62 Gower Street, London,* is to my mind undoubtedly the best way to help a girl to fit herself for the stage as a profession.

Yours sincerely,
Violet Vanbrugh

GEORGE BERNARD SHAW (1856–1950)

Shaw (who eschewed conventional punctuation) was one of the most prolific letter-writers in history; the Post Office must have had no trouble in tracing the great Irish playwright, essayist and critic (ARMS AND THE MAN, CANDIDA, CAPTAIN BRASSBOUND'S CONVERSIOON, MAJOR BARBARA, PYGMALION, HEARTBREAK HOUSE). In the possession of the Theatre Museum, Covent Garden, is an envelope stamped and posted in Turkey, dated 22-11-1916, addressed:

Mr. Bernard SHAW, Esq.,
Somewhere in Great Britain
England

Bernard Shaw hardly enjoys a matinee of CANDIDA on a cold afternoon at the Royal Court Theatre...

BERNARD SHAW TO JOHN E. VEDRENNE [1867–1930], MANAGER OF THE ROYAL COURT THEATRE

10 Adelphi Terrace, W.C.
26th November, 1904

Dear Vedrenne,

Archer came into my box today because he couldnt [sic] stand the cold in the stalls. Four cases of frost bite were treated at the Chelsea Infirmary – one stall and three pit. A man in the dress circle got so rheumatic after the second act that he had to be lifted out by the attendants. *The Morning Post* has lumbago for life. *The Daily Mail* threatens to head his article 'A Frost at The Court'. The fireman caught one man attempting to set fire to the theatre. You will have to warm the theatre and to announce the fact in the advertisements, or the Christmas piece is done for.

There is not a hook or a hat peg in the boxes. You can get excellent ones for three pence apiece. The man in Box B said that if there had been a hook he would have hanged himself to draw public attention to the frightful cold. My wife was affected to tears by the play; and her tears froze so that it took me five minutes to get her eyes open with the warmth of my hands, which are now covered in chilblains. My mother went to sleep; and we are still (6.15) vainly trying to wake her. I think you have done for her. You can get coals and blankets at the Parish Hall, believe. Why not apply?

ever
G.B.S.

In fact, Vedrenne's days at the Royal Court Theatre were numbered, as mentioned in Hermann Vezin's letter which follows...

HERMANN VEZIN (1829–1910)

Actor Hermann Vezin's finest hour was in 1889, when he went on as Macbeth for a week at the Lyceum after Henry Irving lost his voice. For this, Irving presented him with a splendid diamond ring and a cheque for £120. Vezin's great great grandmother was, he was proud to say, Marie Charlotte de Chateauneuf, a leading French actress and grandmother of Rouget de l'Isle, who wrote 'La Marseillaise'.

In a letter to Olive Steltith in 1907 the old man, by now an eminent teacher of Elocution, puts the London Theatre Scene to rights...

November 5, 1907,
10 Lancaster Place,
Strand W.C

Dear Olive,

I registered your letter as ordered. Voici! I did not like Lena Ashwell's piece. I am told it is a success. I can hardly believe it. There is one character in it that I should think would damn any play. It is a sort of Bill Sykes in good society. Likewise there is no sympathy with the woman. Also, except Francis Ivor and my pupil Vibart, there is a general indistinctness of dialogue. I had booked a seat in the gallery. There was no back to it and whenever I tried to sit up I felt the two knees of a clergyman digging into my back.

I liked Horniman's *The Education of Elizabeth* very much. It is immensely funny and clever. Whether a success or not, it is too soon to enquire. *As You Like It* appears to be doing well.

I went to the Court yesterday afternoon to hear the Competition in Elocution. I heard the first batch. They were *Professionals*. Oh! my God! I could not stand any more, so I missed the *Hamathoors*. I'll back one of the young ladies to emphasise more wrong words than all the bad actors in London. The house was *crammed*. Otho Stuart was the umpire. Poor Devil! I wonder what his award was. Not one of the ladies appeared to have had a single lesson. Oh, then I just heard a young man give a speech of Gratiano's and Hamlet's soliloquy, end of Act II. Acton Bond was Master of Ceremonies.

The piece at the Haymarket appears to be what Boucicault [*q.v.*]

used to call 'a Wailing Failure'. I am going tonight to see the first night of *Mrs. Ellison's Answer* at the New Theatre.

It is said that the removal of Vedrenne and Barker to the Savoy 'has been somewhat disastrous *[John E. Vedrenne, 1867–1930; Harley Granville Barker (q.v.) 1877–1946]*. I saw *You Never Can Tell* from a very uncomfortable seat in the gallery and was profoundly bored. But oh! such a cast! I cannot make out why they never had me for Crampton, in which I made such a success. Otho Stuart, I believe, has had nothing but failures at the Court. Serve him right for not doing my Play at the Adelphi.

No, I know no one, Lawyer or otherwise who would lend money as you suggest. I dare say there are lots of them if one only knew. It is sad to read of your troubles and be impotent to help.

There's the Luncheon Bell!

Having finished my Currie – I don't know whether that is the way to spell it – I must finish.

I have read the Reichsbote containing the full account of the Moltke-Harden trial. It is savoury. I wonder the Emperor doesn't resign. It reminds me of two paragraphs which appeared in a Berlin paper when I was there in 1848–9. Von Huelsen was the manager of the Royal Theatres. First par. said how pleased the playgoing Berliners must be that whereas in other Theatres there was generally one Actress who was put forward, not on account of her talent, but because of the affection of the manager, no such scandal could occur in Berlin. The next par. said that the lovers of the Ballet would rejoice to hear that Herr Something, a dancing nobody, had been advanced to the position of Premier Danseur, although they had already two Premiers Danseurs in the company. Oh, Marquis de Sade what you have to answer for!

As to me, I don't know how I am. One day better and next day queer. Still, we live in hopes. I continue the Raphanus Niger, but cannot say whether it is doing me any good. I have lately learned that Horse Radish is even better. May fortune smile on all of us soon.

Yours,
Poppie

GEORGE BERNARD SHAW (1856–1950);
MRS PATRICK CAMPBELL (1865–1940)

George Bernard Shaw enjoyed a number of love affairs on paper; his two most celebrated correspondents, who both returned the affection, were the actresses Ellen Terry (q.v.) and Mrs Patrick Campbell, (given name Beatrice Stella Tanner), his first Eliza Doolittle in PYGMALION...

MRS PATRICK CAMPBELL TO GEORGE BERNARD SHAW

33, Kensington Square, W.
[Postmarked] 29th July, 1912

Both Sir Edward and Lady Stracey were very amused and delighted with your letter and book – Mary Stracey begged me to write and say it would be grand, and that you rather owe it to me, and that chivalrous spirit that dwells somewhere in you to let us have *Liza* to take with us for me to read to her – so that she will hear what the world will never hear now – we would treasure the MS and let you have it back faithfully – and we would let no other soul see it – My Stella used to sing a song which I told her was silly, and she declared was funny – your last letter reminds me more of it than your others –

> He's mad, mad, mad,
> He's clean gone off his nut
> He cleans his boots with strawberry jam
> He eats his hat whenever he can
> He's mad, mad, mad –

– I hope you too will have a lovely holiday and not need our 'cap and bells' all the time – and that bladder-whacking of yours, that makes my dear friend D.D. jump, and imagine it's really a bump!

My address will be:

Hotel Mirabeau,
Aix-les-Bains,
Savoie, France.

I start to-morrow after 8 days in bed – with two black eyes – and some screw-like pains in my shoulder.

Yours affectionately,
Beatrice Stella

Hotel de Russie,
Bad Kissingen,
9th August 1912

Stella, Stella:

All the winds of the north are musical with the thousand letters I have written to you on this journey. But at last the car's gears got jammed at the fall of evening, and as I live (by vegetables)! I *stood* – stood on my straining legs on that hillside for ten hours, keeping up the spirits of my chauffeur and warding off ghosts and foreign devils from him, whilst he took the whole transmission to pieces and put it together again. I found a village and a clean double-bedded room in a gasthaus for Charlotte and her sister; and they slept happily. I and the chauffeur kept up magnificently, and greeted the dawn with the exultation of men who had not turned a hair. And that day we did not turn many hairs. But the next (which was yesterday) – my word! I tell you, my good woman, that if you expect to find any romantic nonsense about me, you are greatly mistaken. My knees are out of order: my calves are like a shop assistant's where there are no seats behind the counter. I shall not feel romantic about you again for at least ten minutes.

But this is not what you want to know. The original manuscript of Pygmalion you cannot read: it is in shorthand. The typed copy with my corrections which I read from at DD's has been through the hands of a compositor's in Edinburgh and would not be fit for your lily-white hands even if it were within my reach instead of – I dash I presume – in London...

Is it Lady Strachey you are with? Your letter reads like Strachey, which suggests nothing to me but a Colonel in the Guards of whom I knew something (in connexion [sic] with a famous opera singer) thirty years ago. If it is Lady Strachey, what will she think of me when you trail your victim before her? I solemnly protest that when I went into that room in Kensington Square I was a man of iron, insolently confident in my impenetrability. Had I not seen you dozens of times, and dissected you professionally as if you were a microscopic specimen,

what danger could there possibly be for me? And in thirty seconds –
oh Stella, if you had a rag of decency it *couldn't* have happened. I
always thought that if I met you I should ask you to play. I looked at
the piano; and I said 'Good God! Fancy listening to *that* when I can
listen to her'. Is this dignified? Is it sensible? At my age – a driveller – a
dotard! I will conquer this weakness, or trade in it and write plays
about it. Oh Lord! I hope it isnt *[sic]* Lady Strachey: she is such a nice
woman; and I had to disgust her before with certain savageries in a
little piece called *Press Cuttings. She* cannot be made the dupe of my
ridiculous illusions about you. I am like the brigand in *Man and
Superman* with his Louisa (who was our cook, by the way). Still, Stella,
I kiss your hands and magnify the Life Force for creating you; for you
are a very wonderful person.

That doggerel of Stella's – Stellinetta's – nearly cost the life of
myself and the three people I was driving; for instead of minding my
work I kept composing millions of additional verses, in proof whereof
I send you three or four of the least poetic and most intelligible. The
one profane rhyme is not my fault: jam inevitably suggests dam.
Stellinetta is rather a wooden little devil, by the way; but perhaps the
baby will wake her up – not that I want her to be wakened up; for she
is rather exquisite as she is. I once puzzled her frightfully by a piece of
Irish folly. We were sitting in the front of a box at the Savoy at some
idiotic performance of *Arms and The Man*; and the audience gave me a
sort of ovation at the end. My impulse was to rise and bless them (I
often feel like a Pope – should have been one), but Stellinetta was
talking to me; and to appear conscious of anything but her would
have been a breach of gallantry. So I betrayed not the faintest
consciousness of the applauding house, and hung on Stellinetta's
words... And Charlotte was furious, and said I'd been guilty of a
gross breach of public manners. But it was pleasanter to be gallant to
Stellinetta than to smile at a mob of gushing Shavians. I am the
servant of the public, but not its adorer. And I will not begin another
sheet or I shall never get to bed.

And so *buona sera* Beatrice.

G.B.S.

[Postscript]

Stellinetta sings to her banjo.

He's mad! mad! mad!
He's gone right off his chump
He cleans his boots with strawberry jam;
He thinks the world of my silly old mam
Who doesn't value his plays a dam
    For they give her the blooming hump, dear girls;
    They give her the blooming hump...

Then hurrah! rah! rah!
He'll never be my Papa;
For however he loves and however he longs,
My mammy and I wouldn't touch with the tongs
Such a silly old man with such silly old songs:
    No, we'd rather marry the Shah, dear girls;
    We'd rather marry the Shah.

(Banjo *ad lib* – Plunk a tunk a bunk chunk etc. etc)

Mrs Patrick Campbell was known for her rebellious temperament, and Shaw often took her to task for this in his letters. Here, he fires off some home truths for another of his favourites:

Ellen Terry (q.v., married to James Carew), at a difficult stage of her career...

Ayot St. Lawrence
Welwyn, Herts.
Station: Wheathampstead, G.N.R. 2¼
Telegrams: Bernard Shaw, Codicote,

10 Adelphi Terrace, W.C.

9th November, 1913

Dearest Ellen,

You fill me with concern – with dismay. What am I to do or say? It's as if Queen Alexandra came to me and asked me to get her a place as cook–housekeeper, except that I'm not in love with Queen Alexandra.

Nobody dare have you in a cast: youd *[sic]* knock it all to pieces. A tiny yacht may throw its mast overboard and end its days quietly and serviceably as a ferry boat; but a battleship cant *[sic]* do that; and you are a battleship.

What parts are there that even the most callous youngster who never saw you could offer you in the ordinary routine of theatrical commerce? Matrons at £15 a week or less. And then the agony of learning a part and being hustled by a producer, and finally overwhelming everyone on the stage by dwarfing them and mopping up every scrap of interest and attention in the house! Can you wonder that we all recoil, and say 'She would be splendid in it'; and then get some estimable mouse who would give no trouble and spread no terror?

Ellen, Ellen, what has become of all the jubilee money? For you *must* be in difficulties or you would never be content with minor work. You are not wildly extravagant: you dont [sic] keep two motor cars and wallow in sables and diamonds. Do you give it all away; or has Teddy a family in every European capital for you to support? Not my business, isnt [sic] it? Then dont harrow my feelings by telling me that you must get engagements instantly. Must we all sink with 50 starving parasites clutching our hair? I have three letters just received from unfortunate people, pitiable people, nice people, whose only≥ refuge is being adopted by me. I *must* turn savage and thrust them from my plank into the waves or I shall presently be as desperate as they are. So must you.

Well, this isnt very consoling, damn me.

If I were you, I should take the Margate Theatre, and set up a school. Teddy's ambition is to be the successor of Sarah Thorne; but as you gave him your forehead without your chin he will never do it: he will only talk and write beautifully about it, and produce nothing but pretty children with stomachs to fill and backs to clothe. You will have to set up the school yourself as you have had to do everything else; and then you can give him parts to play at thirty shillings a week and use up the children for the pantomime.

And James? What's James doing?

Ellen: what a world!

Oh, why cant I write a letter that will make you forget your troubles, instead of rubbing them in?

Oh Lord!

Let us tie ourselves together – close – and give some respectable boatman our last shilling to row us out and drop us into the sea.

G.B.S.

ARTHUR WONTNER (1875 –1960)

I like this good-natured letter, written in all the flurry of a Press Night. The recipient might have been Margaret Fraser, former Gaiety girl, who made her professional début in 1895, and gave her hobbies as 'Shooting and Motoring' in The Green Room Book of 1907...

Savoy Theatre
Strand W.C.
7th January, 1913

Dear Miss Fraser,

It's disgracefully late to write and thank you for your kind Christmas wishes, but I am going to risk it and do so. May I, too, send my own sincere wishes for a very, very happy and prosperous New Year.

You are an Indian and I am a Duke – a love-sick Duke. What the dickens have we been since we met. I don't know, do you?

One of these days I may have the good fortune to run across you.

Till then always,
Yours very truly,
Arthur Wontner

[Postscript] The beastly critics are in front tonight with all force! Pardon if this letter is incoherent or the writing unreadable. Eh! I'm that nervous.

[Arthur Wontner's son, Hugh Walter Kingwell Wontner, who gave 'acting' as his hobby in WHO'S WHO, became Chairman of the Savoy Theatre and was honoured with the title 'Clerk of the Royal Kitchens'.]

VASLAV NIJINSKY (1890–1950)

The Russian dancer's management miss a few heartbeats...

Post Office Telegraphs
Handed in at 2.30 p.m., Oxford St.
Received at 3.06 p.m.

To Gustave de Beer, Pressimus, London,
From Zenon

NIJINSKY LITTLE BETTER
DOCTOR SAY CAN DANCE THURSDAY

Post Office Telegraphs
Handed in at 1.19 p.m., West Strand.
Received at 1.45 p.m.

To Gustave de Beer, Pressimus, London,
From Zenon

NIJINSKY GONE FOR A DRIVE MUCH BETTER

NOEL COWARD (1899–1973)

Noël Coward, playwright, actor, singer, inherited the mantle of Sheridan (q.v.) and Wilde (q.v.), writing witty, perceptive plays: BLITHE SPIRIT, HAYFEVER, TONIGHT AT 8.30, PRIVATE LIVES, etc., and numerous brilliant song lyrics. In about 1911, on holiday by the sea, the 'ever loving sun' wrote to his adoring and adored mother:

Dear Darling old Mother,

Thank you very much for your letter I could not send a card and this was scarcely odd because there were no cards to send I have been out in the yaught this after noon it was very very rough and I was fearfly sea sick and uncle Harry took me ashore and I was going to wait on the beach for 2 hours but a very nice lady asked me to go to tea with her I went and had a huge tea this is the menu 3 seed buns 2 peacises of Bread and jam 3 Biscuits 2 cups of tea when I thanked her she began to Preach and said we were all put into the world to do kind things (amen) I am afraid she did not impress me much but I wished her somewhere I shant go in that yaught again for months and months and months Auntie Laura sent my washing to the village I hope you are not miserable it makes me miserable to think you are I have got to go to bed now so good bye from your ever loving sun Noël. Squillions of kisses to all love to Eric X X X X X X X X X X X X X X X X X X X X X X X X X X X X X X X X X X X X X X X the name of the lady that gave me tea is Mrs Penrose Walter The dogs are so nice down here Nan and Marcus, Marcus sits on a chair and smokes a pipe he looks so funny and if you drop anything anywhere Nan goes and fetches it. I had 3 little boys to tea yesterday each about the size of a flea *I* had to amuse them and didnt enjoy it much Elephant sends her love.

Noël

CONCERNING
HARLEY GRANVILLE-BARKER (1877–1946)

Harley Granville-Barker introduced a new 'naturalism' to Shakespearian theatre, subjugating design and effect to the author's intention – a reaction, perhaps, to grandiose concepts such as H.B. Tree (q.v.) described in his letters to Olivia Truman. In 1912, Allan Wade, irritated by critics of the ground-breaking theatre director's work, wrote to the Pall Mall Gazette, using a cousin's name as a nom de plume:

Pall Mall Gazette
6th September, 1912

THE WINTER'S TALE AND SOME CRITICS

Sir,

It is a little puzzling to the common playgoer who is not a professional critic to observe the state of bewilderment – not to say irritation – into which some, though not, I am glad to say, all, of our dramatic critics have been thrown by Mr. Granville-Barker's production of *The Winter's Tale* at the Savoy Theatre. Surely there is no need for such perplexity. Mr. Barker has simply given us the first adequate Shakespearean production that this generation has seen – that is to say, the first production in which a play of Shakespeare's is given as he wrote it, without cuts, re-arrangements, tedious over-elaborated 'business', and the rest of it. (I need not complete the list, it would be a long, sad tale.) He has invented or revived methods of staging by which we pass rapidly and easily from one scene to the next; and he has chosen two admirable artists to collaborate with him in giving the play a simple and beautiful setting. What is there so bewildering, so disconcerting, in all this?

The decoration of the play has been called Post-Impressionist; it has also been called an imitation of Professor Reinhardt's work… This is an age of catch-words. One uses such expressions as post-impressionists, Reinhardtian, and so forth, a little loosely in conversations between the acts, perhaps, and nobody is a penny the worse; but should not a critic define his meaning a little more carefully when he writes for cold print?

We have been told also that the rapid delivery of the lines renders much of the play unintelligible. Is this really so? *The Winter's Tale* is not a favourite play of mine, and I cannot claim to know it as intimately as the majority of dramatic critics doubtless do; but I can honestly say that I had no difficulty whatever in hearing or following the lines of the play, except in a few instances, where I believe the fault lay in the performer's actual elocution, and not in the speed. On the other hand, the value of this swiftness to the action of the play was immense.

Why is it, then, that our critics are so disturbed? Can it be (distressing thought!) that Mr. Granville-Barker has once more pioneered successfully, and that these gentlemen don't like pioneers? If that be so, why, one wonders, do they attend Mr. Barker's productions at all? Why not, as Mr. W.B. Yeats once suggested, content themselves with those productions which so many clever men have made specially to please them? They have seen Mr. Barker at work for several years, strengthening and revitalising the modern drama and its methods of production; they have been dragged reluctantly to admire him. (Only one critic, I fancy, had the courage recently to reprint his original 1905 'notice' of *The Voysey Inheritance* as though to prove triumphantly that he had not advanced in the interval!) Surely these critics might have guessed that Mr. Barker would be 'up to' something when it came to Shakespeare – and stayed away!

Personally, speaking as one who had hoped, almost despairingly, to see a production of Shakespeare that should not cause one intolerable shame, I am very grateful to Mr. Barker. Thanks to him, we may confidently hope that in a few years' time to attempt to present the plays of our great English dramatist in the form in which he wrote them will not necessarily be stigmatised as 'German'. On the whole, one may say 'It moves.'

Yours, etc.,

(Miss) Irene Dallas

35, St. George's Mansions,
Red Lion Square,
W.C.

SCOTT OF THE ANTARCTIC (1868–1912)
to novelist and dramatist
J.M.BARRIE (1860–1937)

[J.M. Barrie wrote THE ADMIRABLE CRICHTON, PETER PAN, DEAR BRUTUS]
  On January 17, 1912, on his second expedition to the Antarctic, Captain Robert Falcon Scott, 44, reached the South Pole. Returning, his team were stranded in appalling weather. Close to death, Scott thawed out his fingers at an improvised tin and wick lamp to write his last letters...

Near South Pole,
Late March, 1912

We are pegging out in a very comfortless spot. Hoping this letter may be found and sent to you, I write a word of farewell... More practically, I want you to help my widow and my boy – your godson.

Goodbye, I am not afraid of the end, but sad to miss many a humble pleasure which I had planned for the future on our long marches. I may not have proved a great explorer, but we have done the greatest march ever made and come very near to great success. Goodbye, my dear friend.

We are in a desperate state, feet frozen, no fuel and a long way from food; but it would do your heart good to be in our tent, to hear our songs and the cheery conversation as to what we will do when we get to Hut Point.

Later. We are very near the end, but have not and will not lose our good cheer. We have had four days of storm in our tent, and nowhere food or fuel. We did intend to finish ourselves when things proved like this, but we have decided to die naturally in the track.

As a dying man, my dear friend, be good to my wife and child. Give the boy a chance in life if the State won't do it. He ought to have good stuff in him.

I never met a man in my life whom I admired and loved more than you, and I never could show you how much your friendship meant to me, for you had much to give and I nothing.

Robert Falcon Scott

Scott died on or about March 27. The bodies, and papers including this letter, were found on November 12, 1912.

GEORGE BERNARD SHAW (1856–1950)

From George Bernard Shaw to actress Mrs Patrick Campbell (q.v.) on the death of her son, killed in action on 30th December, 1917...

London, 7 January, 1918

Never saw it nor heard about it until your letter came. It is no use: I cant be sympathetic; these things simply make me furious. I want to swear. I *do* swear. Killed just because people are blasted fools. A chaplain, too, to say nice things about it. It is not his business to say nice things about it, but to shout that the 'voice of thy son's blood crieth unto God from the ground.'

No, dont show me the letter. But I should very much like to have a nice talk with that dear Chaplain, that sweet sky-pilot, that...

No use going on like this, Stella. Wait for a week, and then I shall be very clever and broadminded again and have forgotten all about this. I shall be quite as nice as the Chaplain.

Oh, damn, damn, damn, damn, damn, damn, damn, damn, DAMN.

And oh, dear, dear, dear, dear, dear, dearest!

G.B.S.

MARTIN HARVEY (1863–1944)

Actor-manager Martin Harvey was particularly known for his performance as Sidney Carton in THE ONLY WAY, a dramatization of Dickens's A TALE OF TWO CITIES, and for his delivery of the line: 'It is a far, far better thing that I do, than I have ever done; it is a far better rest, that I go to, than I have ever known.' He was a member of Sir Henry Irving's Lyceum company from 1882–1896. Described generally as an actor of power, truth and sensitivity, he was knighted in 1921.

Mr. Harvey gets a fan letter...

Tel. no. Edg. 254
Llantrisant
Yately Road
Edgbaston
Birmingham

Dear Mr. Harvey,

Just a short letter to thank you very much for finding time to write to me, it was awfully good of you, for I'm sure you're a very busy man.

As for my poor little gift I only wish I could have given more.

We *are* looking forward to next time you're in 'Brum'.

Oh! Mother said she would be delighted if you would care to come and see us next time you're here, we should love it if you and Mrs. Harvey could come to lunch or tea.

I must stop now because (as usual) my homework is waiting to be done, and Duty calls. I must obey her demands – I would much rather write letters but I must do my lessons. Besides there are your feelings to be considered in the letter writing question.

So I will spare them and say goodbye from
Mavis Carter

[Endorsed by Harvey: 'Isn't this a sweet letter']

RUTH GORDON (1896–1985)

American actress Ruth Gordon, who determined to be an actress after seeing
Hazel Dawn in THE PINK LADY, writes home with a copy of her review in
the New York Times (Alexander Woollcott – q.v. – wrote 'Ruth Gordon is
ever so gay as Nibs') after her New York debut in 1915 as Nibs, opposite
Maude Adams, in PETER PAN at the Empire Theatre:

December 22, 1915

Dear Mama and Papa,

Well, it's all over and you can be proud of me. I wish you could have
been there. That was truly the only thing missing. It was the worst day of
my life and the greatest night. No matter how old I live I will never
experience such emotions. I'll begin from the worst, it was my period
and, Mama, you know what pains I have, but nothing could equal yesterday. Thank fortune I had a good sleep although how I had the courage to,
the night before my first opening night, I don't know! I really think I am
wonderful. But this horrible pain woke me up. I could just groan and our
good colored maid looked in. She asked me if I ever had gin. Mama, I
didn't drink any. Ida fixed me up some of the Penny Royal tea from
Wollaston. I thought I would throw up, but I didn't and it worked.

That was my terrible day. My night made up for all that and for all
the rest of my life. In a big envelope I am sending you something will
prove why. I don't care how hard it is or how terrible, I would rather be
an actress than live. In other words, if I could not be an actress, I would
gladly take my life. I can say that without fear because I *can* be an actress
and *will* be, as proven by what it says in the other envelope. Papa, I
know you like the Boston Globe, but wait till you see this envelope!

At the Empire Theatre I dress one flight up with Angela Ogden, who
kind of slips me little hints of what to do, without exactly letting on
she's doing it. Also in the dressing room is Miss Keppel, who is sweet
and subdued. They are all too old, except me, to play the Lost Boys, but
most of them are friends of friends of Miss Adams or been with her
since the year one. Angela Ogden is a very wonderful actress, who, they
say, stole the show from Miss Adams when they played *Quality Street*,
so Miss Adams won't put that one on any more, but will revive *The
Little Minister* where Angela has a nice part that's no competition.

Well, I better get back to opening night. Did I write you I wear a suit
of sort of like teddy bear fur? It goes all over me except my face and is

187

quite hot and cumbersome, but the Lost Boys have to wear them. Well, the curtain went up and I thought I would die of fright, but the scenes in the Darlings' nursery are before I come on, so I recovered. Our scene started in the Never Never Land and I was in my place inside the tree trunk when I heard my cue and came out and said my line and got a huge laugh. I was so pleased. They tell me no one ever got that laugh before, so it made quite an impression.

All went swimmingly. It was a very fashionable audience, all the Fifth Avenue set. Miss Adams is a big society draw. They said all the men wore silk hats and white ties and tails and the ladies were quite decolleté and heavily jewelled. After my dance Miss Adams beckoned me to take three bows and our orchestra leader Henri Deering stood up and applauded. Gratifying after all I've been through. And Miss Adams has no jealousy like Alice Claire Elliot says many stars have. My cup runneth over and I guess when you read this yours will, too.

Then came the final curtain with Miss Adams alone in the treetop house after having waved goodbye to Wendy who flew home and everybody including the cast in the wings were crying when down came the curtain to thunderous applause and we all took our rehearsed bows, then rushed back and stood in the wings. That means just out of sight in the scenery. Miss Adams took one of her calls alone then came over and said 'Nibs' and led me on and while the audience applauded she broke off a rose from the immense bouquet that had been passed over the footlights and handed me a long-stemmed American Beauty rose that must have cost I don't know how much and I will treasure and preserve forever.

Well, that's about all. All the people in the dressing room including those I mentioned and Mrs. Buchanan, quite a swell, and Miss Clarens, extremely elegant, told me I had made a most auspicious start. And when you see the other envelope you will note they are right.

Your loving actress daughter,
Ruth Gordon
(a name you will one day see in lights)
December 22, 1915, my favorite day of my life.
R.

56 years later, Ruth Gordon was to refer again to the NY Times *review. (See page 256)*

MARI LOHR (1890–1975)
EDWARD SEYMOUR HICKS (1871–1949)

Mari Löhr made her first appearance in 1901 at the Garrick Theatre in SHOCK-HEADED PETER and THE MAN WHO STOLE THE CASTLE. She was an actress with a passionate following...

London
Nov. 25 *[No year]*

Dear Miss Löhr,

This is a letter from one who can never hope to meet you, to tell you what your acting means to some of your audience – I've sat and watched you so many times at the theatre and have grown so fond of you that I want to tell you about it – perhaps you'll laugh at the idea of a stranger being fond of you but I don't believe you will – leaving the Royalty the other night I overheard a remark 'one may *admire* other actresses but everyone *loves* Marie Löhr' and that's just about what all London feels – it's not only your beauty but it's the soul showing in your eyes we love, and your wonderful voice.

'Times are hard' sometimes for most, and when they are for me I often go and listen to you speaking – Others may have such a voice – I can only say I've never met them. And, so, Princess, carry on your wonderful way – and God bless our Marie Löhr!'

'One of the Stalls'

The great comic actor Edward Seymour Hicks (knighted in 1935) receives some advice:

Thursday
28 Blenheim Road,
St. John's Wood

Dear Mr.Hicks,

I was most interested in the play, and nearly every part was excellently acted, if you will allow me to say so, and also allow me to say to Mr. L. Irving *[Laurence – Henry Irving's younger brother]*, and yourself: Work! There is a lot in both of you. 'Work is worship'.

Always faithfully yours,
Rachel Emily Willard

THE LORD CHAMBERLAIN

Lord Chamberlain's Office
St. James's Palace, S.W.1

To Miss Florence Tench

21st November, 1919

Madam,

With reference to the sketch *A Breezy Honeymoon* which you have submitted for license, I am desired to inform you that the Lord Chamberlain is of the opinion that the ending as at present is slightly indelicate, and suggests that the piece should finish *before* the couple go into the bedroom.

Perhaps you would be good enough to submit a new ending embodying this requirement.

Yours faithfully,
Assistant Comptroller,
Lord Chamberlain's Office

RUDOLPH VALENTINO (1895–1926)

Hollywood actor Rudolph Valentino dresses to kill…

Hollywood
April 26 1921

Nikolaus Tuczck,
15B Clifford St., Bond St, W1,
London

Dear Sir,

To replay [sic] to your last of the 28 of February, I would be very glad if you would send me a sample pair of boots with fancy perforated finish and straight toe caps, bottoms with suede top as per your Batch No. 1.

If you cannot send them C.O.D. kindly inform me by cable, and I shall send the money immediately.

Hoping to hear from you by return mail.

Sincerely yours,
Rudolph Valentino

[Postscript] My new address is: C/o Citizen's Trust and Family Bank, Hollywood Branch, Hollywood, Cal.

THE BARRYMORES

Lionel Barrymore (1878–1954) made his début at the at the age of fifteen, as Thomas in THE RIVALS, in Kansas City. He said 'It was like trying to play a French horn while standing on my head.' His voice was breaking, he tangled his whip in his legs, wore boots that were much too small and a mangy grey wig. He went home to find this dread letter on his bed:

[1893]

My dear Lionel,

I sincerely wish I did not have to write this letter, for I want to spare your feelings. But, dear boy, I am compelled to inform you of the plain facts regarding your portrayal of Thomas. You were somewhat inadequate, and it is with the deepest regret that I convey the news that it is no longer necessary that you appear in the cast.

I shall see you in the morning, dear boy. Until then, good night, and God bless you,

Your affectionate grandmother,

Mrs. Drew

Lionel's brother John (1882–1942) was slow in answering letters. In 1926 the producer William Foss, for whom John had played HAMLET, offered him two months at His Majesty's Theatre, and a film...

JOHN BARRYMORE TO WILLIAM FOSS

1926

The fact of your getting a letter from me will probably establish in your astounded cosmos the basis of an aneurism that might cut short a brilliant managerial career. I have thought of your letters with sporadic frequency, usually before I get up in the morning, each time accruing more and more of a Gethsemanic sweat. I consider it disgraceful, my not having answered you earlier, but by saying so I am merely amplifying my autobiography, which as a phrase is redundant, but which as a fact I have a vague feeling you will understand.

I have been so saturated in cinematic labour (I use the word 'saturated' in the broader sense of benignant actuality) that I have literally had time for no mental reactions away from this line of endeavor...

Heaven alone knows when the vicissitudes of a precarious profession shall land me on your shores again...

Jack

*When VANITY FAIR decided to feature him in its next issue, Barrymore was
unhappy with their choice of photographs, and sent replacements...*

JOHN BARRYMORE TO JOHN CROWNINSHIELD, EDITOR, VANITY FAIR

The pictures the estimable Warners sent you of the younger Don
Juan looked a little like Frederick Warde, made up for James G. Blaine
Sr. In other words, it struck me – and we movie actors still retain our
facial expressions long after every other function has gone back on us –
as a trifle too authentic...

Jack Barrymore

On the night of the Dempsey-Tunney title fight [1926], which Dempsey lost:

Cable
Jack Dempsey to John Barrymore
Handed in Philadelphia   Received Hollywood

DEAR JACK I FORGOT TO DUCK

In a return match the following year Dempsey forgot to duck again.

*On the night of Barrymore's first wedding anniversary (with actress
Dolores Costello), his brother-in-law cabled him:*

Cable
Lowell Sherman to John Barrymore

CONGRATULATIONS ON FIRST YEAR OF THE RUN
STOP IF ANYTHING HAPPENS REMEMBER
THERE IS ALWAYS VAUDEVILLE

*An undated letter from John Barrymore on location to Writer/director (and
later Barrymore's biographer) Gene Fowler in Hollywood (which, in another
letter, Barrymore describes as 'that dermoid cyst, Hollywoodus in Latrina'):*

Limbo – on the Dunes

Dear Gene:

Someone – I think it was Sam T. Jack – the eminent buttock impresario – said 'God works in mysterious ways His wonders to perform'.

As I remember (a thing, thank Christ, I'm not very good at!) it was a

193

farewell banquet in honor of four sisters – large girls all, who, having been, to coin a phrase, the mainstay of the troupe for many years, were laden with honors and hernia. We retired to the patchoulied twilight of the Everleigh Club. It was a really great moment, and reminded one of Napoleon's farewell to the Old Guard at Fontainebleau. (No I wasn't *there*. You bastard – I merely heard about it from somebody who was – a Director.)

I don't know why I ramble on this way, but Elba is kind of quiet today, and the bees are droning lazily around the one-holer. Two dogs of frail parentage are lolling in the stink-weed patch, and all Nature seems waiting with finger on lip for some portentous event or cataclysm to occur. It wouldn't surprise me at all if it were *The Master of Ballantrae*.

Oddly enough, I've always wanted to play the Ophidian and fearless son of a bitch, and went so far as to have a long interview with Lloyd Osborne on the subject... Walker Whiteside did it, and it was a bit of a flop, and *why not?*

Whether or not Lionel can be seduced into playing it, I don't know. Of course that would be great. I have, more times than I can tell you, broached the subject to him, and he has always dexterously evaded it. *You* might have better luck, even intimating it might be a bridge to terra firma for his little brother, who is at present in a state of slightly swirling levitation.

If, however, that combination, which would be imperial, with you and Charlie (MacArthur) writing the script, prove hopeless, and Lionel prove inexorable, the idea is too gorgeous to give up. We could get some swell person to play the other brother. There *must* be more in this than meets the eye, as I have thought about the damned thing so intensively for so many years.

It is a quaint conceit, but I have always regarded you and Charlie as two bawdy and libidinous guardian angels, a proper complement as it were to my somewhat static and sacerdotal self! A sort of *Balance Wheel*, as it were, to phantasmagoria.

I am eating my gruel at regular intervals, and dreaming as infrequently as is compatible with celibacy... Since your letter, oh, Ishmael! – or P—— Pot, as you prefer – I live again!

Love,

Jack

MR DIX, TOUR MANAGER OF LUMBER LOVE

1929. A letter to Mr. Southern at the Garrick Theatre, from an efficient Mr.Dix, tour manager of LUMBER LOVE, currently at the Grand Theatre, Southampton. Mr. Dix seems to have studied the literary style of Mr. Pooter in George and Weedon Grossmith's 'Diary of a Nobody':

Grand Theatre, Southampton
February 20th, 1929

Dear Mr. Southern,

I enclose an exact report of a quarrel which occurred last night between Mr. Woolgast and Mr. Tenant...

Firstly, Mr. Woolgast was obviously in the wrong in accusing Mr.Tenant of loafing. I have never yet found this artist a slacker, and had he been, it would have been the place of the Stage Manager or myself to pull him up, *not* Mr. Woolgast.

Mr. Tenant was, of course, unpardonably wrong in starting a fight in the theatre, however provoked he may have been, and undoubtedly was. Mr. Woolgast has been very bitter against this artist for some time now, and the fact that there are not sufficient dressing rooms for Mr. Woolgast to have one to himself this week had undoubtedly added to this ill-feeling. On the other hand, Mr. Tenant is now reaching that stage in the career of a suddenly-promoted chorus man when the hat gets too small.

This has been brought about mainly by his wife, who is in the chorus and has caused a very strong undercurrent of ill-feeling. She is very proud of this hero husband of hers and uses this to run down the other principals at his glorification. Also she continually forgets her place as a chorus girl, and interferes with the principals. While it would be difficult to get actual proof of this, I do not go about with my eyes shut, and several incidents have convinced me of the correctness of my deductions. She has even refused to leave Mr. Woolgast's dressing room when asked by the management to do so. This sort of thing is utterly out of the question, and I am giving her her notice on Saturday. I expect this will involve Mr. Tenant's resignation, which will be all to the good, as under the circumstances the team work of the show, which was its great and all-important feature, has gone by the board.

Mr. Woolgast has expressed his desire to finish, and asked me to accept his notice – as and from – last Saturday. While we are at it, I think it advisable that we should dispense with both dissentients. I am continually having very strong complaints from the public, via the resident manager, that Mr. Woolgast was no good to us. I wrote to you regarding this at the end of last tour, if you remember, and I suggested changing him. Mr. Dodds did not like the idea, however, and thought he would be O.K. in the South, especially as he went so well at Penge.

This tour, however, I have had complaints from Mr. Fitt at Norwich, Mr. Barnard at Ipswich and Mr. Curry at Grimsby. At Stoke Newington last week he hardly got a laugh, which nullifies the effect at Penge.

Anyway, we cannot afford to sacrifice all our dates for our eight weeks in London, where another comedian will go just as well. We have here, therefore, an opportunity of dispensing with a swelled-headed leading man who can be bettered with ease, and a comedian who has started a nasty breach in the team work, and is doing the box office no good anyway. All of which can be done without compunction or risk of abuse to the firm.

Mr. Tenant will not be at all difficult to replace, and I think I can lay my hands on Reggie Connor, an excellent little comedian who has done some splendid work of all kinds, playing parts played by all the leading comedians from Harry Welden upwards. I hear he has just finished panto., and can get him for £15 instead of the 18 we are playing Mr. Woolgast. I have dropped him a line, quite non-committally, asking him if he is disengaged. I feel sure we shall never do any good while we have the comedy of a very high class musical play played by a low comedian. This is not only my own opinion, but the opinion of the Managers and Public all over the country.

I shall carry on, on these lines, unless I hear from you to the contrary, and can arrange for a new comedian to open at Plymouth and a new Paul at Gloucester. Mr. Tenant is now in bed with laryngitis, and will be there for at least two days, according to the doctor. This was the cause of *The Mountains of My Home* having to be cut last night and incidentally of Mr. Woolgast's quite unjust accusation as to his 'loafing':

REPORT

Mr. Tenant took exception to the remark and high words ensued, during which Mr. Tenant claims that Mr. Woolgast called him 'a bastard'. Mr. Tenant aimed a blow at Mr. Woolgast, and the latter picked up a chair, and hit Mr.Tenant with it. There ensued a nasty brawl, which was heard and witnessed by stage hands, chorus men and other members of the company. Mr. Allen informed me of the trouble and I went down immediately. When I arrived, Mr. Tenant and Mr. Woolgast had been separated by the Chorus Men and Stage Staff, and were still abusing one another. Mr. Woolgast was using very foul language, though several ladies were present. I immediately cleared the room and packed Mr. Tenant and Mr. Woolgast off home, as obviously no good could be got out of further arguments while they were both in fighting mood. Before going, Mr. Woolgast tendered his resignation to me, and told me he was fed up with the show, and would be 'glad to be out of it'.

END OF REPORT

I have no brief for Mr. Tenant, however, who was never really strong in the part but certainly tried his best at all times.

Yours truly,

Dix

J.B. PRIESTLEY (1894–1984)
ANNIE HORNIMAN (1860–1937)

J.B. Priestley (AN INSPECTOR CALLS, TIME & THE CONWAYS, THE GOOD COMPANIONS, DANGEROUS CORNER, WHEN WE ARE MARRIED) keeps his diary free…

3 The Grove, Highgate Village
Telephone Mountview 6603
22nd April 1933

Madam,

I am much honoured by Your Royal Highness's suggestion that I should write a booklet for the Royal Sussex County Hospital. I must beg to decline the invitation, however, partly because I am in the middle of a novel that has to be published this autumn, and partly because I think it would be better – for the Hospital's sake – if you got a writer who was associated in the public mind with Sussex. (I am a Yorkshire man.)

So I venture to suggest one of the following as acceptable in that sense: Hilaire Belloc; Sheila Kaye-Smith; *Beachcomber* (J.B. Morton) or S.P.B. Mais.

I have the honour to be, Madam,
Your Royal Highness's obedient Servant.
J.B. Priestley

Annie Horniman, who established a pioneering repertory theatre at the Gaiety in Manchester, often casting the young Sybil Thorndike (q.v.), writes very precisely to the Secretary of the Shakespeare Reading Society:

1H Montagu Mansions, London W1
November 28th, 1927

Dear Mrs. Leon,

Of course I will talk to you all for 7 minutes on Dec. 10th. That is the correct length in which to propose a toast – may the other speakers follow my example! As I know nothing of your aims, I'll speak at random and so may tread on people's toes, and hereby make it cheerful for the other speakers.

Yours sincerely,
A.E.F. Horniman

JOHN GIELGUD (born 1904)

Shortly before her death, Ellen Terry's sister Marion (1852/6–1930) writes to their brother Fred, about their great-nephew John Gielgud as Hamlet:

MARION TERRY TO FRED TERRY

Bayswater
[1930]

I have been to three of John Gielgud's performances of Shakespeare's plays at the Old Vic, and I can't say how really thrilled I have been with the work he does: Macbeth – Oberon – Hamlet – the last without cuts!!

I was in the *uncomfortable* stalls for *Hamlet,* for just *five* hours, and didn't *want* to move (tho' I'd have liked to do so but couldn't, the place was crammed), I wanted to go tomorrow, the last of his performances, but there is no seat to be had, and I hear today it's going to the West End in a fortnight, so I'll see it then – it's *very young*, very thoughtful (without dragging it with long pauses and mouthing), graceful without effort and every word distinct; and of course he looks charming – I told him I was proud of my nephew; he replied he 'was proud of knowing he had some of the Terry blood in him, and hoped to go on doing better'.

Marion

JOHN GIELGUD TO WRITER W. GRAHAM ROBERTSON

7, Upper St Martin's Lane
Temple Bar 5175
December 6th, 1934

Dear Graham Robertson,

Thank you for your very nice letter – I am so delighted that you enjoyed the performance – People do seem to find it stimulating and controversial, and that is very important.

I am apt to be swayed in my views about certain details, both by outside criticism and my own judgement, and I suppose one cannot hope ever to play the part entirely to one's own satisfaction, or anyone else's either, which gives one impossible ideals to strive for, and is very exciting.

I did so very much enjoy lunching with you the other day and seeing your lovely pictures – and shall greatly hope to renew my acquaintanceship at a not too distant period – Siegfried Sassoon, the poet, whom I met the other evening, was so enthusiastic about you both as a writer and a conversationalist, and I felt very proud to say that I had the pleasure of knowing you too.

> Thank you again for troubling to write.
> Very sincerely yours,
> John Gielgud

In 1945 Gielgud played HAMLET again, at the Haymarket Theatre.

JOHN GIELGUD TO KERRISON PRESTON

> John Gielgud
> Park Lane
> February 28th, 1945

Dear Preston,

It was a quiet pleasure to receive your letter, and to know that Hamlet gave you so stimulating an evening – It is a great *adventure* every time one plays it, and one is never sure of the success of its effect – so much depends on one's own *personal* mood – the *reactions* of the audience and the other actors too seem to matter more than in other plays – But I hope you saw us on a good night – certainly you contributed greatly by your own enthusiasm and sensitivity – I hope you will come round again and see me if you are at The Drama.

Kindest regards to you and your wife –

> Most sincerely ever
> John Gielgud

C.B. COCHRAN (1872–1951) and NOEL COWARD (1899–1973)

*In 1931, Noël Coward (q.v.) was planning an extravaganza with a cast of 300:
CAVALCADE. He asked C.B. Cochran (q.v.) to secure the Coliseum, with its
huge stage....*

TELEGRAM
Handed in New York   Received London
C.B. COCHRAN to NOEL COWARD

NO CHANCE OF THE COLISEUM STOP DRURY LANE ONLY
STAGE LARGE ENOUGH AND HOLDING ENOUGH MONEY WILL NEGOTIATE IF
YOU THINK STAGE POSSIBLE

TELEGRAM
Handed in London   Received New York
NOEL COWARD to C.B. COCHRAN

PART ONE SMALL INTERIOR TWO DEPARTURE OF TROOP SHIP THREE SMALL
INTERIOR FOUR MAFEKING NIGHT IN LONDON MUSIC HALL NECESSITATING
PIVOT STAGE FIVE EXTERIOR FRONT SCENE BIRDCAGE WALK SIX EDWARDIAN
RECEPTION SEVEN MILE END ROAD FULL STAGE BUT CAN BE OPENED UP
GRADUALLY AND DONE MOSTLY WITH LIGHTING PART TWO ONE WHITE CITY FULL
SET TWO SMALL INTERIOR THREE EDWARDIAN SEASIDE RESORT FULL SET BATHING
MACHINES PIERROTS ETC FOUR TITANIC SMALL FRONT SCENE FIVE OUTBREAK OF
WAR SMALL INTERIOR SIX VICTORIA STATION IN FOG FULL SET AND LIGHTING
EFFECTS SEVEN AIR RAID OVER LONDON PRINCIPALLY LIGHTING AND SOUND
EIGHT INTERIOR OPENING ONTO TRAFALGAR SQUARE ARMISTICE NIGHT FULL
STAGE AND CAST PART THREE ONE GENERAL STRIKE FULL SET TWO SMALL
INTERIOR THREE FASHIONABLE NIGHT CLUB FULL SET FOUR SMALL INTERIOR FIVE
IMPRESSIONISTIC SUMMARY OF MODERN CIVILISATION MOSTLY LIGHTS AND
EFFECTS SIX COMPLETE BARE STAGE WITH PANORAMA AND UNION JACK AND
FULL CAST STOP NECESSITATES ONE BEST MODERN LIGHTING EQUIPMENT
OBTAINABLE TWO COMPANY OF GUARDS THREE ORCHESTRA FIFTY FOUR
FACILITIES FOR COMPLETE BLACKOUTS FIVE FULL WEEK OF DRESS REHEARSALS SIX
THEATRE FREE FOR ALL REHEARSALS SEVEN ABOUT A DOZEN RELIABLE ACTORS
THE REST WALKONS A FEW STRONG SINGERS EIGHT FOG EFFECT INDIVIDUALS
NECESSARY ONE FRANK COLLINS STAGE SUPERVISION TWO DAN O'NEIL STAGE
MANAGEMENT THREE ELSIE APRIL MUSIC SUPERVISION OF COSTUMES AND
SCENERY AND YOUR OWN GENERAL SUPERVISION STOP THIS SYNOPSISIS MORE
OR LESS ACCURATE BUT LIABLE TO REVISION STOP PLEASE TAKE CARE THAT NO
DETAIL OF THIS SHOULD REACH PRIVATE OR PARTICULARLY PRESS EARS
REGARDS NOEL

GEORGE S. KAUFMAN (1889–1961)

John Steinbeck (q.v.) called George S. Kaufman (see also Alexander Woollcott) 'the greatest director of our time'. Kaufman was a famous wit, playwright (collaborations with Moss Hart include ONCE IN A LIFETIME, THE MAN WHO CAME TO DINNER, YOU CAN'T TAKE IT WITH YOU), director, journalist, card player, actor... Kaufman wrote forty five plays and won two Pulitzer Prizes. He writes to his friends Augustus and Ruth Goetz:

> George S. Kaufman
> 410 Park Avenue
> New York City
> Tuesday

Dear Goetzes,

I had a chance to dispose of the movie rights to *Franklin Street* the other night, so I thought I'd better do it. This was in a dream induced by two sleeping pills, which is the reason I went right ahead without communicating with you.

This was in a large store which seemed to handle a good many things besides movie rights – shirts, nails, custard. Everything. I had a good deal of trouble getting waited on. 'Miss, would you mind... Miss, I've been waiting longer than... I think it's my turn now, Miss.'

But once I got attention everything went very nicely. I sold it an act at a time, which is a new idea that I rather like. The first act went for $30,000, and the second act for $60,000, which I thought was doing pretty well. The girl who was waiting on me knew all about these two acts, but the third act was all new to her. However, she took my word for it. I said there were two very nice situations in it, and that it should bring $35,000. I remember her saying, 'Well, as long as we've got the other two...'

Don't bother to thank me for this – anyone in my place would have done the same. I imagine they're delivering the money, like Saks.

And incidentally, how's tricks?

> George

JOHN STEINBECK (1902–1968)

Author John Steinbeck (THE GRAPES OF WRATH, EAST OF EDEN, OF MICE AND MEN, TRAVELS WITH CHARLIE) sends an appreciation to George Kaufman, who has just directed the stage production of OF MICE AND MEN:

Los Gatos

Nov. 1937

Dear George,

As the reviews come in it becomes more and more apparent that you have done a great job. I knew you would of course but there is a curious gap between the thing in your head and the thing set down and you've jumped the gap. It's a strange kind of humbling luck we have. Carol and I have talked of it a number of times. That we – obscure people out of a place no one ever heard of, should have our first play directed and produced by the greatest director of all time – will not bear too close inspection for fear we may catch the gods of fortune at work and catching them, anger them so they hate us. Already I have made propitiation – thrown my dear ring into the sea and I hope no big fish brings it back to me.

To say thank you is ridiculous for you can't thank a man for good work any more than you can thank him for being himself. But one can be very glad he is himself and that is what we are – very glad that you are George Kaufman.

It doesn't matter a damn whether this show runs a long time. It came to life for one night anyway, and really to life, and that's more than anyone has a right to hope.

Sometimes – in working – the people in my head become much more real than I am. I have had letters. It seems that for two hours you made your play far more real than its audience so that Mr. Black's loss in the market, and Mrs. Klick's hatred of the Vanderbilts, disappeared from them and only the play existed. I wish I could transpose, into some mathematical equation, my feeling – so that it might be a communication unmistakable and unchanging.

And that's all.

John

Kaufman treasured this letter. Steinbeck, however, never came to see the stage production of OF MICE AND MEN, despite its success. Kaufman, furious, decided not to speak to Steinbeck again. It is reported that Steinbeck finally bearded Kaufman: 'George, you haven't spoken to me in twelve years.' Kaufman replied,'Then it's about time. How about dinner next Tuesday?'

Kaufman to his main collaborator, playwright Moss Hart (1904–1961):

> George S. Kaufman
> 17, Blomfield Road
> London, W.9
> Cunningham 4411

June 28

Dear Mossie (and especially Kitty. Aside to Kitty: Save your money from that television show – we're all going to need it someday),

Well, you have been through something, and I can only say that it takes a strong man. We all (certainly I) have a way of clinging to shows with a sort of lightning-may-strike point of view, even when we feel dubious or disinclined, but eventually the axe must fall. Me, I've done it again and again. In fact, I may be doing it now – I have an uneasy feeling that the show I'm on with Alan is rather dated – those twin targets at which I have aimed so many times – business and politics, whereas they want pyjamas and baseball. I know that doesn't make sense, but you can't have everything. Hell, you can't have *anything*. But you will go down in history – maybe ahead of it…

I mean it when I say I think our show may be old-fashioned – it is hard to change one's style. On the theory that credit should be given where credit is deserved, I have prepared a credit list for the program, as follows:

By George S. Kaufman, plus glucose, lecithin, Bemax, Serpisal, Anesolysene, nutrilite, lipotaine, Equanil, Empirin, Veganin, Codeine, dramamine, Doctors E.B Greenspan, L.S. Kubie, John Janvrin, C.L.

Johnson, Vitamins B1-2-3-4-5-6-7-8-9-10-11 and 12, Laboratory staff of Mt. Sinai Hospital, phenobarbital, seconal, nembutal, tuinal, and **FUCKITALL**

– AND –

Alan Campbell

...It's now nine o'clock, and we'll go down and pick up a cold supper – it's the staff's night out, and anyhow there is a small crisis there – they must go back to Italy and the sun for four weeks because the cook is ill. This is after all winter as a vacation. Oo-la-la, or whatever the Italian for oo-la-la is. This is rather a pedestrian effort after your throbbing letter, Mossie. If I am not being impertinent I hope you are going to write a straight play now – I like to think of you being at work and I like to think of eventually seeing the play.

George

Kaufman was a ladies' man, and had many relationships. Early in his love affair with actress Leueen MacGrath he cabled her:

WHERE AREYOU?	WHERE ARE YOU?	WHERE ARE YOU?
WHERE ARE YOU?	WHERE ARE YOU?	WHERE ARE YOU?
WHERE ARE YOU?	WHERE ARE YOU?	WHERE ARE YOU?
WHERE ARE YOU?	WHERE ARE YOU?	WHERE ARE YOU?
WHERE ARE YOU?	WHERE ARE YOU?	WHERE ARE YOU?
WHERE ARE YOU?	WHERE ARE YOU?	WHERE ARE YOU?
WHERE ARE YOU?	WHERE ARE YOU?	WHERE ARE YOU?
WHERE ARE YOU?	WHERE ARE YOU?	WHERE ARE YOU?
WHERE ARE YOU?	WHERE ARE YOU?	WHERE ARE YOU?
WHERE ARE YOU?	WHERE ARE YOU?	WHERE ARE YOU?
WHERE ARE YOU?	WHERE ARE YOU?	WHERE ARE YOU?

GEORGE

Leueen McGrath was with him years later at his death, holding his hand.

ALEXANDER WOOLLCOTT (1887–1943)

Alexander Woollcott was a playwright, critic, broadcaster and journalist who worked relentlessly and still enjoyed a dizzying social life. He was friends with Dorothy Parker, Moss Hart, Charlie Chaplin, Walt Disney, Harpo Marx, Noël Coward (q.v.) and literary/theatrical Society on both coasts of America. He collaborated with George Kaufman (q.v.), most famously on THE MAN WHO CAME TO DINNER, in which he was persuaded to play the leading rôle – a caricature of himself. He was an inveterate gambler...

Alexander Woollcott
Hotel Carlton
London
April 26th

My blossom,

Noël is the only gamester I ever knew with my own whole-heartedness. We played backgammon or Russian Bank all the way over. I had never before crossed the Atlantic without once laying eyes on the darned thing.

The other passengers were mysteriously angered by this singleness of purpose. They would stop by and say: 'Don't you two ever tire of that game' or 'Still at it?' or, in the case of the German passengers, they would merely say 'Immer!' to each other in passing. We finally devised an effective rejoinder, merely singing in duet:

> We hope you fry in hell
> We hope you fry in hell
> Heigho
> The merry-o
> We hope you fry in hell.

I did not have much luck. Paid for my passage but not much over. *Cavalcade* last night. Noël's party in the royal box. A convenient arrangement with a salon behind it for coffee and liqueurs and an adjacent room for the occasional relief of the royal kidney.

A.W.

ALEXANDER WOOLLCOTT TO HARPO MARX

New York City
March 24, 1937

Dear Harpo,

This is the reminder I promised about Helen Keller. She and Polly Thompson will sail April 1st. from San Francisco on the *Asamu Maru*...

Have you read *Of Mice and Men*? Just your dish. Just your length.... One of the characters is an amiable and gigantic idiot, so tender that he has to fondle everything he likes and so clumsy that eventually he breaks their necks – mice, puppies, rabbits, tarts – whatever he happens to be petting at the moment. I tried to get Broun to take this part and he was very hurt.

I've forgotten what you look like. I guess that's a good break for you, at that.

The Prince Chap

[Postscript] Come to think of it, Helen would prefer a bottle of bourbon or scotch to a bouquet any day.

A.W.

ALEXANDER WOOLLCOTT TO WALT DISNEY

Bomoseen, Vermont
January 12, 1942

My dear Disney,

This is a letter of thanks from the bottom of my heart. Having been over to England, done a dozen broadcasts there, come back and delivered half a dozen lectures here, I blew myself to a spot of rest. In fact, during the Christmas holidays, I did nothing but sleep, dine with Frank Sullivan, listen to Churchill, and go to see *Dumbo*. That's what I call a good life.

After seeing *Dumbo* for the third time, I suspect that if we could get far enough away to see it in its place, we would recognise it as the highest achievement yet achieved in the Seven Arts since the first white man landed on this continent. This cautious tribute is paid by one who was several degrees short of nuts about *Snow White* and a little bored by *Pinocchio*. I was as afflicted by what went agley in *Fantasia* as anyone in this country, with the possible exception of yourself. But *Dumbo* is that once far-off divine event toward which your whole creation has moved.

After some thought, I have decided that you are the most valuable person alive, so for God's sake take care of yourself.

Yours to command,
Alexander Woollcott

ALEXANDER WOOLLCOTT TO MARIAN STOLL

The White House
January 21, 1942

Dear Marian,

Under separate cover (which has always been our life in a nutshell) I have sent you two packs of playing cards because:

(a) you said you wanted some

(b) these, which were given me for Xmas, are not the kind I like, and

(c) they can be washed with soap and water.

Personally I prefer washing my hands instead of the cards. I never soil cards because my hands are always pure, like my thoughts.

Your old playmate,
Alexander Woollcott

Alexander Woollcott died after a fatal heart attack during a live radio broadcast.

ATHENE SEYLER (1889–1990)

In a correspondence contrived with Stephen Haggard, who has written asking if she will explain 'The Craft of Comedy' for a friend of his with theatrical ambitions, 'William Eager', Athene Seyler sets out her credo in a collection of letters which the two published, more or less as a text book for actors, in 1943:

17th June, 1939

Dear Athene,

Your extremely interesting and prompt reply leads me to hope that this correspondence may develop into a spirited epistolary bombardment; I only hope I shall be able, with scarcely more than a couple of unremarkable stage cannon for my defence, to hold my own against your accurate and quick-firing comedic guns. Perhaps I'd better take each shot as it comes...

I suppose the truth is that there are many different kinds of comedy acting, ranging from the unconscious humour of an Epihodov to the 'conscious' humour of a George Robey, and that the art of acting comedy consists in choosing just the right balance between the conscious and the unconscious which each character demands...

Would it be presumptuous of me, Athene, to suggest that the choice of emphasis should rest rather with the author than the actor? And is one not being slightly unfaithful to an author if one singles out certain characteristics for special comment at the expense of others?

I realise, of course, that this (perhaps rather irritating) suggestion is all very well in an academic argument about comedy, but that it completely disregards the personal – or perhaps I should say the personality – element in acting. That is something upon which you do not touch in your letter. I look forward to hearing what you have to say about it. I suspect that, in the last resort, comedy acting, much more than straight acting, is bound up with the actor's personality, and that it is the actor's personality which unconsciously chooses the bias he will put upon a part. This might explain too why you, who are so kind a person, insist that comedy should be inspired by only good-natured laughter, when for me, who am of a less generous nature, irony and especially satire may contain much that is bitter and yet not be tragic.

209

All this is by the way, however; what really matters is whether William can make head or tail of it or not. I shall send your letter on to him and see what he says.

Yours ever,
Stephen

30th June,
1939

Dear Stephen,

Your letter makes me think twice if not three times! I must make myself a little clearer about 'standing outside a character' in comedy acting.

Of course one must be lost in the personality one is playing, and when you say that the comic characters of Tchekov need complete reality you have only stated the fundamental law of all acting, comic or serious. Surely all artistic creation must be founded on truth; but one can regard truth from different angles, I should have said.

Should we not first agree on the basic principles of humour? Having done that we can then examine a part in the light of them; we can stand outside the character when studying it and measure the truth by the comedic principles. This sounds very solemn and is of course a clumsy attempt to analyse what every natural comedian does instinctively – but it may be valuable to try to lay down some rules.

What, then, is at the root of comedy? The essentials are: lack of balance, distortion, over-emphasis or under-emphasis, and surprise. Now, all these things are only relative to something else: the truth. So that you must first see the truth of a character before you can upset its balance. But you must *believe* in the distorted view of the truth that you have discovered. Having drawn the character a little out of proportion you must passionately believe in that measurement as the correct one. I think that your true comedian does both of these things at once; that is to say, he is aware instinctively that the emphasis he is laying on one side of his portrait distorts it, and yet he offers it as a true likeness. The 'standing outside' – the approach to the character – is the first process. The second process is concerned with presenting this view, and depends on what we call *technique*. It is the craft of appearing to believe in the balance of a thing that one knows is out of balance. This sounds like a theory of tight-rope walking! And indeed I think it is mental tight-rope walking, in which the slightest slip ends in disaster…

I remember a very great comedian, James Welch, playing in a play called *The New Clown*. He was *[playing]* a little man who joined a circus because he was starving and, if I remember correctly, was not a real circus performer, but tried to do the job without any training or knowledge. As the time of the performance drew near, he was seized by panic, and the manager, fearing he would run away, locked him up in a small room.

The audience saw the 'clown' trying to escape from this room so as not to have to perform; and his growing fear and inability to tackle the situation, his final hysteria and suggestion that he would throw himself out of the window, kept the audience in a continuous roar of laughter.

I saw the play many times – but, far from laughing, I always wanted to cry in that scene. James Welch used the comic effect of over-statement, for the situation was not as frightening or hopeless as he thought it. But he must have lost this outside knowledge for a few moments, and allowed himself to believe in the character's own fears for me to have felt terror and pity instead of laughter. Now the actor should hold these two aspects of a part in his mind at once: he and the audience both share a secret from the character itself. If the actor is really frightened, the audience will be frightened too; but if he knows sub-consciously that this fear is out of proportion to the danger, the audience will enjoy it…

This letter is getting too bulky for the post, so I will leave you here to send me your reactions.

Athene

RUTH GORDON (1896–1985)

One of the most admired stage and film actresses of her time, Ruth Gordon never lost her drive, or her humility. Four letters written by the 46 year old American actress in 1942:

Dear Mr. Shumlin,

Is there a part for me in any play you are doing?

Yours truly,

Ruth Gordon

60 West 12th Street

Gramercy 7–2748

Dear Max,

If you read a play with a part for me, let me know.

Love,

Ruth

Dear Mr. Wyler,

I read that you're going to direct *The Little Foxes*. Would you consider me for Birdie? My address is 60 West 12th. Street, New York. The phone is Gramercy 7–2748.

Best wishes,

Ruth Gordon

60 West 12th Street,

New York

Dear Lawrence,

Is the Guild doing any play I could be in? I hear Sam Behrman's play is great. Is there a part for me?

Ruth

MICHEL SAINT-DENIS (1897–1971)

Many a career was cut short or interrupted by the Second World War. The French actor, dramatist and producer Michel Saint-Denis was called up in 1939...

London Theatre Studio
Providence Place
Upper Street
Islington N.1

Directors
IAN E. BLACK Chairman
BRONSON ALBERY * JOHN GIELGUD
TYRONE GUTHRIE * LAURENCE OLIVIER

Managing Director
MICHEL ST-DENIS (French)

Manager
GEORGE DEVINE

2nd September 1939

To the Chairman of the Board of Directors of London Theatre Studio:

I had to repay the sum of £72.14.3. to the Studio; this sum was going to be repaid on the 21st. August when the rehearsals for *The Cherry Orchard* started and when by contract I was going to have £150.0.0. I have to leave at short notice because of general mobilisation in France, and the abnormal circumstances have naturally stopped the management of the Globe Theatre paying me the £150.0.0. I am, therefore, unable to repay the Studio, at present, and I will be during the length of the war, because I have only my salary as a French officer to live on.

M. St.-Denis

213

SYBIL THORNDIKE (1882–1976)

As a student in London, I did a morning job delivering household groceries for a Chelsea shop. Dame Sybil of Swan Court, SW3, always tipped me a florin.

Dame Sybil Thorndike (DBE in 1931) graciously answers criticisms by a Miss Janet Long of her war-time (1943–4) touring production of MACBETH.

Porth Cawl
Oct. 21st

Dear Miss Long,

Forgive me for not having answered your letter before – we live a very hectic life, and there is hardly any leisure, but it's very exciting and interesting, even if letters have to be shelved!

Forgive me too if I don't answer all your criticisms satisfactorily. I'm so very sorry you didn't like our performance at all. The standard of stage production is bound to be different *[from]* that of the Old Vic where they have a big stage and room to dress in etc., but we do adapt ourselves to war conditions – we had the production designed for tiny stages of all shapes – designed or rather adapted from Elizabethan cum Japanese cum Greek cum modern methods!: We were specially asked *not* to do it in just curtains which my husband *[Sir Lewis Casson]* and I had wanted to do, knowing the great difficulties of transport and stages.

I'm sorry you don't like the Prologue – it was commended to us by a very great Shakespearean scholar who said he felt something of the sort was implicit in the texts of *Macbeth* – by the way a 'straightforward' *Macbeth* as you suggest is rather a difficult thing to find! I have played it in about 10 different versions all claiming to be the authentic version – it's the most corrupt text of all the tragedies and this particular scholar – a very well known and deeply respected man of letters – thought we might ease things with a Chorus. (We've had many letters thanking us for the Chorus.) Lionel Hale, whose original play work is very able, has, as we have, the deepest veneration for the scenes of *Macbeth* – some of which are the *most* superb writing in our language – other scenes which are now attributed to Middleton and various other writers after Shakespeare we felt at liberty to cut and to interpolate, tho' L.H. has written only a *little* – the 4 biggest Choruses are straight out of *Macbeth* and given to them (the Chorus) in place of 'Old Man' and Lennox etc., etc....

This good scholars have felt legitimate and I do not apologise. Anyone who has played in *Macbeth* knows only too well its vast difficulty.

Audibility: no, we've no business *not* to be heard, that's terrible – and the 1st. Witch's adenoids were on purpose!! I think the 1st. Witch *did* have adenoids – nasty old woman, she was!! But she must be heard. It was *I* that played her. As we can only travel a certain number of actors we have to 'adapt ourselves' – and I love playing that hateful old crone – she's just like an old governess I knew with adenoids who I always felt *was* the 1st. Witch and I never heard a word *she* said either! Still that's my excuse. The Tredegar Hall was the most difficult place I've ever had to speak in – we were warned before and thought we'd been careful, but the chattering of 4 or 5 people near the front made things *very* hard and called forth that remark from my husband. Several people thanked us for it as they had been much disturbed. Also the Ice Cream selling during the 'Murder scene' – we mentioned that on purpose as someone had complained about it from the front – and it certainly was horrible in the midst of that lovely blackness of the audience to see brightly lighted Ice Cream signs! Anyway that was settled and a very just complaint from a very interested audience otherwise was put right as it never happened again.

I know the Welsh audiences very well – my home is Wales. My husband is Welsh – and we love the people dearly and would never dream of not giving of our very best to the most intelligent public we have ever played before. People have been so generous to us and I'm glad to say have enjoyed the play, as we have enjoyed playing to them!

You'll never read this letter, it's much too long, and as incoherent and badly written as the 1st. Witch! Please forgive. I am so *very* sorry you and your friends were disappointed. We were so happy in Tredegar and enjoyed the audience so much, with the exception of our 'chatty friends' who I don't believe had ever known a real play or know how to behave; it's so hard playing when there is a continuous stream of conversation going on to which *we* as players are more sensitive than the audience, who *only* realise if they don't hear that something is amiss.

It did hurt a lot when you said 'insult' – no one loves Wales or the Welsh more than we do – from our families and years of Welsh living – to the lovely intelligence and sensitiveness of them.

Forgive this rigmarole!

Yours very sincerely,

Sybil Casson

[Postscript] I wonder if you know the stage at Tredegar – the amateurs implored us to complain as the putting on of a play is *so* hard there and the dressing rooms – well they aren't!! But this is going to be altered I believe.

RUTH DRAPER (1884–1956)

'I have always felt that Ruth Draper was (with Martha Graham) the greatest individual performer that America has ever given us, and I count myself infinitely fortunate to have known her a little as a woman as well as having been given so much joy by the extraordinary and unique subtleties of her art.'

John Gielgud (q.v.)
London, 23 April, 1978

'I want to declare Miss Draper open to the new generation of playgoers, and to trample on their suspicions, which I once shared, that she might turn out to be a museum-piece, ripe for the dust-sheet and oblivion. She is, on the contrary, about as old-fashioned and mummified as Spring... she works her miracles benignly and unfussed...'

Kenneth Tynan (q.v.),
London Evening Standard, 23 May, 1952

The American 'monologuist and mono-dramatist' Ruth Draper, on tour in rationed Britain just after the war, writes to her friend Grace Martin:

June 23, 1946

The food situation is bad, but in the country, easier, and I have been spoiled – a friend in Sussex sends me a little butter each week which I have for my tea, and everywhere people have given me eggs, one for every day at tea time, for the theatre hour is 6.30 (too early to dine, so I have a good tea at 5 and something at 9.30-10 before I go to bed). At the hotel I've had *nothing* but cabbage and potatoes *every* day at lunch – my main meal – and generally fish, meat perhaps twice a week (and a small portion), chicken *never*, except at private houses, and I think I've had it six times in four months. I got *desperate* for vegetables in Manchester last week (they're lovely in market now, but very expensive). I bought a bunch of asparagus for 7/- one day and cooked the tips in my room, (gave the rest to my grateful 'dresser') and had a feast, with lovely butter. Another night I had peas at 6/- a pound and another, carrots at 2/- a bunch – tiny ones. But oh, so good! My kitchen is a joy! I have a darling tiny Sheffield tea pot I bought for £1/-/- in an antique shop in Bristol and I make my own tea (some China I brought over), save a little milk from breakfast, and with my own bread and butter and egg and jam, I have a perfect meal. I hide my stores and have not been discovered yet.

In less difficult times (though rationing continued until 1954), two letters to her sister Dorothea Draper (Mrs Henry James):

May 9, 1953
Cambridge

Too beautiful for words here; and, oh, the boys – in their sloppy gowns – so young and beautiful – with books, hurrying along on bicycles or on foot – in punts – lying under trees; the magic precious heritage of scholars creates such an atmosphere of hope and faith in values we cling to. Lists of names of the fallen, crosses and monuments remind us how futile our efforts are, but youth and books and beauty go on forever in spite of losses. I'm off to the Fitzwilliam to see, as on each visit, Keats' manuscript of *Ode to a Nightingale*. It makes me cry and fills me with such awe – like what a devout person feels in a church...

Ruth

May 17, 1953
London

Thanks for your good letters – I've had excellent care – a wonderful man in Bath whose father was Queen Mary's dentist, and who also cared for the royal jaws. Of course I'm sorry now that I didn't plan to stay *[for the Coronation]*! Excitement grows and it's all thrilling. The young Queen is a wonder, and I don't see how she can sustain the burden of her job and the love showered on her.

My heart is heavy over lovely Kathleen *[Kathleen Ferrier, the singer, 1912–1953, dying of cancer]*. Her beauty and goodness and marvellous voice all to be sacrificed to this evil thing. She's so brave and keeps cheerful – and one only hopes for a miracle. They continue to try and hide the truth but all who love her know...

Ruth

GEORGE BERNARD SHAW (1856–1950)

When he was a young actor, the playwright Arnold Wesker (born 1932) wrote to George Bernard Shaw asking for advice on playing Marchbanks in CANDIDA. The reply was on a postcard...

10th June, 1949

It is a curious part, clever experienced actors fail in it. Novices succeed in it.

Take care to make your lines heard. Leave the rest to luck.

Advienne que pourra.

G.B.S.

Shaw was a busy man and a prolific and generous correspondent. But he knew how to be terse:

William Turner Levy
Department of English,
The City College of New York
Convent Avenue and 139th Street
New York 31, N.Y.

15.iii.48

Mr. George Bernard Shaw
Ayot St.Lawrence

Dear Mr. Shaw:

I am writing a critical biography of the Ballyshannon poet, William Allingham, who died in 1889; there are few people alive today who recall him as either man or poet. If you have an [sic] recollection of meeting him, or of being impressed by his work, I would be most grateful for your comments...

[At this point, Bernard Shaw has underlined 'William Allingham', and, for return of post, endorsed the letter in the margin:]

Never heard of him.
G.B.S.
18/3/1948

...A word of thanks for your consideration – and for the great pleasure your plays are providing us with this season on Broadway!

Yours most respectfully,
William Turner Levy

ELEANOR FARJEON (1881–1965)

Poet and author Eleanor Farjeon with some home truths for an ambitious young Czech refugee Otto Lampel (his wife was held in a concentration camp at this time) who performed songs in French and Czechoslovakian at the piano. The tone of the letter is harsh, but Miss Farjeon is known to have been very charmed by him:

20 Perrins Walk, N.W.3
Feb. 14th 1942

I want you to read every word of this letter, long as it is.

Dearest Otto,

The concert is over for which many of us worked so hard to the exclusion of almost everything else – time, health and our own work and private affairs. Real affection for you, as well as a belief in your gifts, made all the others go on indefatigably after I had to drop out. The great hope on which we were all set was that real professional work and recognition would result from it. When you told me last night that the Phoenix [*Theatre*] was offering you £30 a week, my heart jumped for joy. When you went on to say that you were demanding double, it sank terribly. Once again I felt that you were inflating your value beyond its real worth. And Otto, my dear, I do not mean only beyond its worth as an unknown artist here; I mean – and I hope you can take this – your *actual* worth as a performer in the eyes of us who know something about it. You are often very, very good indeed; you have sudden moments of being almost inspired (when your Daimon gets you unawares); but you are too often below your best; you can be mediocre, and no £60 artist, who has not made his name here, can dare to be that, or he will soon drop out. After an artist has become a national favourite, he can go on being downright bad for a while (vide Evelyn Laye), but that is a point I hope you will never reach.

Please be clear about this; the concert was not a very great success. You never once 'blew them to pieces'. You were not nearly your best. You had many admirers… But I have not heard one professional opinion which was hopeful, and I made a point of asking everybody who could tell me the real truth of their reactions and those of the audience; and I have built up a pretty clear idea of what really comes across the footlights…

It was your personality that persuaded Holt [*Harold Holt, theatrical manager*] but he won't be doing anything more for you, dear; you didn't impress him enough. And from the point of view of Bertie and Bronnie Albery, both of whom were seeing what you could put over in a theatre, you did not succeed…

Look at it like this; if what you want is to play in a London Theatre before full houses, the Phoenix gives you that, whether you get £30 or £60. If the job itself is good enough, believe me, £30 is not to be sniffed at.

Meanwhile, you can polish your performance, and become so sure of yourself with your material that you will grow easy and gay, as well as grim. You were neither easy nor gay at Wyndham's, and one of your best assets was dimmed. When you spoke to me about your performance on your return home on Monday night, you seemed to me to speak with sense and judgement, and on Tuesday when you came here you talked as though you had given your best show, and swept the audience away. Dear, dear Otto, when you do this so excessively, it seems to me you are like a small boy who has no self-confidence, and is boasting very loud to delude himself…

How much of this can you take? I write it because I am your loving

Eleanor

Eleanor Farjeon's nephew, Gervase, never got as far as needing home truths from his aunt about his performing – he became a theatrical manager. But at the age of seven he slipped a letter under his parents' pillow:

Mummy Daddy

Do let me be
an <u>actor</u> I would
like to be one
so much
but you must
tell me first
you know best
I fell shy

to say this.
Even to you.
Please do
not laugh
at me or
tell any one.
With love
from your
son who
Loves you

GF

DONALD WOLFIT (1902–1968)

The actor-manager Donald Wolfit (knighted 1957) presented 112 performances of 'lunch-time Shakespeare' during the Battle of Britain, and 100 full-length performances of Shakespeare's plays at the Scala Theatre in 1944. He writes to Oliver Savage on the subject of his Shakespearean mentor, theatre director and scholar William Poel (1852–1934):

Donald Wolfit
Scala Theatre
Charlotte Street W 1
17. 4. 44

Dear Mr. Savage,

I am indeed grateful to you for sending me those collected letters of *that great* William Poel. The reading of them is giving me the greatest pleasure and revives many treasured memories of the work I did for him twelve or fourteen years ago.

Often and often my mind has gone back since I have been in management to the long discussions we had at Putney on the Elizabethan theatre, and I used to go down to him and encroach on his time and leisure whenever I had a new part to study. Whether it was Shakespeare or not it made little difference. His interest was always the same, with a keen eye to detect the spurious and always with a great touch for the essential word or stress of a line.

I worked with him in only two productions and these at the end of his distinguished career, but he lit a torch for the simplification of the plays in production, and a direct attack, which is still burning.

Thank you once again for thinking of me, and the book will go into my most used shelf to be taken down whenever I need the inspiration which his work always gave to those who knew and loved him.

Yours sincerely,
Donald Wolfit

ANDRE HUGUENET (1906–1961)
SIEGFRIED MYNHARDT (born 1909)

The two doyens of South African theatre before, and for many years after, the Second World War, were Siegfried Mynhardt and André Huguenet. Both men played in major productions in Britain and were recipients of the Queen's Coronation Medal. Mynhardt played in HAMLET, directed by Tyrone Guthrie (1900–1971, knighted in 1961), with Alec Guinness (born 1914, knighted 1959) as the Prince, and Huguenet played Hassan in HASSAN at the Festival of Britain in 1951.

The two men were good friends. When Huguenet died, Mynhardt, travelling on the Orange Express one night from Durban to Bloemfontein, wrote this farewell letter to his dead friend:

Orange Express
Sunday, July 1961

Dear André,

Recently I bumped into Will Jameson in Capetown and he told me just how much he loved directing you in *Lear*, what a magnificent performance you gave and that you hope to be doing it in Johannesburg. I do hope you will and that I shall be able to see it. In my opinion Lear is the most demanding of all the classical parts. Despite his age he somehow has to have the passion and vitality of a young man – an almost impossible combination. You are the only Afrikaans actor with the physical capacity to do so...

My most vivid impressions of, and associations with, the theatre, are those concerning you. It is now late at night, the train chugging onward, but I am wide awake and feel rather nostalgic. I was a schoolboy when I attended my first play. It was Paul de Groot's production of *Nora*, and you were the young man. I was enraptured... I realised I simply had to become an actor.

Four years later I joined your company in Kroonstadt. We rehearsed in the town hall. You were a bundle of energy, impulsive and short-tempered. We were terrified of you – you would insult us one moment and the next have us collapse with laughter. We were a young group, working very hard, but no one worked harder than you... I realise now how much you did for Afrikaans theatre, and how indebted we all are to you.

You were two people: the one fiery, inspired, liberal... and always with one single aim: the best, only the best for the theatre – the play, the players, costumes, decor, publicity; everything critically, strictly and tastefully executed. Over the years our small group of young players came to appreciate and accept each others' weaknesses as well as attributes. We toured and lived together, sweated together, cried and laughed together – the result was co-operation, interplay and ensemble work of the highest quality.

You know, André, your *other* ego is your worst enemy – that hasty, almost cruel, sense of humour. What you do and say is legendary across this vast land of ours, and the end result is a colourful, dramatic personality, which no other actor can equal or surpass.

We never had contracts. Wasn't necessary. I know of no actor who was ever diddled by you. Oh yes, I do recall a contract. Overnight you decided to have them printed in Cradock *[the setting for Olive Schreiner's STORY OF AN AFRICAN FARM]* and one clause stipulated we had to attend church every Sunday. Did we kick against that! It was no use. The purpose most likely was twofold: you are a deeply religious person, you love your church and attend regularly; but it was also wonderful publicity – our little smartly-dressed group would wait till the service was about to start, and then with excellent timing we would march down the aisle, the whole length of the church, and sit down in the front row. I can still hear the whispers of the congregation as we made our entrance, and parsons often offered up prayers for us. There certainly was method in your madness! If I remember correctly, you provided us with your own money for the collection...

Little did we realise then that twelve years later you would be opening the new His Majesty's Theatre with your Hamlet. Hamlet in Afrikaans! One of the world's greatest plays in a great language but now in the world's youngest language. Hamlet! It really was a sensational success... Will we ever again be able to recruit such a wonderful group of players? – You as Hamlet, Anna *[Neethling-Pohl, actress and director]* as Gertrude, Bernadine Grunewald as Ophelia, Gideon Roos as Claudius, Philip Burgers as Polonius, Jan Schutte as Horatio and I as Laertes. Indeed we can be proud of that milestone in our theatrical history. Then came the prestige of getting our very own National Theatre, the first in the British Commonwealth. I remember you so well in your parts there... Hassan will always remain, for me, one of your best parts. Did you also enjoy it so much? That reminds me – it's years since we did something together... You know I should love to act in Afrikaans again. After all, that's how we all started with you... What about us all getting together again?... What do you think? Perhaps *Lear*?

Yes, dear André, we went through a lot together, and we have so much to be grateful for. Thank you. I'm becoming sentimental again, but it's late, I'm tired, and in 20 minutes we arrive in Bloemfontein.

Sleep well, old friend.

Siegfried Mynhardt

BERNARD MILES (1907-1991)

Bernard Miles (knighted in 1969, made a Life Peer in 1979) produced Purcell's DIDO & AENEAS as a fund-raising event for his new Mermaid Theatre. The soprano Kirsten Flagstadt (1895-1962) always insisted that for her the following letter from him and his wife Josephine Wilson was a binding contract:

Mermaid Theatre
Duff House
Acacia Road
London N.W.8
19th April, 1951

ARTICLES OF AGREEMENT between KIRSTEN FLAGSTADT, Soprano, hereinafter called 'the Singer' and THE MERMAID COMPANY, hereinafter called 'the Management'

The Singer undertakes:

1. To sing for 20 (twenty) performances the part of Dido in the opera DIDO AND AENEAS.

2. To assist in the production of the opera and to lend all such aid, help and assistance as may be deemed necessary to the successful presentation thereof.

3. To use only her best quality voice, fully supported by the breath throughout the performance.

4. To sing all her notes in time and in tune, but not to add any notes, grace notes, acciaccaturas, appoggiaturas, upper and lower mordents, shakes, trills, turns, titillations or other embellishments.

5. To let the management or any part thereof look down her throat with laryngoscope whenever they need encouragement.

6. To sing to the Management or any part thereof any or all of the songs of Schubert, Schumann, Beethoven, Handel, Bach, Grieg as often as requested.

7. To be obedient, tractable, sweet-tempered and helpful in every possible way, and not to brag about the Vikings.

On their side the Management undertake:

1. To treat the Singer in the manner worthy of her great name and fame, to look after her, to nourish, cherish, care for and make much of her. Also to hold her dear, to prize, treasure, cling to, adore, idealise and dote upon her.

2. To appoint as her personal slaves their three youngest members, to whit, Sarah, Biddy and John, who shall wait upon her hand, foot and finger.

3. To supply the Singer with all necessary scores, bars, notes and parts of notes, key signatures, ledger lines, etc. as shall be deemed necessary for the adequate interpretation of her rôle.

4. To find her in board-lodging throughout the run of the opera.

5. To supply her with two pints of oatmeal stout per diem, at the following times and in the following quantities, viz. lunch one half pint, dinner one half pint, and one pint following each performance.

6. To give her plenty of little surprises, presents of flowers, fruit, fish and fresh foliage; to recite to her; to write letters and little poems to her; also to take every opportunity of making her laugh.

Given under all our hands and with all our hearts, this tenth day of February, one thousand nine hundred and fifty.
Sealed with a kiss.

227

NOEL COWARD (1899-1973)

NOEL COWARD TO TOLETTE LA BLANCHE

1573 Sunset Plaza Drive
Beverley Hills
[Christmas 1955]

BOULEVARD NOWHERE

Tolette,

This is going to be a curious letter as I am doing it on the new Tippa Tappa et je ne suis pas certain of it. The house is sweet and when the fog lifts the view will be gorgeous. Oh dear there is so much to tell you that I don't know where to begin...

The cocktail party yesterday was a riot of fun and fancy and the girls *[Erica Marx and Elizabeth Taylor]* came and Erica was mistaken for Millie Natwick by Betty Bacall who congratulated her on her performance in something. Erica finally said, 'who do you think I am?' Where upon Betty said, 'Mildred Natwick Jesus Christ have I put my fucking foot in it!' and it all passed off in gales of laughter. Rock and Phyllis *[Hudson]* appeared and were very sweet. Marlene gave me a wonderful set of black silk pyjamas and dressing-gown to match. The Nivs also very sweet and send you particular love and so do Betty and Bogey *[sic]*.

Havana was unnoted by me on account of the Ambassador giving an enormous buffet dinner party for all the nobs the majority of whom were called Gonzalez-y-Lopez except for a few who were called Lopez-y-Gonzalez. They were all Sugar Barons.

Mexico City was almost complete disaster... V. was playing the Dauphin in THE LARK in the Round and I had to go and sit through it wrapped in a rug with a flask of brandy and it was a bugger to end all buggers. So bad indeed that I was bereft of speech. My only comfort was when Joan *[of Arc]* said something about not fearing the flames, a small, miserable boy in front of me let out such a loud fart that it nearly blew the brandy flask right out of my hand. She, Joan, was a bright amateur with her arse resting on her heels and a boyish manner. I expected her to say, 'Mumsie, can't I play just one more set with Roger?'... V. camped about and was quite inaudible and the whole thing was very very dreadful.

My maid is called Fredda. She has Sugar Diabetes and comes from St. Ann's Bay. She is very sweet, not only because of the diabetes. I have not yet got a secretary but one I believe is coming which all points to the fact that I miss Tolette La Blanche but on the whole I am happy as a bird-dog, perched in my little housie, and mercifully alone, and with a great great deal to look forward to.

Love Love Love...

Master

[Postscript] My Spanish lessons stood me in good stead, I found myself gabbling away like crazy and making witty little jokes...I hate Christmas...

Did I mention that Mexico City is a cunt?

The nicest Mexican I met was Boulting. Bogey, justly celebrated for his Dix-Huitieme manners, said to Clifton at the party apropos their own projected Christmas Eve rout, 'Bring your fucking mother and she can wipe up her own sick!' Clifton was not pleased.

Alec Guinness was very pleased and we bowed low to each other like characters in a Restoration comedy...

Betty Bacall passed out on Mabelle's bed for three hours. All of this surprised the Rock Hudsons who are perhaps unused to high society.

Betty Bacall called Hedda Hopper a lousy bitch and kicked her up the bottie under my very eyes...

Comme la vie est étonnante, n'est-ce pas?

Voilà c'est tout.

EDITH SITWELL (1887–1964)

After forty years of quasi-feud, Noël Coward and the poet Edith Sitwell (DBE in 1954 – FAÇADE, STREET SONGS, SONG OF THE COLD) finally became friends late in life, when he sent her a flattering message and she answered with a telegram:

DELIGHTED STOP FRIENDSHIP NEVER TOO LATE

Coward couldn't make her 75th Birthday celebrations, but she dropped him a line after:

[1962]

Dear Mr. Coward,

...Osbert and I were so very sorry you couldn't come... The concert and supper party were fun, in a way. But it was all like something rather macabre out of Proust. The papers excelled themselves – the *Sketch* particularly. I had never met the nice well-meaning reporter who 'covered' the event, but according to him he sat beside me as my weary head sank into my pillow, and just as I was dropping asleep I uttered these

Famous Last Words:

'Be kind to me! Not many people are! '

Very moving I think, don't you? ...please don't forget that if you can spare the time, you are coming to see me when you are in London.

Yours very sincerely,

Edith Sitwell

[Postscript] Osbert sends his love.

Edith Sitwell was a delicious correspondent. Here is her last letter to Coward, shortly before she died:

March 3rd, 1963

Dear Mr. Coward

I was so delighted to get your postcard...

A Club here have seized a poem of mine, *Still Falls the Rain*, without my permission, and have recited it with their heads out of a window! Evidently they don't know it is a poem about the bombing, but think it is an advertisement for mackintoshes! Some people might be rather cross. Osbert has just been here and sends his love. I look forward so much to seeing you when we both get back to England.

Your *ancient* friend (ancient God knows),

Edith

SPIKE MILLIGAN (BORN 1918)
FLORA ROBSON (1902–1984)

When Film Actor and Comedian Peter Sellers (1925–1980) had his first heart attack, and survived, his friend and fellow-Goon Spike Milligan sent him a telegram:

SWINE BLOODNOCK HAD YOU INSURED

In 1966, Flora Robson (DBE in 1960) wrote to the young Clive Francis:

Dear Clive,

You could not do better than to go to have your classical training; it will *enlarge* you as an actor. Olivier, after his first Old Vic season, had to use an extra size collar.

With love,
Flora

LAURENCE OLIVIER (1907–1989)
CHRISTOPHER FRY (BORN 1907)

Playwright Christopher Fry sends his new play VENUS OBSERVED to the most influential actor of the twentieth century: Sir Laurence Olivier (knighted 1947, created Life Peer 1970), act by act...

TELEGRAM
29 OCT. 1949
Handed in West London 5.21   Received Shipton under Wychwood 5.39
LAURENCE OLIVIER to CHRISTOPHER FRY

DEAR FELLOW ACT ONE PROVOCATIVE SO EXHILARATING SO DELICIOUS CANNOT RESIST WITHHOLDING MYSELF IN TINGLING RESISTANCE FROM THE JOYS OF ACT TWO BY PAUSING TO SEND YOU THIS WIRE WITH LOVE LARRY

TELEGRAM
1 NOV. 1949
Handed in West London 5.11   Received Shipton under Wychwood 5.50
LAURENCE OLIVIER to CHRISTOPHER FRY

DEAR FELLOW FORGIVE ME NOT ACKNOWLEDGING THIRD ACT AT ONCE EST EST EST LOVE LARRY

The 1950 London maiden performance of VENUS OBSERVED, starring Olivier, was a success. Two years later Olivier directed the same play in New York, with Rex Harrison (1908–1990, knighted 1989, described in Chambers Biographical Dictionary as 'An urbane light-comedian and roguish leading man') in the lead. Casting had not been easy. Laurence Olivier to Christopher Fry:

LAURENCE OLIVIER PRODUCTIONS LTD.
St JAMES'S THEATRE LONDON SW1
Cables: VIVIER, LONDON
Telegrams VIVIER, PICCY, LONDON
Telephone WHITEHALL 3944
25th August 1951

Dear boy,

Lunt has turned down *Venus*. Langner *[the producer]*'s next choice is Rex Harrison and then John Gielgud.

Let me know tout de suite if you have any objection to this. I personally think that after this we will be getting a little bit sticky on it.

Love –

<u>L.</u>

CHRISTOPHER FRY TO LAURENCE OLIVIER

27 Blomfield Road
London W9
August 27th 1951

Dear Larry,

No, no objection. What happened to Frederick March? Did he say 'no' too?

With love from us both to you both,

Christopher

First by cable and then from his dressing room in New York (where he is playing Shaw's CAESAR AND CLEOPATRA and Shakespeare's ANTONY AND CLEOPATRA in repertory with Vivien Leigh) Laurence Olivier reports on the first night, the reviews, the casting and the cutting of his American production of VENUS OBSERVED to Christopher Fry...

THE WESTERN UNION TELEGRAPH COMPANY
VIA WESTERN UNION CABLES
1952, FEB. 14   6.46 P.M.

CHRISTOPHER FRY, 27 BLOMFIELD ROAD W9:

DEAR BOY WONDERFUL RECEPTION LAST NIGHT PRESS WHICH AM SENDING YOU IS MIXED WITH UNHAPPY IMPLICATIONS THAT I AM TO BLAME FOR FAULTS I DONT HONESTLY THINK YOU WOULD AGREE HOWEVER WRITING FULLY NEXT WEEK WHEN A BIT CLEAR THANKS SWEET CABLE DEAREST LOVE BOTH LARRY

THE WESTERN UNION TELEGRAPH COMPANY
VIA WESTERN UNION CABLES
1952, FEB. 19   6.52 A.M.

CHRISTOPHER FRY, 27 BLOMFIELD ROAD W9:

DEAR KIT HAVE HAD FOLLOWING TELEGRAM FROM LANGNER QUOTE DEAR LARRY CALLED TO MEETING OF GOVERNMENT INVENTORS *(sic)* COUNCIL...GOOD POSSIBILITY OF RUN IF WE CAN CUT PLAY AS SUGGESTED BY REX AUDIENCES NOW LEAVE OVERTIRED AND DONT RECOMMEND PLAY TO FRIENDS SHALL GUILD CABLE FRY OR DO YOU HAVE AUTHORITY UNQUOTE HAVE I YOUR AUTHORITY TO DO WHAT I THINK BEST THE FEELING SEEMS TO BE PRETTY GENERAL LOVE LARRY

My dearest Kit,

Here at last, at long last. It is not going to be *v* easy, first because I am now a bit tired out with it all, and then because it is rather like a boxer being asked to describe a fight in which he feels he has been knocked about a bit, and consequently feels a bit disheartened about making the full report on it; however darling Boy, such is at the least what you are due, and so here is the best I can do.

The casting was of course a problem right off. And the chief mistake, if such it can be called, lay always in the relative ages of the players.

With Rex and Lilli *[Lilli Palmer, one of Rex Harrison's 6 wives]* playing together, the desire on the part of the audience is very much to wish them together, so that Edgar is apt to appear as the interloper, rather than the Duke in the symmetrical wishes of nature. Against that we have the box office advantage of that particular team, which we were prepared to settle for.

Had Rex and Lilli *both* been on the old side, then the age scaling could have fallen naturally into place, and providing always the right expert players were free and willing to be engaged no incongruities need have been apparent – but as things are – Rex is on the *light* side and Lilli (German too) is on the heavy side, and no such simple method of approach was useful.

The feelings of an actor of Rex's calibre and position naturally had to be taken into consideration, and he had a great phobia of having 'a lot of old women' round him, in spite of his wish not to make Lilli look foolish.

Now as one can *never* cast a play absolutely perfectly it always seems sensible to me to land the incongruity onto the actor who by his virtuosity is best able to look after himself, and by the nature of his popularity with the audience, is most likely to be accepted for what he is *meant* to be.

As an example of this, had I cast the film of *'Hamlet' round* myself – then Aubrey Smith would have played the King and Lillian Braithwaite the queen, and that whole part of the story would have seemed ridiculous, so I cast the whole film as acceptably and logically as I could (there were one or two mistakes I know) and offered my own face to look the only miscast one, because I thought I was the most likely person to be accepted for what I was meant to be, rather than for what I *looked* to be.

In our case this person is Lilli.

This situation was somewhat precipitated by the Guild finding no Rosabel in N.Y. and my having to fix the best actors I could find (Rawlings couldn't come) in the last two days before I left London.

John Merivale is *first class* as Edgar and is a much better age weight for Lilli than your 'Sleep of P.' boy who couldn't get free.

The three women are all well cast in themselves.

Your wire to Leah Salisbury would have tickled me, darling boy, had I not been so wrought at the time. 'Light, mercurial, adorable.' Baby boy I must put it to your sense of fairness that it is the writing rather than the casting that is the problem there. The part was always a bit of a teaser to both of us. It is, I'm afraid, one that requires the big, big star who could never dream of playing it, to achieve all qualifications.

However, we have not done too badly here. Joan Haythorne has some beautiful qualities – she is not persuasive enough to look at, but that is not her fault; she was the best actress I could get in the time.

This letter is bound to be a bit jumpy as it has to get written, when and how. I am just dec'd as Antony, and Vivien is doing her stuff.

The *Jessie* – Claudia Morgan is excellent and has achieved enough cockney accent to get well by here, and what is more important has got the *character* entirely – warm, adorable and very funny.

Hilda – this is a wee bit disappointing. Eileen Peel started well enough, and seemed to understand the kind of empty countyness that I required, then slipped off it and went hopelessly wrong, and became just actressy and rather over-actressy at that. It has calmed down now into a perfectly decent, but quite 'straight' performance.

All of them, without exception, managed to get their characterizations either entirely ironed flat, or else distorted and overemphasized, by finding themselves accused constantly of inaudibility, half on account of the huge theatre in Philadelphia, and half by the audiences' difficulty in following the dialogue, and *thinking* that they couldn't hear it. (We get 'heard' in the Shaw, but *not* 'heard' in the Shakespeare!)

Stuart Burge is very nice indeed as *Bates* – a little on the grotesque side perhaps but only a little; it is somewhat of a Shakespeare comic rôle – both Bates and Reddleman are prone to appear as things rather 'familiar' – 'Eccentric Servant types', and one can only play them as that.

Both Rex and I had high hopes of our *Reddleman* – James Westerfield – but he has turned out to be absolutely lousy, inaudible and still muddles his lines, and is quite damaging to the show – this is really another of those 'star' parts that you cannot cast for the price commensurate I'm afraid, unless you are lucky enough to unearth a dormant genius. Well, we have been unlucky again.

Hurd Hatfield is a very decent *Dominic*, inclined to be heavy, but it is I think more your idea of the part than we had in London.

John Williams is absolutely first class as *Reedbeck* and has made a great whacking success. I don't know if you know what an awful and unlooked for situation I found myself in, in having to decide to change the Reedbeck after two precious weeks' rehearsal; there's no sense in going into all the details when I can tell you so much more than I can in a letter, when I get home. Suffice it the change was all for the very best. Strangely enough tho' he is a very good comedian, he implored me to cut what were to us a couple of his best lines, because he could not get them over: 'the rain and the firemen's hose' – they just didn't take at all.

Lilli now. She really gives a pretty jolly good show of *Perpetua*, and does the 'Sentence' quite beautifully. (Yes – standing quite still darling boy). The only trouble is that – not that she looks – but she *is* a bit too old for the part – that shouldn't matter too much I know, but she is also unmistakably German – this matters more to the English ear than the American, but it does some indefinable mischief to the part. Tho' she managed brilliantly to eradicate all traces of European *experience* from her moments of pathos she still exudes a certain toughness of personality which is not exactly the fortitude of a white crocus that I feel Perpetua has got. It has much to do with the way she stands, and her sleek, but unmistakably 'Kleines mädchen' figure.

Now before I start discussing my job I know you are most anxious to hear about the crits.. They are *not*, I think, savage, and knowing that you must realise that universal opinion holds that your plays are prone

237

to be too verbally rich for the modern ear, it is to be hoped that you may appreciate that, though cutting may not do you good service as a poet, it may as a dramatist.

I have not said anything about Rex as *the Duke* yet, because he is bound to come into a great deal of what follows.

For instance the first baby cut is in Hilda's introduction 'There will only be the appearance of people being near to us.' Rex thought he could never get over to the audience what that was meant to say – and why bemuse them, or make them feel unintelligent, and I must say I agree with him.

No change now, except that Edgar piles a second apple onto Rosabel which goes better for 'plying Rosabel with fruit'.

When things got good-and-panicky just after the N.Y. opening, I tried a cut in the Duke's speech from 'the dark tree' to 'unattractive beam'. It seemed to take all the brilliance out of the speech and I couldn't stand it and so put it back.

After trying it in and out we finally did make your suggested cut in Rosabel's 1st. Act speech. I didn't like the cut because it seemed to diminish her case as well as leaving out an important exposition of the Duke's character, but without moving her around during it, which she tried but didn't do very convincingly, the thing does seem rather a set speech, and the act is better for it being trimmed...

In Act II we took out the little image of 'the year, whose arrow Singing from the April bow' etc...

I used to enjoy it heartily myself, but Rex found it too difficult to convey, and, now this is the point which will explain to you a little of what is lacking, did not *enjoy saying* it, which means you see that the Duke who is not only in love with words for their own sake, but who is even more in love with his own use and manipulation of them is not there as he should be. Please understand that there is a wealth of stuff that is. He is the most attractive actor imaginable, has a style, presence and personality, that is most original, brilliantly amusing, extraordinarily winning in its individuality. I really love his performance and I know you too would be captivated by it. If one wished to be scathing, which I really do not, the worst one could say would be that it smacks of Berkeley Street rather than St. James's Street. The wine in his blood is champagne-like rather than the *more* fruity kind that I myself felt in it. His lack of vocal range and equipment makes it very hard for him to keep the sound of the part rich and always refreshing in tune and tonal idea. Repetitious inflections, sheer running-out of vocal ideas, cause some of the highest flights of poetic imagery to flatten out into tired shallow cadences that have fallen weakly away to one side of the rip-roaring current that should be hurtling them ever changeably along.

(This is all very poetic, but what I really mean is at times it's a little boring to listen to.)...

The *Sentence* – standing stock still is very successful and Lilli pulls it off brilliantly with only a little too much gesticulation and she is cutting this down all the time. I'm not really sure that I am entirely happy about the stillness – it is even more blatantly a tour de force, but when my beloved author says do something I certainly will do it unless it kills me... By the way I do remember at our first reading in London during Heather's 'Sentence' turning to you and whispering 'alright to move her around?' – and you nodding your head in vehement approval. Darling boy I bring this up in no recriminatory vein just a point of interest, I don't see why you shouldn't change your mind if you want to!

But here was the difficulty. Perpetua's speech – stock still – set piece. The Duke's Halloween also stock still – set piece. The scene becomes a goddam spelling bee you see. I tried moving the Duke around – it was horrid... it makes it pixillated and unconfident – all wrong. The way we had it in London did work alright – Perpetua swishing around and then the Duke stock still rang a change and the audience was held – anyway until the 'rigid winter' which was too much for them. I cut that bit anyway for New York because I knew it would be too much for them and poor Rexie was frankly dismayed by it...

To digress a little. You know darling boy if you would act some of your roles, which I am sure you could as well as any of us, you would find out so much that would cause you some constructive pondering. *Please* don't think I am being impertinent enough to preach at you, it is only my duty as a 'theatrician' (which they call me here!) and as a devoted friend, to offer you any conclusions that experience has brought me to. It cannot ever be right or desirable in the theatre that we should *lose our audience. Sound* for its own sake can be a property I know, but a very esoteric one; to be sparingly used in my considered opinion only when the audience is *fresh*. Their intellectual receptiveness gets tired as the evening wears on. W.S. was brilliantly conscious of this, and I think that is why he always manages to excite.

All the tragedies show him gradually relaxing his call upon the intelligence as the evening progresses until he finally says 'Alright, you see it's quite easy now' and sometimes 'Here you are groundlings – here's a damn good *fight*'.

The *Emotions* of the audience last the longest of the contributions that they bring to the theatre. *Intellect* wears out quickest. After all they have paid their money to enjoy themselves.

Time and time again in *Venus* in London, I would have the brutes in my hand like baby mice, and then out would come something *difficult* again, or obscure, or too clever, and it would be suddenly like playing in a hospital for croup – impatience had seized them and they were gone for a while. And they got more and more sensitive during the evening. When the play was really over after the general exit when I was alone with Georgie Relph, there would be the most sublime atmosphere of glowing emotional quietude, and then even not so difficult a word like 'desuetude' would send them crestfallen back their bronchitis.

Be a bit easier on them cockie will you? Don't Tease the poor bastards too much. Exercise is good for them but they've paid mostly for relaxation...

It seems to me that you have intrigued and provoked basic emotions, a). by the love scene and b). by the fire, and then you say now listen to these *words* and get a kick out of them for your curtain – and I think you have asked too much of people in a place of entertainment. The situation you've introduced is amusing enough – their quarrel I mean – and it's piquant at this point, but it somehow don't do no good boy. The words aren't strong enough (though I can't think *any* words could be better than yours) and the jokes aren't funny enough to win over this occasion, and the spectators feel cheated and unsatisfied and your little friend feels frustrated and defeated...

Now as to the production. I can't honestly feel that the criticisms are justified; I was thoroughly hauled over the coals in the Sundays. *Most* of it is a great deal differently done; this is a natural procedure when dealing with quite a different actor, one moreover of such an establishment as Rexie-boy.

I didn't realise before I started what an extremely delicate (and interestingly so) job it was to direct another actor in a job one had done oneself.

There is always the wish in any star actor to have his own ideas, and in this sort of case there is the very natural, if minutely truculent, desire to do everything as much unlike the other fellow as possible. This works equally for good and ill. Sometimes the new thoughts, moves, positions, work well and interestingly, and sometimes the old ones – amazingly enough – turned out to be the best. It never seemed proper to insist even on these, as it was *his* performance up for judgement, not mine; but it did seem dutiful to offer them when I genuinely thought it was for the best...

I got the lighting very beautifully, I think, for a time – but then had to spoil it with a lot of extra front light as these folk here can't see unless there's a *blaze*.

I really think this letter has gone on for long enough, don't you? It is now Tuesday night (4th.) and I am between Acts 2 and 3 of *Caesar*... I told Ruth Gordon about the length of this letter, and she said that you should give it a title and we should put it on.

I must stop, I am being called...

See you, dearest Kit, not too dreadfully far ahead – all love from Vivien to you and Phyll,

And from Your

Larry

Olivier was a generous man who enjoyed great loyalty from his colleagues and never failed to support them. Laurence Olivier and his third wife Joan Plowright to Brenda Bruce on the occasion of her first night in Tourneur's THE REVENGER'S TRAGEDY *for the Royal Shakespeare Company in 1966:*

Darling Brenda,

Oh so much love and *oh* such tremendous wishes for your absolute socking smashing belting *triumph* darling –

Your friends

Joanie and Larry

KENNETH TYNAN (1927–1980)

In 1962 the journalist, critic and deviser/author of the musical OH CALCUTTA Kenneth Tynan, whose declared intention was to unnerve a nation 'fearful of bad taste', joined Sir Laurence Olivier (q.v.), artistic director of the newly-created National Theatre, as dramaturg and consultant. Tynan's relationship with Laurence Olivier was based on terrific mutual respect...

20 Thurloe Square
April 28, 1970

Dear Larry,

This is just to thank you not only for giving by far the best performance of Shylock I've ever seen but also for the privilege of watching some of it take shape.

I think it is one of the most astonishing things you have ever done – and, as always, you do something with the part so shatteringly and obviously right that one wonders why nobody has thought of it before. *You show us Shylock turning into a Jew before our eyes.*

The man at the beginning of the play is a businessman first and foremost, only secondarily a Jew. When the Christians steal his daughter, he begins to realise what it means to be Jewish, and by the end of the trial he knows it through and through – so indelibly that no-one in the theatre will ever forget it.

You do not need luck or prayers or good wishes tonight. All you need is an audience.

Love,
Ken

In 1976 Tynan, with lungs weakened through emphysema, moved to California for his health. From here he wrote a regular column for the New Yorker magazine.

Kenneth Tynan to actress Marlene Dietrich (1904–1992), who had just sent him a draft of her autobiography for appraisal:

765 Kingman Avenue
Santa Monica
January 27, 1977

Dearest M –

Much as I'd love to come to Paris, my *New Yorker* work will keep me here until at least April; and in any case my health won't let me return to Europe before then. But I'm usually awake and functioning by 10 a.m. California time, which is 7 p.m. your time, so after that hour you can normally reach me.

A few more notes on what you sent me, some important, some trifling, in no particular order:

A. Insist on your $50,000 immediately. Tell Nizer [*Louis Nizer, her lawyer*] that if he won't, you will, and shoot off a firm note to Putnam's [*her publishers*] asking why they have failed to fulfil their obligation...

B. Page 1 of the preface: 'I, personally, am not interested to tell about my life. But as there seems to be a vast interest... 'Dear Marlene, please do not sound so grudging. You really cannot start out a book by saying you have no interest in writing it. The reader's reaction will be: 'So why should I be interested in reading it?' Also, if you'll pardon the expression, it sounds a touch arrogant.

C. AVOID PRINTING WORDS IN CAPITAL LETTERS. It's too melodramatic. If you want to add emphasis, just underline the key words or put them in quotes. (E.g. 'fame,' not FAME; *no diaries*, not NO DIARIES.) This is important.

D. Contrary to what you say, the facts (not FACTS) do matter. Part of the purpose in writing the book is to set the record straight.

E. Page 2 of preface: '... the white skin that is the red-head's priority.' I think you mean something like 'birthright.' I mention this because there are hundreds of little wrong notes of this kind in the text, all of which could easily be put right by a good editor...

F. Try not to have paragraphs that are only one or two sentences long. Run them together into longer blocks of prose. It looks less scrappy. Here again, any competent editor could do this for you with no difficulty.

G. You say you 'hate anecdotes.' Please don't. One's life is an extended anecdote. And you can tell good anecdotes very well, such as the story about the Texan and the crabs.

H. A personal note: I'm sorry you admire Richard Burton's writing so much. I promise you it's really flabby, like Dylan Thomas with all of the alcohol and none of the genius. However...

I. Childhood section: I liked all this very much. It was new to me and beautifully remembered. But there are certain essential facts we need to know from the beginning – what city we are in, what your father's job was, and (yes) when you were born.

J. Page 43: 'I often think that being revolutionary is just a matter of no opinion at all.' This simply doesn't hold water. Whatever you may think of Lenin or Brecht or Rosa Luxemburg, they certainly had very strong and precise opinions, and not just negative ones, either. This passage makes you sound politically a bit naive, which is a pity. You say: 'Don't just destroy what you don't like.' But surely it would have been worthwhile to 'just destroy' Hitlerism in 1939? This brings me to a general point. Later on, when you describe how you always did exactly what the dictator von Sternberg told you, and how the actor's job is to obey the supreme commander, people may draw a parallel between your *artistic* obedience and the *political* obedience the German nation gave to Hitler. I think you should be careful of this. Perhaps add something to the effect that the German quality of respect for authority has its bad side.

K. When you decided to go on the stage, didn't your socially well-connected family raise any objections?

L. Similar to (C): never use more than one ! or ? at a time. It's over-emphatic.

M. About the matter of 'no trespassing' (on your private life)... I am *not* suggesting detailed descriptions of erotic wrestling matches, etc.. But there are discreet ways of indicating that your relationships with (say) von Sternberg, Remarque and Gabin were different from your relationship with (say) Paustovsky. You tell me: 'Nobody of any stature ever related with whom they slept'. Well, Stendahl did; and so did Boswell and Samuel Pepys and Jean-Jacques Rousseau and Bertrand Russell. It's true that some of these were writing private journals, not intended for publication; all the same, their candour has not injured their reputations. You will help us to understand you if we know the kind of men who attracted you physically as well as intellectually. You will also help us to like you. Otherwise we wonder: why so much space on a writer like Remarque? What is she hiding? And we may start to imagine things much worse than the plain romantic truth. 'He attracted me because' is just as respectable as 'I admired him because...' So why not say it? I remember one evening you told me the depth of your feeling for Gabin and how much you agonised over his demand that, if you were to stay together, your career must come second to his. It was a very moving story. Your book needs it.

N. I stupidly stopped making notes of page numbers, but somewhere you name Phyllis Haver, Evelyn Brent and Georgia Hale among the *stars* created by von Sternberg. I've never heard of any of them. Another trivial point: you describe Orson as 'Young' when in fact, incredible as it may seem, he is now 62!

O. Elsewhere you launch a tough attack on 'bookworms' and 'professors.' I have forgotten the context; but the attack sounds somehow unpleasant, especially coming from someone like you, who admires intelligence so whole-heartedly. One of the best editors I ever worked for once warned me: 'Never take the anti-intellectual side in an argument. You'll find that most of the people who applaud you will be the people you hate.' He was quite right.

P. Tiny point: I didn't understand why you were so scared by dancing with Walter Wanger at the speakeasy. This isn't clear.

Q. The whole portrait of von Sternberg is superb and definitive. Your picture of him is better than the one in his own book.

R. I can't recall whether you mention the Lubitsch film 'Angel.' (I mention this for no other reason than that I'm going to see it again next week. There's a Dietrich movie playing somewhere in L.A. every night of the week.)

S. Putnam's may be worried about what you say apropos of the G.I.s feeling let down by the country to which they came back after the war. Don't let them influence you on this. It's a powerful argument and well worth stating, even though it may not endear you to the great American public. Finally: a little more about people you didn't like or admire would not come amiss! A pantheon of gods is very nice, but there's room for a rogues' gallery as well. (The portrait of Jannings, for instance, is wickedly good.) I know you didn't dislike Garbo, but a word or two about her would be very illuminating: the pair of you reigned side by side, and to leave her out would be like a book by Duse that didn't mention Bernhardt.

No more to say, except that I can't wait to read PART TWO.

If I can find a reasonable villa, I hope to spend May-to-October in South East Spain. Perhaps I could pass through Paris en route.

Meanwhile, continue to hit those keys, avoiding only the capital shift-lock and restraining the temptation to multiply ? into ???

Kathleen joins me in sending mega-tons of love

Ever,

Ken

In 1979 the American television personality Johnny Carson threatened to retire from hosting his celebrated show...

1500 Stone Canyon Road

Bel Air

April 22, 1979

Dear John,

What follows is sheer impertinence on my part; all I can say in its defence is that it is well-meant. When I read in the paper that you might be quitting *The Tonight Show* in the fall, I felt a twinge of quite definite grief, and suddenly realized how much it meant to me, when contemplating a trip to this country, to reflect that whatever else might have dried up or degenerated, one sparkling fountainhead of pleasure would still remain – Carson at 11:30. Here at least was something I couldn't get anywhere else in the world. I cannot tell you how many bad days you have saved, and good days you have improved, by simply being there on Channel 4, doing what nobody else can do anything like as well.

And now I hear talk of Specials. Dear John, *all* your shows are Specials. I hear, too, that you are bored. Was Dickens bored after writing novels for seventeen years? Did Matisse burn his brushes after seventeen years' daubing? Did you never hear the great remark of the painter Delacroix: 'Talent does whatever it wants to do: genius only what it can do'? What other TV format would give you the freedom to improvise, to take off and fly, to plunge into the unpredictable? Carson script-bound would be Carson strait-jacketed. We all know you are like a great dish that combines all your flavours. It resembles the pressed duck at the Tour d'Argent in Paris: the recipe hasn't changed in my lifetime, yet it tastes as inimitably fresh every time I order it.

Was it unadventurous for Astaire to stick to tap-dancing instead of venturing into ballet? On the contrary: it was brave, and it was what made him (and will keep him forever) a classic. Similarly, I honour Cary Grant for never having played *Macbeth* and Muhammad Ali for keeping out of the Wimbledon championships.

I wouldn't insult you by supposing that you haven't thought along these lines yourself. I'm sure you are convinced that there is a new Carson ready to emerge from the old and stagger us all once again. And your track record is such that you may well be right. But I beseech you – as Oliver Cromwell said on a famous occasion – to consider in the bowels of Christ whether ye may not be wrong. (I may have misquoted Cromwell but I hope ye get my drift.)

No need for a reply. This is an impulse letter that I simply had to get off my chest. In terms of entertainment, to lose Carson would be like erasing a star from the flag.

Yours sincerely,
Kenneth Tynan

RALPH RICHARDSON (1902–1983)

Sir Ralph Richardson (knighted in 1947) turns down a part; a letter to Michael Meyer, who had translated Ibsen's WHEN WE DEAD AWAKEN:

Majestic
New York
10 Mar 63

My dear Michael,

Thanks very much for your letter and the copy of *When We Dead Awaken* with the excellent preface.

Wish that the play was all that the preface leads one to hope for– although it is extremely well translated.

The first act is fine, although a little more humour in the sculptor's make up might lead one to expect more of his masterpiece.

The second act is good – reflective, poetic, but one waits for the trail – at least for the dynamite to explode.

The third act opens with a scene which is rather silly in my opinion, but, when the sculptor comes on and one thinks 'at last we are going to have a scene' – nothing whatever new happens!

There is a re-statement of situation – new development in the sculptor's character – but a hell of a lot of stage difficulties – a situation which poor old Richardson could not untangle.

I am very grateful to you for thinking of me and I wish to God I could find a part to play – but I could not play this. Ninety per cent of what this play has to say has been already said with magic, charm, whit *[sic]* and humour and mystery in *Peer Gynt* don't you agree? No – you don't – I am very stupid I am afraid!

EVER,
Ralph

HAROLD PINTER (BORN 1930)

One of the strongest features of Harold Pinter's plays is the quality of mystery and enigma. It was reported in the Daily Mail *of 28th November, 1967, that he had received the following letter...*

Dear Sir,

I would be obliged if you would kindly explain to me the meaning of your play *The Birthday Party*.

These are the points I do not understand:

1. Who are the two men?
2. Where did Stanley come from?
3. Were they all supposed to be normal?

You will appreciate that without the answers to my questions I cannot fully understand your play.

Yours, etc.

Pinter is reported to have replied as follows:

Dear Madam,

I would be obliged if you would kindly explain to me the meaning of your letter. These are the points which I do not understand:

1. Who are you?
2. Where do you come from?
3. Are you supposed to be normal?

You will appreciate that without the answers to my questions I cannot fully understand your letter.

Yours, etc..

ATHOL FUGARD (BORN 1932)

The leading South African playwright of his time (BLOOD KNOT, BOESMAN AND LENA, THE ROAD TO MECCA, HELLO AND GOODBYE) writes to Mary Benson – novelist, biographer and friend of the great African leader Nelson Mandela – about his latest play...

S'kop 7th July, 1973

Dearest Mary,

John and Winston [*John Kani and Winston Ntshona, leading actors*] and I went down to Capetown to the Space Theatre to open *Die Hodosha Span*. Yes Mary, we finally took on Robben Island. 'Success' is not a word to use in this context. It's holy ground. As much as I made it, it is possible for me, here at S'kop, to stand back from it and say objectively that what we 'made' was no more than a vehicle for the truth.

The Island is two men (khaki shorts, bald heads), one sentenced to life, the other to ten years. They work in the quarries; every morning they leave their cell and run to a cycle of soul-destroying labour under the hot sun, with the evil hum of the Hodosha, the carrion fly, and the plaintive scream of their wheelbarrows as the only accompaniment to that day in their lives.

In the evenings they run back to the cell. While they run, handcuffed together by wrists and ankles, they pray and cry and try to keep in time, because to run with three legs is not easy.

They arrive in the cell more dead than alive. They piss on each others' wounds because water alone will not disinfect them. And then they start to live again. Slowly, painfully, they pull themselves together – find the tobacco hidden in the cell, talk a little, start to laugh, and before bed that night they enact a daily ritual...

One of them picks up a mug and puts through a long-distance telephone call to New Brighton [*a native African 'township' in Port Elizabeth*]. They talk to family and friends – they 'celebrate' themselves, they refuse to part with the world. They go to sleep bruised and sore and lonely – but not defeated...

Then one day the man serving ten years is called to the office and returns to tell the other that his sentence has been reduced. Three months to go. And so starts a confrontation of the two aspects of the human dilemma – the hell of Hope (92 days to go) and the hell of Despair (a lifetime on the Island – and what is the Island finally except possibly the most brutal metaphor I know of for the space and time any life can occupy?)

Despair is jealous of Hope. It also wants to count. But How? And What? How can you count the days that stretch between you and the end except on the basis of: 'One....another one....another....'? Not only jealous. Mad as well. Because Hope stinks – of poes [sex], people, beer, freedom. Finally, despair accepts and understands. Even as his friend will leave and forget, he too will forget. We die alone.

They collect the few crops for their turn at the prison concert. Despair turns to Hope; 'Come, they're waiting.' (Hope doesn't move.) 'Come, we'll be late for the concert.' They leave their cell and present their 'turn':

The Trial and Punishment of Antigone
Presented for your Entertainment by Die Hodosha Span.

Antigone wears a wig made out of rope; Creyon a crown and pendant fashioned out of jam tins. The trial proceeds, Antigone and Creyon clash – a clash between the laws of Men and those of God. Finally Creyon passes sentence: 'Take her to a desert island and there wall her up within a cell, with enough food to acquit our hands of the taint of her blood.'

Antigone takes off her wig and says goodbye to her land, her people: 'I go to buy my living death because I honour those things to which honour belongs.'

The final, fading image is of two men, handcuffed together at wrist and ankle, running to the quarry. They pray, cry, and try desperately to keep in time. It is not easy for two men to run on three legs.

We made what I have just tried to describe to you in two weeks.

All for now,
Athol

['Die Hodosha Span' – literally 'The Carrion-fly Team' – is named after the labour camp workers on Robben Island. Lawyer and politician Nelson Mandela was imprisoned here by the white South African government for 26 years before emerging to become President.]

251

PATRICK MYNHARDT (born 1932)

Another South African actor, Patrick Mynhardt, who works in both English and Afrikaans, describes a primitive experience on tour with his celebrated one man dramatisation of the Herman Charles Boesman short stories...

Norwood, Johannesburg
1st December, 1980

My dear old friends,
    Now at last a letter with a bit of news, and one of my very worst experiences... Please don't condemn me if aspects of this story revolt you. It is the absolute truth!
    ...I was to do my Bosman show in the beautiful brand new Masonic Hall in Vryheid. I was taken there by one of the conveners... To my horror I saw no stage whatsoever; instead, two tied-together tin trestle-tables, about five feet by five feet, had been placed there to serve as my stage. Because I had foolishly told the conveners I could do my shows almost anywhere, in fact even on a small tin table, they actually took me literally and supplied precisely that!... Before I could throw the full drama queen temperament I was calmed down and assured the situation would be rectified by the evening. I unpacked my trailer and proceeded to move into the dressing room, and of course was confronted with the same old story which had bugged me for so many of my touring years: no toilet facilities. Actors, it seems, have no need ever to do either number one or number two. There wasn't even a washbasin... In a corner I discovered a cardboard box with lots of old bottles – empties, I thought. So I knew that if the worst came to the worst I could pee in one of the bottles and surreptitiously pour the contents out of the window into the empty parking lot.
    My show was to commence at eight thirty. I had a Chinese meal and got to the hall about six thirty, where I found to my great joy that my stage now consisted of *twelve* tied-together tin trestle-tables. Boy was I in business! I went to the dressing room to make up and after that I still had plenty of time to snoop around and furtively peep into the Masonic literature and prayer books. By eight thirty I was raring to go,

and still no beginner's call; the diners hadn't finished guzzling. All this time the convener kept plying me with more and more coffee and coke... slowly but surely the endless drinks were beginning to make me want to do number one. So off to the cardboard box in the corner. Disaster there wasn't an empty bottle in the box; they were all at least three quarters full: whisky, brandy, gin, vodka and cane. As a very heavy ex-drinker myself (alcoholic, if you like) and having loved it, there was no way I was going to pollute or dilute the Masons' medicine, so I had to do it in stages into a glass and pour it out of the window into the empty parking lot.

By now it was nine o'clock and my apprehension and nerves were beginning to play havoc with me. Suddenly at nine fifteen, without any warning, I heard the pre-curtain music playing loud and clear. Thank God. I was fully dressed, made-up and ready, and about to make a magnificent entrance onto my twelve tied-together tin trestle-tables. Suddenly I got the most agonising cramps, the worst I have ever had. At the same moment I was overcome with an awful sense of guilt for having sacrilegiously paged through those little bibles and booklets, convinced the cramps were my punishment! I was all curled up with pain; if I did not relieve myself at once and do number two I would explode. By now the convener was banging on the door. I shouted: 'I am in a crisis situation. Rewind the tape and repeat the music!' But Oh my God the cramps were getting worse. I was beginning to feel borrels wanting to bubble out of every orifice of my body...

And then, praise God, in the corner I saw a bright yellow Clicks [South African chain store] plastic bag with its bold Clicks name emblazoned across it in blue. Pinching for all I was worth, pigeon-toed and knock-kneed, I succeeded in slithering to the corner. I plucked off Oom Schalk's waistcoat, sliding the braces over my shoulders, off with the belt, the veldtschoen shoes and the corduroy trousers, grabbed the bag and then... For this relief, dear Clicks, much thanks.

By now the audience was slow-clapping and tapping their feet, the sound tape seemed to be suffering from stretch fatigue (and so was I) and the convener was banging on my door in a mad panic... Within a flash I was dressed. I left the bag on my make-up table and entered the hall to thunderous applause, mounted my stage of twelve tied-together tin trestle-tables and gave the performance of my life...

During the interval I gathered up the yellow and blue plastic bag and tossed it out of the window into the parking lot – horror, horror, horror! – onto the black bonnet of a Mercedes Benz with little triangular flags of coat of arms on each front fender – the number plate VRYHEID 1. The Mayor's car!!

I have never been invited back to Vryheid.

I must end. Please write back when you can but not anything the length of mine as I certainly would never have the energy to wade through it all!!

Love to you both,
Patrick

P.S. I have been a very grateful Clicks customer ever since.

JACK LEMMON (born 1925)
RUTH GORDON (1896–1985)

In 1982 Hollywood actor Jack Lemmon sent a cable to British actor Alec McCowen, who was just about to perform his solo THE GOSPEL OF ST. MARK in Hollywood:

FOR GOD'S SAKE ALEC DON'T SCREW IT UP

In 1956 Alec McCowen worked with Ruth Gordon (q.v.) in Thornton Wilder's THE MATCHMAKER. He writes: 'After six months of watching her extraordinary performance with awe, I wrote her a rather embarrassing fan letter. I said words to the effect that she made hard work look like a miracle of freshness'...

CLARIDGE'S
Brook Street, W.1
Friday

Dear Alec,

It *is* hard work – and also a miracle. The miracle is when you get the job. The hard work follows the miracle... I think acting is so hard to do – at best – that everybody ought to tell everybody all they know about it.

Alec, your letter was as rewarding a reward as one can get. To please other actors gives me the most pleasure next to one – to please myself. I guess in the end the real secret of acting is to get through rehearsals and remain *intact* – not a piece of your conception *and* the author's *and* the producer's *and* God knows who else – to get through rehearsals and wind up doing it the way you want it, that's paradise. *And* the secret of freshness. The way *you* want it. Otherwise I think it's an un-adult occupation and a *bore*!

Ruth

RUTH GORDON (1896–1985)

Fifty six years after her début in New York [see page 187] the distinguished Ruth Gordon fought, audition after audition, test after test, to secure the marvellous rôle of Maude in the film HAROLD AND MAUDE...

TO THE DRAMA CRITIC, NEW YORK TIMES

244 Ladera Drive
Beverley Hlls
California 90210
22 December 1971

Dear Mr. Canby,

What a disappointment to read your review. I know people aren't supposed to write a critic and the last time I did was fifty-six years ago today. I got a good review in the December 22, 1915, TIMES and wrote the critic. It was my first time on the stage and I didn't know you shouldn't. Today I know, but I'm doing it.

I wish you'd liked *Harold and Maude*. They said you saw it in a screening room with a dozen other critics. I wish you could have seen it with an audience. Maybe you wouldn't have liked it then, but then I'd feel you saw it the way it was meant to be seen. Shoulder to shoulder with people is how a play or film is written to be seen and I wish you'd seen it that way.

Maybe you think this is about as important as what Lillian Lorraine said was wrong with her life when the lady reporter came to interview her. Lillian Lorraine was old and broke and living up Broadway at 96th. Some paper sent the lady interviewer up to do a piece: 'What do you think happened, Miss Lorraine? Ziegfeld said you were the greatest beauty he ever had in the Follies. What went wrong?'

'He was *right*. And he was crazy about me. He had me in a tower suite at the Hotel Ansonia and he and his wife lived in the tower suite above. And I cheated on him, like he cheated on Billie Burke. I had a whirl! I blew a lot of everybody's money, I got loaded, I was on the stuff, I got the syphilis, I tore around, stopped at nothing, if I wanted to do it I did it and didn't give a damn. I got knocked up, I had abortions,

I broke up homes, I gave fellers the clap. So that's what happened.'

'Well, Miss Lorraine,' gasped the lady reporter, 'if you had it to do over would you do anything different?'

'Yes,' said Lillian Lorraine.

'I never shoulda cut my hair'.

Well, seeing *Harold and Maude* in a projection room may strike you as no more relevant than she shouldn't have cut her hair. Forgive the letter. Maybe it's all right to do if you only do it every fifty-six years.

Ruth Gordon

TENNESSEE WILLIAMS (1911–1983)

Playwright Tennessee Williams (given name Thomas Lanier – THE GLASS MENAGERIE, A STREETCAR NAMED DESIRE, CAMINO REAL, CAT ON A HOT TIN ROOF, SUDDENLY LAST SUMMER) to Estelle Kohler who was playing the lead in his THE RED DEVIL BATTERY SIGN at the Phoenix Theatre:

THE BERKELEY
LONDON
SW1X 7RL
7/7/77

A very Early Poem for Estelle

All roses are enchantment to the wise,
The veil of sophistry drawn from the eyes,
The heart washed clean of an accustomed stain
By gusts of memory as fresh as rain.

In gardens or in vases or grown wild,
They are the crystal vision of a child,
Untaught by craft, undisciplined by grief,
Sweet as child's laughter and as wild and brief.

Love always,
Tennessee

[Postscript] I write them while stoned, drunk, totally mentally incompetent – but! – apologise? No! Jamaisss!

Ma chère Estelle,
Toujours,
Tennessee Williams

SOURCES AND BIBLIOGRAPHY

I have edited spellings, paragraphs and punctuation where necessary to ease the flow of reading, and occasionally edited within letters where trivia, verbosity or contextual irrelevance make sections less readable, always marking the cuts with three dots. I have not used footnotes. John Barrymore said: 'A footnote is like having to go downstairs on the first night of your honeymoon'. Of course he was talking of editions of Shakespeare's plays, and I disagree with him – like most actors I find footnotes can be very helpful; but for this collection I have preferred brief interpolations and introductions.

I have used headings, addresses, salutations and signatures where available and legible; I have given dates whenever I could trace them or, in the case of undated letters, calculate them exactly; otherwise they are marked 'undated' and placed approximately. However, I refer readers wishing to study individual letters in manuscript to my sources. Where letters have also appeared in accessible publications I add those titles, and refer readers to the scholarship of the scores of biographers who have been so useful to me. In a few cases where I have transcribed from a scrawled, worn or smudged original manuscript I have had to guess a word.

In cases of copyright material from published works or private collections, permissions have been sought. If there are missing acknowledgements please accept sincere apologies; errors brought to the publishers' attention will be corrected in future editions.

IN ORDER OF APPEARANCE

The Alleyn Letters MS The Henslowe Collection, Wodehouse Library, Dulwich College; also quoted in supplement to Foakes/Rickert *Henslowe's Diary*, CUP 1961

Jones Letter MS The Henslowe Collection, ibid; also quoted in Chambers *The Elizabethan Stage*, Vol II, Oxford Clarendon Press 1923

William Birde letter MS The Henslowe Collection, ibid; also quoted in Chambers *The Elizabethan Stage*, Vol II, Oxford Clarendon Press 1923

Burbage & Co. letter Chambers *The Elizabethan Stage*, Vol II, Oxford Clarendon Press 1923

John Field letter Chambers *The Elizabethan Stage*, Vol 4; also quoted in Yates *Theatre of the World*, Routledge Kegan Paul (1969)

Philip Gawdy letter MS *Letters of Philip Gawdy, of West Harling, Norfolk and of London, 1579-1616* originals in British Museum; also quoted in Jeayes *Letters of Philip Gawdy*, Roxburghe Club; also quoted in same title, Edited for J.B. Nichols, London 1906; also quoted in Chambers *The Elizabethan Stage*, Vol II, Oxford Clarendon Press 1923

Greene's Groatsworth *Mediaeval & Renaissance Texts and Slides*, ed Dallen Carroll, British Library; letter to Marlowe and friends quoted in Schoenbaum *William Shakespeare: A*

Compact Documentary Life, OUP 1975

Aphra Behn letters Behn *All the Histories and Novels Written by the Late Ingenious Mrs. Behn, Entire in One Volume*, Fifth Edition ('Printed for R. Wellington at the Dolphin and Crown in St. Paul's Church-yard: 1705')

Arlington/Haughton letters Rosenfeld *Some Notes on the Players in Oxford, 1661-1713*, Review of English Studies 1943, XIX; also in Nicoll *A History of English Drama 1660-1900* Vol I

Betterton letter Rosenfeld *Some Notes on the Players in Oxford, 1661-1713*, Review of English Studies 1943

Coling letter ibid

Pope letter *The Correspondence of Alexander Pope*, ed Sherburn, Oxford 1956; also in *A Book of Condolences From the Private Letters of Illustrious People*, ed Harding/Dyson, Continuum NY 1981

Swift letter *The Correspondence of Swift*, ed Williams, Oxford 1965; also in *A Book of Condolences*, ibid

Garrick/brother Peter letter Molloy *The Life and Adventures of Peg Woffington*, Downey & Co. London 1897

Garrick/Sheridan letter *The Lives of the Sheridans* Vol I, Richard Bentley 1886

Sheridan/Wilson letter MS Theatre Museum Collection, Covent Garden (V. & A.)

Sheridan/Mrs. Sheridan 'Hecca' letters *The Letters of Richard Brinsley Sheridan* ed Price, Oxford Clarendon Press 1966

Woffington's letter Augustin Daly *Woffington - a Tribute to the Actress and the Woman*, published by the author, limited edition of 25, 1888, edition 17 in the possession of the British Library

Garrick/Woffington letter MS Every Collection; also (transcript) Theatre Museum Collection

Clive/Garrick letter 1774 Ingpen *Women as Letter-Writers*, Hutchinson 1909

Clive/Pope letter ibid

Clive/Garrick letter 1776 ibid

Clive/Garrick letter 1778 *Some Unpublished Correspondence of David Garrick*, ed Baker, 1907

More letter Ingpen *Women as Letter-Writers*, Hutchinson 1909

Voltaire letter *Lettres Choisies des XVII et XVIII Siècles*, ed Lanson, Librairie Hachette 1932, transl Bill Homewood

Fanny Burney 'Etiquette' and 'by the seaside' letters Ingpen *Women as Letter-Writers*, Hutchinson 1909

Wewitzer letter MS Theatre Museum Collection

Cherry letter (and Mathews quote) Clark Russell *Representative Actors*, Frederick Warne 1888

Jordan 1791, 1809, 1811 letters Aspinall *Mrs. Jordan and her Family Letters*, Arthur Baker, London 1951

Jordan letters 'My mind...' and 'Though I did not see...' *Our Old Actors* Vol II 'The Kemble Period', undated publ Bentley

King letter Folger Library MS Box 1; also quoted in Price *Theatre in the Age of Garrick*, Blackwell 1973

Siddons/Pennington letter *An Artist's Love Story - Told in the Letters of T. Lawrence, Mrs. Siddons and her Daughters*, George Allen 1904

Colman letters MacQueen-Pope *Haymarket: Theatre of Perfection*, W.H. Allen 1948

Sumbel (Wells) letter: MS Theatre Museum Collection; also *Memoirs* II

Siddons/Mathews letter: MS Theatre Museum Collection; also Macqueen-Pope *Haymarket: Theatre of Perfection*, W.H. Allen 1948

Siddons/Fitzhugh letter Ingpen *Women as Letter-Writers*, Hutchinson 1909

Lamb letter Ibid
Kean letters Playfair *Kean: The Life and Paradox of the Great Actor*, Reinhardt & Evans 1950
Examiner **letter** ibid
Powell letter MS (Private collection) **Frances Hughes**
Vestris letter MS Theatre Museum Collection
Grimaldi letters Findlater *Joe Grimaldi - His Life and Theatre*, CUP 1978
L.J.B. Booth letters, E. Booth washing list, War Dept. bill, Stoddard letter Ruggles *Prince of Players* Norton Inc. NY 1953
Jarrett/Booth letters Asia Booth Clarke *The Unlocked Book – A Memoir of John Wilkes Booth*, MS in private collection; also Faber and Faber 1938/Putnam's, N.Y. 1938
J.W. Booth/Phil. Enquirer letter MS USA National Archives, transcr. Arthur Kincaid
J.W. Booth/Mary Ann Booth letter MS USA National Archives, transcr. Deirdre Barber; also quoted in Lincoln Log 11 (4)
Booth quote 'I don't think John will startle the world...' Ruggles 'Prince of Players' Norton Inc. NY 1953; also Wilson *John Wilkes Booth* Houghton Mifflin 1929
Brontë letter Ingpen *Women as Letter-Writers*, Hutchinson 1909
Charles Kemble letter Clark Russell *Representative Actors*, Frederick Warne 1888
Fanny Kemble letters (i) Kemble *Record of a Girlhood* Bentley 1878; (ii) Kemble *Records of Later Life* Bentley 1882; (iii). Kemble *Journal of a Residence on a Georgian Plantation 1838-1839*, Harper NY 1863; also Meridian NY 1975; also quoted in Ransome *The Terrific Kemble*, Hamish Hamilton 1978
Baillie letter Ingpen *Women as Letter-Writers*, Hutchinson 1909; also in Clayden *Rogers and his Contemporaries*, Smith Elder
Macready/Serle letter MS Theatre Museum Collection
Dickens waistcoat letter MacQueen-Pope *Haymarket: Theatre of Perfection*, W.H. Allen 1948
Dickens Paris letter MS Theatre Museum Collection
Webster letters MacQueen-Pope *Haymarket: Theatre of Perfection*, W.H. Allen 1948
Keeley/Webster letter MS Theatre Museum Collection
Lind letter Ware/Lockard Jr. *P.T. Barnum Presents Jenny Lind*, Louisiana S.U.P. 1980
Peabody (Cushman) letter Stebbins *Charlotte Cushman: Her Letters and Memories of Her Life*, Houghton, Osgood (Boston) 1879
Cushman letter ibid
Collins letter MS Theatre Museum Collection
Boucicault letter MS ibid
Boucicault article *North American Review*, Sept.,1877; quoted in Matthew/Hutton *The Life and Art of Edwin Booth and His Contemporaries*, Page (Boston), 1907
Hugo/Bernhardt letter Verneuil *La Vie Merveilleuse de Sarah Bernhardt*, Brentano's NY 1942, transl Bill Homewood
Bernhardt/Sardou letter *A Treasury of the World's Great Letters*, ed Schuster, Heinemann 1941
Phelps letter MS Theatre Museum Collection
Fanny Kemble letter (Home Rule in Ireland) Kemble *Further Records 1848-1883* Vol I, Bentley 1890; also: Blom NY 1972
Fitzgerald Letter *Letters of Edward Fitzgerald to Fanny Kemble, 1871-1883*, ed Wright, Macmillan 1902
James letter *Henry James – Selected Letters*, ed Edel, Rupert Hart-Davis 1956; also quoted in Ransome *The Terrific Kemble*, Hamish Hamilton 1978
Tennyson letter MS (typescript) Theatre Museum Collection
Edw. Willard letter MS ibid
Ward letter MS ibid

261

Duse letter Rheinhardt *The Life of Eleonora Duse*, Fischer Verlage (Berlin) 1928; also Secker (London) 1930, transl Muir

Irving Telegram MS (Private collection) **Frances Hughes**

Clarke letter MacQueen-Pope *Haymarket: Theatre of Perfection*, W.H. Allen 1948

X/Miss Bertrand/Her Father exchange Hyman *The Gaiety Years*, Cassell 1975

Ruby Miller note ibid

Twain letters *Mark Twain's Letters*, ed Bigelow Paine, Chatto & Windus 1920; also in *A Treasury of the World's Great Letters* ed Schuster, Heinemann 1941

Wilde letters *Sixteen Letters from Oscar Wilde*, ed Rothenstein, Faber 1930 (Limited Edition of 550)

Cochran/his Mother/his Sister Min letters Heppner *Cockie*, Frewin 1969

E.Terry kiss letter Auerbach *Ellen Terry, Player in Her Time*, Dent 1987; also quoted in Brown *Reflections*, Hutchinson 1988

E. Terry 'Amuse me?' letter/Macbeth letter Auerbach *Ellen Terry, Player in Her Time*, Dent 1987

E. Terry/Shaw 'begging letter' exchange *Ellen Terry and Bernard Shaw - a Correspondence*, ed St. John, Putnam's NY 1932

Truman/H.B. Tree letters Truman *Beerbohm Tree's Olivia*, ed Wigram, Deutsch (1984)

Yeats/Campbell letter MS Theatre Museum Collection

Gregory/Synge letters *Theatre Business*, ed Saddlemyer, Smythe 1982

E. Terry autograph with instruction MS Theatre Museum Collection

E. Terry/Nettleship letter MS ibid

E. Terry 'Sir Henry' note MS (Private collection) Clive Francis

Irving/Heilbron letter MS (Private collection) Vivien Heilbron

H.B. Tree/Shorter letters MS Theatre Museum Collection

Duse/Bernhardt letter Rheinhardt *The Life of Eleonora Duse*, Fischer Verlage (Berlin) 1928, transl Bill Homewood; also Secker (London) 1930

Melba letters, memo, note Hetherington: *Melba*, Faber & Faber 1967

Norton Open Letter ibid

Williams letter MS Theatre Museum Collection

Vanbrugh letter MS ibid

Shaw unaddressed envelope MS ibid

Shaw/Vedrenne letter MS ibid; also in *Collected Letters 1898-1910*, ed Laurence, Reinhardt 1972

Vezin letter MS Theatre Museum Collection

Campbell/Shaw 'Lady Stracey' exchange *B. Shaw and Mrs. Pat. Campbell: Their Correspondence*, ed Dent, Gollancz 1952

Shaw/Terry 'You fill me with concern...' letter MS Theatre Museum Collection

Wontner letter MS ibid

Zenon (Nijinsky) telegrams MS ibid

Coward 'Dear Darling Old Mother' letter Lesley *The Life of Noël Coward*, Penguin 1978

Wade (n.d.p. Irene Dallas) letter Wade *Memories of the London Theatre 1900-1914*, Society for Theatre Research 1983

Scott letter *The Book of Condolences from the Private Letters of Illustrious People*, ed Harding/Dyson, Continuum NY 1981

Shaw/Campbell letter on the death of her son ibid

Carter letter MS Theatre Museum Collection

Gordon/Mama and Papa letter Gordon *My Side*, Harper & Row 1976

Mari Löhr letter MS Theatre Museum Collection

Rachel Willard/Hicks letter MS ibid

Lord Chamberlain/Tench letter MS (typescript) ibid

Valentino letter MS ibid

Barrymore letters Fowler *Good Night, Sweet Prince*, Viking 1944
Dix letter MS (typescript) Theatre Museum Collection
Priestley Letter (MS Private collection) Peter Dunn
Horniman letter MS Shakespeare Reading Society Archives, London
Cochran/Coward exchange of telegrams various; quoted in full in Heppner *Cockie*, Frewin 1969
Marion Terry letter Steen *A Pride of Terrys*, Greenwood Press, Connecticut 1962
Gielgud/Robertson letter MS (Private collection) Frances Hughes
Gielgud/Preston letter MS ibid
Kaufman letters, Steinbeck letter and telegram Teichmann *George S. Kaufman an Intimate Portrait*, Atheneum NY 1972
Woollcott letters *The Letters of Alexander Woollcott*, ed Kaufman/Hennessey, Cassell 1946
Seyler/Haggard letters Seyler/Haggard *The Craft of Comedy*, J. Garnet Miller 1958
Gordon 1942 messages Gordon *My Side*, Harper & Row 1976
St-Denis letter MS Theatre Museum Collection
Thorndike letter MS ibid
Draper letters Warren *The Letters of Ruth Draper, 1920-1956 - a Self Portrait of a Great Actress*, Hamish Hamilton 1979
Shaw/Wesker letter MS (Private collection) Arnold Wesker
Turner Levy letter MS (Private collection) Peter Dunn
E. Farjeon letter Farjeon *Morning Has Broken*, MacRae 1986
G. Farjeon letter MS (Private collection) Anne Harvey
Wolfit letter MS Theatre Museum Collection
Siegfried Mynhardt letter MS (Private collection) Patrick Mynhardt, transl P. Mynhardt
Miles letter of agreement MS (typescript) Theatre Museum Collection
Coward/Tolette letter Lesley *The Life of Noël Coward*, Penguin 1978
Sitwell telegram/letters Lesley *The Life of Noël Coward*, Penguin 1978
Milligan telegram *Independent on Sunday* (London) 11/12/1994
Robson letter MS Private collection) Clive Francis
Olivier/Fry cables and letters MS Theatre Museum Collection
Olivier message MS (Private collection) Brenda Bruce
Tynan letters *Kenneth Tynan - Letters*, ed Kathleen Tynan, Weidenfeld & Nicolson 1994/Random House USA 1995; quoted in *The New Yorker*, Oct. 31 1994
Richardson letter Meyer *Not Prince Hamlet*, OUP 1990
Pinter exchange *Daily Mail* (London) 28/11/1967; also recorded in Esslin *Pinter the Playwright*, Methuen 1982
Fugard letter MS (Private collection) Mary Benson
Patrick Mynhardt letter MS (Private collection) J. Mynhardt
Lemmon telegram MS (Private collection) Alec McCowen
Gordon/McCowen letter MS ibid
Gordon/Canby letter Gordon *My Side*, Harper & Row 1976
Williams poem/letter MS (Private collection) Estelle Kohler

N.B. Anecdotal and historical material as credited or from the above list, especially C18 and C19: Clark Russell: *Representative Actors*, Frederick Warne 1888; H. Barton Baker: *Our Old Actors*, undated publ Bentley C19/early C20; Bentley: *The Jacobean and Caroline Stage*, Oxford Clarendon 1968; Matthews/Hutton *The Life and Art of Edwin Booth and His Contemporaries*, Page (Boston) 1907; also Lloyd Evans *Everyman's Companion to Shakespeare*, Dent 1978 and standard biographical reference sources.

INDEX

'That's rather a sudden pull up,
ain't it, Sammy?' inquired Mr Weller.

'Not a bit on it,' said Sam; 'she'll vish
there wos more, and that's the great
art o' letter writin'.'

Charles Dickens
The Pickwick Papers

Christopher Fry

Herbert Herbert Tree

S. Siddons

Terry

Bransby Williams

J. Garrick

Sybil Thorndike

'the Stalls'

Seymour Hicks

C. Kemble

Rudolph Valenti[no]

Edmund Kean

Chris...

...ble.

...es Cox

Helen Vanbrugh

...ennessee

W. C. Macready.

...athews.

Martin Harvey

Syb...

S. Siddons

G. Coleman

Ellen Terry

John Tussud.

J. Garrick